THE **EXPLORER RACE**

COUNCIL OF CREATORS

AND ZOOSH
THROUGH ROBERT SHAPIRO

LIGHT Technology
PUBLISHING

ISBN 1-891824-13-9

Published by
Light Technology
Publishing
P.O. Box 3540
Flagstaff, AZ 86003
1-800-450-0985
e-mail: publishing@lighttechnology.com
www.lighttechnology.com

Printed by
Sedona Color Graphics
■ ■ ■ PRINTING SPECIALISTS
2020 Contractors Road
Sedona, AZ 86336

THE *EXPLORER RACE*

COUNCIL OF CREATORS

AND ZOOSH THROUGH
ROBERT SHAPIRO

Other Books by Robert Shapiro

THE EXPLORER RACE SERIES

1 · *The Explorer Race*
2 · *ETs and the Explorer Race*
3 · *Explorer Race: Origins and the Next 50 Years*
4 · *Explorer Race: Creator and Friends of the Creator*
5 · *Explorer Race and Particle Personalities*
6 · *Explorer Race and Beyond*
7 · *Explorer Race and the Council of Creators*
8 · *Explorer Race and Isis*
9 · *Explorer Race and Jesus*
10 · *Explorer Race and Lost Civilizations*
   (available 2002)
11 · *Explorer Race: ET Visitors Speak*
12 · *Explorer Race: Techniques for Generating Safety*
13 · *Explorer Race: The Ultimate UFO Book*
   (available 2002)

THE MATERIAL MASTERY SERIES

Shamanic Secrets for Material Mastery
Shamanic Secrets for Physical Mastery
(available 2002)
Shamanic Secrets for Spiritual Mastery
(available 2002)

The Sedona Vortex Guidebook
(with other channels)

SHINING THE LIGHT SERIES

Shining the Light
Shining the Light II: The Battle Continues
Shining the Light III: Humanity Gets a Second Chance
Shining the Light IV: Humanity's Greatest Challenge
Shining the Light V: Humanity Is Going to Make It!
Shining the Light VI: The End of What Was . . .

AUTOBIOGRAPHY

Robert Shapiro: The Man who Moves Hurricanes
Training of an American Shaman
(available 2002)

Contents

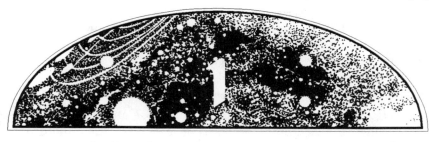

Council Spokesperson and Specialist in Auxiliary Life Forms

March 25, 1997

 speak for the Council of Creators. What would you like to know?

The Council of Creators

How much territory does the Council of Creators take in?

Overall, it has been created by that which has created it, plus we have two members beyond that. We hear from them but cannot see them; so they can see us [chuckles] but we can't see them. We consider their points of view especially valuable because they have a vision, perhaps, that we do not have. They are a little circumspect when communicating with us, but we are happy to have their input at all.

Can we talk to them sometime?

You can request it. I do not know whether they will comply, but it is a worthy request.

How many members are there in the Council? How does it work? How long do you stay? Do you come and go between creations?

You have to ask one question at a time.

How many members?

About two hundred.

And is it through a lifetime or do you come and go?

We do not sit in a room. All of the members in the Council are involved in their creations at this moment, but they can spare moments to conduct business of the Council. But no one is in a given place; they're all over.

Are you elected, appointed or self-chosen?

Well, no one on the Council of Creators can *sit* on the Council without having produced and completed at least one creation and now being involved in the production or creation of another. So there has to be a minimum of that, and many of our people have had five or more creations. So it isn't an election, but more of a volunteering, with a certain minimum requirement.

How far back does this go? When did it start?

I am not aware of it ever having not existed in this All That Exists. I believe it was always involved, which of course makes an obvious suggestion to you, does it not?

That they came here from someplace else?

Not only that, but that they produced their creations somewhere else or, in the case of all these creators, even if they produced their creations somewhere else, they had to have been involved in the creation process here as well, so that there would be a very clear understanding of how things work here.

Do you know where this someplace else is?

Well, I think it is further up the line, since that's the term we're using. Up the line before this.

Are you a spokesperson or a conglomeration?

I'm a combined voice.

How long do you sit? Is it a revolving group?

No. It is something that we "sit on." It is a volunteer situation, and you never stand down from it unless you are asking to be excused. So you volunteer and it's permanent.

There's not much room for new ones, then, if it seats around the same number.

Well, there is no need for new ones, because any being who is a new creator will have sprung forth out of one of these creators anyway.

Ah, I see. What are some of the things that are brought to your attention?

Usually we are asked for advice. We do not sit in a circumstance to give or not give permission. If we suggest that something not be done, it usually is not done, but usually we are asked to advise in creations. Once or twice we've been asked to advise in the procedures of an uncreation. There was quite a large creation in a prototype orb that was discovered to be flawed. The flaw in this particular orb, which did not have very many lobes, was that once it expanded to a certain point, it tended to fold in on itself. This was noticed, fortunately, very early on, and the creators involved asked our advice as to whether (and how) to move the beings and universes or uncreate them. It was decided, after a quick discussion, that because of the imminent collapse, an uncreation would be the quickest possible way, and then realign the individual souls into a new creation once an improved orb system was created. The problem with this particular orb system is that it wasn't really a living being, but more of a construct, not unlike a machine. Therefore it had no reason for being. It didn't feel that it was a portion of the creation, and after a certain amount of stretching it just collapsed. So there was a very rapid uncreation, with the assistance of the Council of Creators, and an almost as rapid re-creation within a functional, soul-oriented orb. This I mention to you because the orbs in which you are within at this time are a result of that improvement. Thus the orbs themselves in which you are living are living beings. That was perhaps the fastest thing we ever had to do.

The Council and the Explorer Race Experiment

How did you feel when you were first approached about the idea of the Explorer Race? What were some of the discussions and some of the thoughts about that?

Almost everyone was interested and intrigued by the idea until the details and ramifications of the project were fully expressed, and then I think that we had just about a ninety-nine percent agreement that it should not go forward. This project has really gone forward only because the beings involved in it were willing to commit vast amounts of their time and experience to the infinitesimal details that would be involved to uncreate such a project from "X" point, whatever that point might be, all the way back to before it was noticed as an idea. It was only this that was able to get conditional approval. The Explorer Race project has never had more than conditional approval from the Council of Creators. So even though it seems to be working well, I know of no being on this council who would retract conditional approval.

Has there ever been another conditional approval given about something?

I'm not aware in this All That Is or at all of there ever having been such stringent conditions. I think there have been very minor conditions, with a one percent potential for their ever having to be exercised. When it started out, the Council of Creators felt that the likelihood of the conditions of uncreation for the Explorer Race experiment being called into play was over ninety percent. It just goes to show that long odds can pay off. It also shows what a tremendous risk it was. The Council of Creators was expecting to jump in at any moment and assist in the uncreation of the experiment, but as it turned out, the experiment created its own percentage. It created its own motivation, so the longer the experiment was in existence, the better the odds were for your survival and your ultimate achievement. But when you began, it was a long shot.

Did even the Council of Creators not know that the Explorer Race was going to be separate from the Creator? I mean, the Creator didn't know.

Well, I think we perceived the necessity for you to be ultimately separate, because your Creator wanted to create something for which he could not contribute everything. Spontaneity grows out of an interaction with various things that are present, but it does not work if things are not present. So I think we realized quite early on that your Creator was going to have to have beings at the root of the Explorer Race that had experience other than your Creator, meaning potentials other than your Creator. I think we realized that early on.

How did you come to settle on the two choices, the ones who tell stories and the Temple of Knowledge?

We didn't do that. That was your Creator. Your Creator simply sent out the call for participants.

And they answered.

Yes. It is interesting to note, however, that even creators have what amounts to an unconscious. Your Creator, in order for the core beings of the Explorer Race to arrive in time, had to have a dreamlike vision. Creators do not sleep, but they are almost always calling for visions. That's how they get going on a given creation. Your Creator called for a vision to give It something to do, a reason to be. The motivation to be came first, and that's when your Creator broke off from Its creator and started Its journey. Before that motivation to be, there was the reason to be, though your Creator did not need to know that reason at that time. But when that initial motivation took place of the reason to be, that's when the unconscious call went out to the roots of the Explorer Race to come. In this way, the vast journeys involved over immeasurable space (in terms of your numerical system) could be undertaken, because your Creator would have to birth itself, travel around and so on. Thus by the time the idea came to your Creator consciously, the roots of the Explorer Race were practically there.

Always before this experiment you could ask the All That Is for advice, right? Did you ask the All That Is when something came up?

Did we as the Council ask?

Yes.

No. Our job is not to disturb that . . . [chuckles] our job is to advise.

So you didn't previously consult with them on other issues before the Explorer Race issue came up?

No.

Oh, I thought you did.

Communicate, yes, but not consult.

Beyond the All That Is

You said two of the members of the Council of Creators conversed with you from what we're just calling beyond. Does the All That Is know that? Did he talk to these beings?

Oh, I'm sure he must know.

He didn't seem to feel, or at least he didn't say or act like he knew what was up there.

He doesn't know what's up there. The beings are not revealing anything that is there. They are simply advising and involved in what we are doing, but they do not . . . well, they do not tell.

So it wouldn't do any good for us to talk to them?

What I'm saying is that they won't tell what's there, and I'm sure there's a good reason for that.

So which ones on the Council came from someplace else, the earlier ones?

Came from someplace else?

You said they'd already created creations someplace else.

Oh, everybody on the Council has come from someplace else. You have to remember that when the All That Is started all of this, we needed to have a council almost immediately, because one of the first things the All That Is created was obviously creators. If you are going to start even the biggest business, or some big project, you don't go from one end of the project to the other making it yourself. You immediately delegate. So the first thing that All That Is did was to create creators for quite some time. We as the Council of Creators were called to come from other places to advise them on how to create, because when the All That Is created creators in this place or space, they had not had creation experience before, so they needed advisors. Thus early on we were simply advising creators. That's why we have such a good working relationship with them. I'd say that early on, we were two hundred then. I think some of the creators who are in our council . . . it depends on how you count it, but the bottom line is, we're two hundred now.

Where did those who came from someplace else come from?

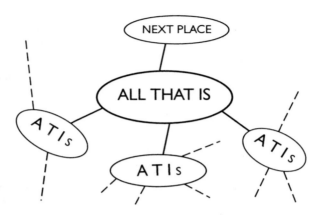

A moment . . . [draws].

All That Is is going to end up being like a circle of light?

You're not surprised, are you? This is the place where the All That Is is going to, the next place the All That Is is going to. Most of us . . .

. . . came from Pittsburgh. [Laughs.]

Some of us came from St. Louis, but you know, it's a matter of taste, isn't it? Nobody came from Malibu, though. There are three other places, I think. Most of us came from here.

Those are just strings of connections, they're not subsidiaries?

No, these are other All That Is's [ATIs]!

You have made three circles, but does that mean there are only three other All That Is's?

No, this is just the three we came from. That's a good question; let's just do this. [Draws.] Dotted lines. The dotted lines, however poor they are illustrated, indicate, of course, other places, yes?

I had to make sure.

Oh certainly, a good question. Worthy.

The All That Is, then, is in a position . . . what are we going to call this All That Is space? Similar to a creator, he just had the idea first, right?

No, he had the idea in this space first, but he didn't have the idea first. I do not want to discourage you, but in a way it might encourage you if we consider the mass of the All That Is that is here and then we consider the masses of some other places that would be equal to that, as in the illustration. There are many others that are significantly larger.

And much older?

Yes, and still in existence. You have to understand that it's a system. If you pull back, if you go in and you see the atom, then the nucleus, then the particles, it's as if you can go inward infinitely and continue to find smaller and smaller. It's exactly the same in the system if you go outward. If you go outward, you will continue to see other large creations, and that is infinite also within that system, within that construct.

Then there are other systems—we're now getting into an area that is a little hard to understand intellectually, but if you step aside from that system entirely, where you're not dealing with objects of magnitude, if I may call it that, you might then feel, strictly on the feeling level, all that exists everywhere that exists. I do not think you can see it all with the eye, even the perceptive all-knowing eye. You certainly can't *think* it all; even the best creators I've met cannot think it all at the same time. As far as I know, the only way you can experience, within the context of all, is feeling.

You know the feeling you get if you're at a theatrical production where there is a magnificent choir; perhaps they're singing Handel's *Messiah*, where you have many, many individuals singing the same part of the music and also many variations. You might have subtle variations of those who can sing different parts, and then if you go beyond the veils here, you hear the universal choir singing, the angelic chorus, as people say. What happens is that there are more tones available and more feelings available with those tones, and you feel like that is the ultimate chorus. Yet when you can feel all that exists all places, as in my example here, there is yet more. So we're really talking about orders of magnitude.

Could we make it analogous to dimensions. Are all these Isnesses on a similar plane, on a similar level of evolution?

No, we cannot. A simple no there would suffice. It's not analogous to dimensions or time or planes.

So when you go to the beyond, which we're calling "up," is it more rarefied? What is your conception of that?

My conception at this time is that it would have everything available to it that it is connected to; it would have everything available to it from this All That Is and every other All That Is it is connected to, which ultimately means, since all All That Is's [chuckles] are connected, it would have everything available to it, period. That does not mean that it would have what is here, but it would have that available. It might be entirely different.

But there must be more too, to make it so . . .

The one rule I have discovered in creation that is absolute is that there is *always more*. Interestingly enough, while there is always more (and this is necessarily paradoxical), there is never less. If you count the components of more (if you were able to count that high), and then said you were going to compare that number of individual components, say, the components that make up a single atom, you would have to count exceedingly high indeed, for the components that make up the atom (if you could count them all—and I'm not saying there wouldn't be more components in a vaster amount), no matter how simple it might seem, number at the very least in the billions.

The Effect of the Explorer Race Expansion

Will the ten-times expansion we are attempting to create affect all the other All That Is's and beyond?

I don't think it will.

How far do you think it will go?

I think it will initially affect all that is in your orbs; then I think we'll wait.

You mean in what could be sixty-two circles of creation?

No, just in the orbs of which you are a portion.

Just this one circle of light?

Yes. I do not think it will go to all the others immediately. I know others have said so, but I do not think so. I think we have to wait and see how it works. It seems like such a wonderful idea, but suppose it is *not* a wonderful idea, and we don't find out about it until much later? If it needs to be "fixed," then it would be better to have to fix something less complex. So I think we will wait a generation or two, roughly equal to 2500 years, before we allow the expansion. If after 2500 years or so there is no deleterious side effect, then I think we will allow the expansion to continue for a ways and then wait again.

So you have the ability to determine how the expansion goes out?

Oh, certainly.

I thought it was an explosion.

Oh, no. Nothing is absolute like that. If it were, lots of mischief could take place. If the mischief that takes place on your planet were radiated out to all planets everywhere, the universe would be a mess.

I understand. It's just that so many people have talked about this being built up and then just went . . .

No, I do not think so. I can see the value of looking at it that way, and outside the context of time it would certainly appear that way, but I'm putting it into the context of time so you have a frame of reference.

And is a consensus a majority? Does everyone have to agree, or fifty-one percent—or how does the Council of Creators work?

Absolutely everyone must agree. There is never a majority. We all agree, or that's it. If one person/creator says no, then it's no.

So all of you feel that you must contain the expansion?

Oh yes, we're all agreed.

Can we get one person's experience or sort of a combination of some that are similar? Where did you come from? How was it different from this All That Is?

Oh, I see what you want. You want an individual creator . . . hold on, I will see if you have a volunteer. [Pause.]

Specialist in Auxiliary Life Forms

I am the creator of all the helpful, auxiliary or ancillary life forms. On your planet that would be plants, animals. I do not create the plants and animals on your planet, but it is my job to provide suggestions, guidance and advice to other creators, should they wish to create beings such as this for any given planet.

Welcome.

A Road Map of the All That Is's

Can you remember the All That Is you came from?

I can, but since I must hold the hands like this, someone else will have to draw it. I cannot speak for too long. The energy is too much for this body.

Tell me what to draw.

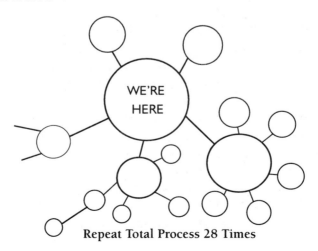

WE'RE HERE

Repeat Total Process 28 Times

Draw a small circle in the center of the paper, then draw spokes coming out from it to five or six other circles, then another series of spokes coming out from each one to five or six other circles, all being All That Is's. If you continued that process twenty-eight more times, I would come from that rim of All That Is's, but I cannot point it out more specifically because I must hold this position exactly.

Are we one of these now? Is where we are now one of these?

Your All That Is is in the center, for the sake of the mapping. It does not mean you are the center, but it is a portion of a greater map.

How can we use you best? Were you called here? How did you come to this one and not one of the others?

I was requested to come, since this All That Is was going to contain many different creations that would have great abundance of variety. As it turned out in the case of your Creator, who is exceedingly fond of variety, it is a good thing. I did advise, as a simple example, that fish not have tails. [Chuckles.]

How did you come upon this great connection to all the variety? Did the one you come from have great variety? Or the one you created?

I had a creation in existence, which is still in existence, now supported by three creators. The entire purpose of the creation was to generate variations of all life forms that could be considered embodied or encapsulated, anything. This would exclude life forms such as mass creations, but include all you would call encapsulated beings—a dog, a cat, a human, a Martian, what-have-you.

You were generated from within that All That Is and then became a creator within that All That Is?

When the need for variety became louder than it had been, I felt myself emerge from what I can only call a quagmire, not unlike a swamp, of varietal cosmic organisms. Having been a portion of such a concentrated mass of entirely individual and unique organisms, it was in my nature to be used to, and even accept and approve of mass variety. I might add that it was my idea that no two snowflakes be the same.

I love it! And there are billions of those circles, millions beyond number, right?

Quite beyond number in your numeric system, though not beyond number in the musical octave system, each octave expressing different characteristics of a given All That Is.

Would it be presumptuous to do a book on the Council of Creators and talk to different creators about these other creations?

Oh, I think it would be a good idea. It might have to be done at times in some different way, because the energy is imposing. But I think it is a good idea to remind people of the infinity of which they are a portion.

I wanted to road-map infinity, but I didn't know it was this big! Are you still connected to your original creation and yet always available? Or are you stationed here, is your essence here?

I am connected to my original creation in long distance only, because it is supervised and taken over by three other creators.

So your beingness is here, then?

Yes.

Does every All That Is have a council of creators like all of you?

As far as I know, but I have not personally been to them all.

But it's your understanding that that's part of the governance, you might call it, or the maintenance, or the . . .

. . . the support.

Support system, right. Someone goes out to create in a space and then puts out a call for a council, for beings to come to the council?

Or to communicate with the council. We do not necessarily go there. Very rarely do we go there, but communications at great distances are easily done.

Is this like a replication and a continuous creation? Is there one creator who created all these or created the beginning?

I think, from what I have been able to observe, that there is no beginning and no ending, but a constant expansion. It is natural in the linear construct in which you now exist briefly to think of things beginning and ending, yet I know of nothing in the place you now exist in that has begun or ended there. It only seems to be so. In truth, a child is born, but does that child's life begin when it is born? Certainly not. That child has had previous lives and energies and ongoing existences. It simply focuses as that child for a time while doing other things. So beginnings and endings are a temporary illusion to support and sustain your lessons.

By analogy, then, would an All That Is creator or a creator like you go through cycles of coming from someplace and existing, and then being birthed?

If they are cycles, they must be very slooooooow. [Chuckles.] Now I must go.

God bless you, thank you.

So that is one of our beings. Perhaps some other evening you can hear from others, but I think perhaps we need to end now.

What would you think of that? Could we actually do a book? It might have shorter sections; I don't want to hurt the channel.

I think that if you are open to briefer segments, it might be of interest, especially since some readers might feel more attracted to one than another and thus be able to generally extrapolate their own source.

Are you saying that within what we call the Explorer Race there are beings from these other All That Is's who are here?

There is, as far as I know, no beginning and no ending, so I must assume yes.

Thank you so much. Perhaps we will talk to you as a group again, and then as individuals.

Good. For now I will say good night.

Thank you very much.

Specialist in Colors, Sounds and Consequences of Actions

January 6, 1998

I am one of the sitting members of the Council of Creators. The Council, as we call ourselves since we advise and counsel other creators, is at various times made up of anywhere from 187 to 200 different creators. The members ebb and flow according to the demands placed on them by their creations, or demands that have to do with their cooperation with the creations of others. So it is going to be a little difficult to create insignia, as it were—names for each of us—but since several of us will make individual contributions for this book, I will simply say that I am the first one.

My expertise lies in the realm of colors and sounds, and also in the realm of the consequences of actions. As my creations and my observations of the creations of others progress, I would have to say that my knowledge of colors, sounds and consequences of actions has been most useful. It has provided not only a focal point, but a basis by which I am able to understand the purpose for my own existence.

I First Became Aware on Level Four

When I first became aware of my existence, I was beyond this level in which you find yourself, on what I can only term level four. It is a level where nothing has form and where a thought does not exist. The only thing reminiscent of your life here that you could relate to would be sensations of touch that would be familiar in the context of standing outside on a windy day. It's not windy there, but there is a steady sensation of such motion. It is my understanding that this motion is the precondition of form.

I became aware of myself in motion on this level, so rather than it being a gradual dawning of awareness in which I had the opportunity to explore the immediate environs and my place within it, I simply became aware of myself while I was traveling. I was in this motion for quite some time and experience. After this time, which I would have some difficulty converting to years, I moved for a short stay to level two, thence to level one, where the action is. In level one you have applications, lessons, opportunities, growth, interaction and so on. The levels above that usually have to do with some form of precursor to these things.

When I arrived in level one, I already had a small creation on level two. Level two's creations are usually impermanent, meaning that it is a place where one can try things out, but where any form of permanence is usually fleeting. If it is something worth doing, it would be reproduced on level one, but not transferred. In this way it is like creating a prototype and then creating the actuality.

So when I got to level one, I reproduced on a larger scale a place where all beings had a direct, felt connection, and anything that any one being did would be instantaneously felt by the other beings. You can see how it would relate enough to your world, since I am one of the beings who consults and advises with the Creator of your universe. I have observed since its beginning the creation of the universe in which you find yourselves—actually a little before, in terms of the rendezvous your Creator had with the elements that came to be the Explorer Race and the conclusions that might ideally be wrought by its application.

The Council Admonishes Your Creator

The Council has, in recent times, had to admonish your Creator, having to do with your Creator's innocence and Its tendency to overdelegate. Your Creator is very enthusiastic about variety. As a result, delegation would fit into that, because your Creator can not only let others do certain things for which they might be more prepared than Creator, but It can also surround Itself with different beings, advisors and councils, even teachers and experts, which suits this particular Creator because of Its enthusiasm for variety.

But some short time ago, the Council felt that your Creator was not taking enough of a personal involvement in Its creation. We feel that the evidence is the level of discomfort manifested not only on your planet, but on the recently retired planet in the galaxy of Sirius. (By "retired," I mean that to Sirian individuals it would have seemed to be destroyed, but from our perspective it was retired from its physical function and has gone into a quiet period of rest at higher dimensions, where it can rebuild itself in its own image rather than be subject to the will of perhaps less-evolved beings.)

Thus, from our perspective on the Council, your Creator has been slightly admonished—meaning advised that it would be better to take a personal interest in the creations and what is felt by the individuals in the creations. Since your Creator is not prepared to feel discomfort, It has been working in close counsel with beings who can expose Him/Her (however you wish to phrase it) to discomfort in ways that your Creator can fathom. As a result, your Creator has begun to have some sensation of this discomfort. On the one hand, it is good for your Creator to know of such things; on the other hand, it will undoubtedly speed your Creator's desire to hand over the reins of this creation to the Explorer Race when you remanifest as one being and as a creator.

Explore Race Timetable Speeded Up

This has speeded up the timetable to some extent, and this is why you sometimes feel overwhelmed on your Earth at this time—not by lessons, but by superimposed experiences. You will talk and listen at the same time, and it will seem normal. Yet after you are done communicating, you will also sometimes feel the memory of conversation that you are mentally quite sure did not take place. These would have been the subconscious—and in some cases the unconscious—thoughts of your own and of those to whom you are talking. This kind of overlay experience comes about as a result of speeding up the timetable.

I mention this because I want you to understand that it is felt by the Council that you can not only survive this experience, but that for many of you the sudden onset of this experience will not be maddening, but in reality remind you gently of your multidimensional capacities. Your Creator does not feel that this is the best thing to do, but the Council has recommended it. If your souls linger in the level of discomfort (which you are getting used to) for as long a period as the original plan by the Creator, the temptation of your souls to re-create yourselves (as you say, reincarnate) in past scenarios where violence and excitement and adventure are experienced in the extreme might become addictive. We feel that the intention of the experience is Creator School, not an addiction to the demands of the courses of the school.

So we have suggested this. (I grant that for you a suggestion does not indicate a demand. On our part, a suggestion to any creator also does not indicate a demand, but it does suggest that action take place on some level of our suggestion.) Your Creator has taken action by speeding up the timetable. As a result, even before many of you read this book, you will have noticed things that sometimes seem to blur an experience. For instance, you will drive somewhere, and for a moment you will be unable to remember your exact route. You will think of it one way, then realize a little later that it was a different way. This will have been an experience of possible routes you might have taken. In some cases, it will play out even further. As you return from a trip, for instance, you will be surprised to see the scenery, thinking that perhaps you had driven through a forest with trees, yet discovering that it is really a highway through cities. And it will be surprising.

Again, you are not going mad, but experiencing multidimensional possibilities. If you notice and understand it, these overlays will not disturb you. That is another reason this material is valuable, since I and some of the other creators intend to make it topical.

Imitations of This Creation Are Emerging

I feel that your creation, as your Creator is involved in it, has great merit. It will most likely be imitated in part by other creators—not to the extreme of this creation, perhaps, but already the Council has been consulted on three other creations in progress that have to do largely with the imitation or duplication of some facets of this universe. One of the creations in progress has to do with the duplication of the variety of life forms in another universe, but without discomfort.

Another creation has to do with the element of adventure, but without discomfort—what you would call, perhaps, intellectual adventure, but it is also going to be experienced by some beings as physical adventure without danger. It may seem tame to you by comparison, but it also has fewer consequences, whereas the adventures you have are often fraught with consequences.

The third creation under way is in the early stages and is likely to express itself along the lines of cultural similarities, meaning that aspects of different cultures now being demonstrated in this universe will be imitated in that creation.

This is fairly unusual amongst creators; most often any creation is the result of a unique idea, perspective or even application. Here we have three creations that clearly involve applications, yet those applications are not unique. I mention this here to let you know that already this universe is making its contributions. I have noticed that your Creator, while not being prideful, is pleased that other creators find this creation worth imitating.

The Council Instructs Creator to Have
Greater Personal Involvement

What was the specific suggestion to the Creator about His feeling humanity's discomforts?

We felt that because your Creator had delegated much of the discomforts to beings such as the Master of Discomfort or to beings who had a wide range of capacity, these experts in their fields were so used to dealing with such levels of discomfort (to even greater extremes than you feel) that the discomfort you and others were feeling here on this planet and on the recently retired planet was not sounding alarm bells with them; rather, it was just another function of what they were used to. I'm not saying here that they were inured to discomfort or able to turn a cold eye on it, but that because they were used to it, they were not likely to react to a more extreme level of discomfort that ought to have been blended with something less challenging.

Therefore the Council felt that your Creator must experience greater growth than It was experiencing, and it could be done only through greater personal involvement. So it was simply stated to your Creator, as close as it can come in your languages, "You are not involved enough. Become more involved with those who experience discomfort so that you can achieve your own lessons as well as completely satisfy the requirements of your core lesson."

What is His core lesson?

Compassion. Your Creator has mastered well all shades of things associated with compassion, including enthusiasm and even sympathy. But compassion is something your Creator has not mastered yet, and It perhaps felt that this mastery would take place in a less complicated circumstance. But in our experience, once you have created something, the motivation to accomplish your lesson within your own creation is much stronger than in the creations of others. You can put a man in a maze of his own creation, and he will enjoy finding his way out; but put him in a maze in the creation of another, and he will become frustrated trying to find his way out. We felt that your Creator would achieve Its mastery on creation levels, you understand—not just the levels of mastery known to the human or the spirit being, but on the creation level, where levels of mastery are a bit broader. We felt that your Creator was more likely to achieve creation-mastery compassion within Its own creation. This is why this was stated. It is also more likely that your Creator will become increasingly involved now with Earth and the Explorer Race as well as with those coming from the recently retired planet in Sirius, who are coming to a denser vibration [3.0] of Earth to manifest.

Now, your Creator will do something different with those beings from Sirius than It has been doing with you. When the average citizen from the negative planet on Sirius (that exploded recently)—presently incarnate at a lower dimensional level on your Earth now—cries out for guidance, your Creator is much more likely to send a representative to have actual communication that the being can understand, not unlike what has been written in your holy books, how communication is experienced between a citizen and God's representative in one form or another. In this way, their level of discomfort, which is much more than your own at the moment, will be soothed more quickly. It will also allow them to develop the applied version of their spiritual sides more quickly than was originally planned.

In your experience on Earth at your dimension, you are all now likely to have more visions associated with the capacity to see and understand. Right now you have many visions: some are dreams, some are spiritual visions, some are even fantasies. But you often do not understand the meaning and will frequently misinterpret the meaning or even believe the misinterpreted meaning of another person. This has sometimes created unnecessary complications, in our view.

Your Creator will now [within about two and a half years from this conversation] help you to be inspired to know the actual meaning. This means that when you had dreams before, the true interpretation was there for you but was mixed with thought interpretations. So it has been hard for you to differentiate which is the real interpretation as it relates to you, your life or those for whom the vision was intended. What occurs now [by the time this is read] is that when you scan quickly through thoughts and have the feeling of the inspired meaning of the vision, when you touch on the mental level or on the inner-vision level (what you see in your mind's eye) and touch the true meaning of the vision, you get a warm feeling in the chest/solar plexus/upper part of the body. Thus, whether you have been trained in this method or not, you know that there is some significance to the particular meaning you are scanning in your thoughts and feelings [see Appendix for Love-Heat Exercise].

In this way the Creator will touch you. It's as if the Creator reaches a finger toward you and touches your chest to say, "This one, not that one." In this way the potential is for you all to be touched by the Creator, making benevolence much more likely for you as well as more personal interaction between your Creator and you. Some of you do not remember your dreams, but this does not mean you don't dream. So the chances of feeling that touch and thence becoming more quickly evolved toward your natural state of being is more likely.

This will not feel to you like a process so greatly speeded up in the next few years; it will initially seem like there is more going on than you can think about. That is why it is valuable at this time to begin using the physical feelings in your body to explore what is true for you, as has been discussed in previous books. The value of such applications is that your brain will not have to feel as if it is being overwhelmed.

Your brain is not unlike a computer in that if it is overwhelmed, it will simply retreat, urging you to back away into a simpler life. Some individuals would experience this as a nervous breakdown or a need to simplify their lives, going from a corporate position to becoming a fisherman, for example. (Not that being a fisherman is uncomplicated, but it concerns varieties of the same thing rather than the multifaceted tasks a corporate executive might have.) Such experiences will allow the mind to feel supported by the body and by the feelings, and thence feel comfortable with inspirations and instincts. They are, in that sense, a bridge for the mind.

Creator Authorizes Greater Benevolence

Okay, I understand how we will gain from the Creator having more contact with us, but how is He experiencing discomfort from us? When He touches our chest, does He feel our discomfort?

He feels all of you; He feels the total being of you. Of course, one might say that He feels this anyway, but when He touches you as an individual, He will feel you as an individual in His entirety. Now the Creator experiences all of you as a whole being; Creator does not experience any of you on a singular level, but as a whole. The predominant energy you experience between sleeping people and people having plus or minus experiences would still allow Creator to get the impression of relative comfort, feeling you as a whole. But when Creator touches you individually and fills Itself with the individual experience of a person, Creator will then become personally aware of individual discomforts without necessarily being impacted by those discomforts. In this way Creator will develop compassion and have a greater capacity to interact with the individual.

A compassionate individual can feel compassion for the many; but to feel compassion for one being requires the ability and the experience through application of one to one rather than one to many. On the creator level, it is experienced more as an authorization. If Creator feels great discomfort in any given area of a person's individual life, that authorizes (you might wonder at the use of permission with Creator) Creator to interfere with your potential future to help you to achieve greater benevolence for yourself, in this way interfering with Creator's own plan, from your perspective. That is how lessons on the creation level work. Normally a creator sets something in motion and then steps back to some extent, allowing its creation to fulfill its own destiny. But here, because of the unusual circumstances, your Creator will be prompted by its interaction with you to authorize change.

That's wonderful for humanity and for Creator.

Yes, so we can hope that your Creator will not do it for you directly, but help you, perhaps by increasing your level of experienced instinct or understanding (to interpret your own instinct, for example) to achieve greater benevolence for yourself.

Since we **are** using the example of the heat in the physical self, maybe your Creator will deign to allow you to feel greater heat, meaning something that would be noticed as a significant event in the physical self of even the most jaded individual. In a more spiritual or benevolent individual, it will be a lingering feeling, meaning something that does not pass quickly but is enjoyable for a longer time. This is an example of what your Creator might do to increase the benevolence of your life. And when that benevolent energy is present, in the physical heat there is described the greatly expanded potential for your life to be improved, both inner (inside your physical body) and outer (the manifestations in your world).

People can ask for this interaction with the Creator in a way they haven't done before?

Yes; ask out loud for Creator to touch you. It may or may not occur in ways you will remember and it might simply occur in the way I described before, but you can ask.

Living Color and Living Sound

At what point did you gain your experience in color and sound? Are color and sound related to the consequences, or are they two separate things?

They are separate things, yes.

How did you gain your experience with color and sound?

I gained almost all my experience in color and sound by passing through the harmonic waves that separate the levels. I went from four to two to one, but did not pass through three; it is not a highway [chuckles]. But between the levels there are vast experiences of what I can only describe for your benefit as living color interacting with living sound. You understand sound now as an effect, something that happens after something else happens, yes? But in these places I passed through, sound is alive; it is not generated by anything else. Sound is alive in its own right and color is alive in its own right.

The first time I passed through that from level four to level two, I chose to stay in that harmonic area for some time (I will relate it to you in terms of experiential years, as your Zoosh has used this term), about a thousand years. Then going from level two to level one, I stayed in that harmonic for about ten thousand years. It had much more variety. Within that zone I was able to understand the living qualities that make up color and sound; I was able to appreciate that sound and color exist without reaction or interaction with anything.

Even on this level, the sounds you make are present before you make them; you simply interpret them—or focus them, you might say— through a means by which you can appreciate the result. Imagine this sound: [claps hands] the clap of the hands. It would seem to be, for all intents and purposes, a result of the hands coming together; the hands come together and seem to make the sound. The hands coming together creates a sequential event. For you, living in this experience of sequential time, you cannot utilize in any way a linear mind without having a logical predecessor to anything that takes place. The linear mind requires a predecessor to all things, even if they are things that do not manifest physically, such as a daydream.

For instance, an individual who has the same daydream over and over again and is perhaps upset by it might ask an analyst or even a trusted friend: "What does it mean?" That simply means, what is the predecessor to this experience? The mind requires this on the linear level. But on the vertical level of the mind (meaning what you need to know when you need to know it), sound or whatever it may be is its own experience. It is not in any way related to the act that, on the linear level, would seem to precede it. It is simply an expression, in that sense, of living sound. There is no criticism; one way is fine, another way is also fine.

It was then my pleasure to experience this color and sound as *someone*, which has allowed me to appreciate the facets of your experience of interacting with color and sound as expressed through your Creator's pleasure, which you know as variety in your world. As such it has given me a unique ability to advise and consult your Creator in these matters, as your Creator wishes.

Is each color an entity within itself—red, blue, green, purple, yellow?

Yes, and all other colors beyond your visual light spectrum and every infinitesimal shading and variety of color within your visual light spectrum. Although you understandably need to refer to red and look at the color wheel (as an artist might do) and say, "Red," all the shadings of red are also unique. Red on the color wheel would be, in the level of master color creation, simply an arbitrary color-reference root. So it would be a *shade* of red, meaning one being of red.

Do the colors that flow between levels four and two continue to flow down to level one and form the basis of our colors here?

From four, one passes through a membrane. One skips level three and thence passes through the membrane that leads to level two. So rather than saying from four to two, it's out of four and into two, for the sake of precision.

Do the colors we see here in level one originate in level four?

They do not originate in four; they do not even originate in these harmonic zones between the levels. The colors, in my communication with them, have stated that they exist everywhere, even beyond levels. The sounds have also said that their experience of creation goes beyond levels. I would suggest that at some point you do a book in which the colors and/or the sounds are channeled. Imagine what they can tell you!

It was long before this creation that you tried out on level two, right?

Yes. I passed out of four, went into two and then did my creation on two. Then I passed out of two into one, experiencing the zone, and then re-created the creation. That is the timetable.

As you know, I'm looking for a road map for infinity.

Yes. Infinity is not fully understood by your minds, but conceptually it is understood. When the colors and sounds informed me that their existence is beyond all levels, they informed me of something for which I did not have personal experience. Yet from my perception I would still consider that where they are from is part of infinity.

So we had a horizontal infinity and now we have a vertical infinity going up the levels?

Well, of course you have a spherical infinity as well as an inside-out one; maybe (or maybe not) you'll get to that. It may be unnecessarily complicated to get into that.

Then we discovered the levels.

Yes, the levels would be vertical infinity. That is a sufficient way to put it, I feel.

My Creation on Level One

So you came to level one. What drew you to that place? I know you can't put it in relation to where we are, but is there any way for us to call that place something or equate it to anything we know?

What drew me there is that there was nothing there. There is something everywhere, but the area was as devoid of creations and experience as possible. Since I was going to try something relatively new, I wanted it to have as little impact on the creations of others as possible. So I went to a place that was [chuckles], simply put, far away.

It was not part of someone else's creation?

It was beyond orbs and all of this, but it was still on level one. This might amuse you: Everything that has ever been described to you that is in level one would be equal to my taking a pin and making the size of a pinprick in the oceans of this world. That pinprick is where things are that you've discussed, and the rest of level one would be all the rest of the ocean mass. This means that there is so much in level one, it is not possible to cover it all in the next twenty years, but we can make generalities.

[Chuckles.] Okay, are you going to hang around with us for the next twenty years?

Much longer than that.

What was this new thing you were going to do?

In the experience of all beings connected to each other, whatever any one being did would be felt immediately by all other beings. This is true for your world now, but because of the veils, you feel this only unconsciously. Even that unconscious feeling has consequences for all beings. Sometimes it is in the dream state for you; most often it is on the feeling level. If some great cataclysmic event were to happen, everyone on the planet, no matter where they were, might get an uncomfortable feeling for at least a moment, which they might relate to this or that around them.

To give you a dramatic example, the atomic bombing of Hiroshima was felt at the exact moment of the flash (the initial explosion) by everyone all over—all people, all animals, fish, trees, gases, air, lightning, rain, everything. It was felt by everyone as a moment of discomfort; in the case of human beings it was ofttimes misinterpreted, and the feeling quickly passed. However, at the moment of the explosion, some sensitive beings, about ten percent of the population of the Earth (not referring, of course, to the people in the area of the explosion), got sick for about three days. One could say, "Well, at any point on the Earth there might be two or three percent of the people who would get sick with a cold or the flu." But ten percent got sick for a while because the sensitive people were a little overwhelmed by such a catastrophic happening. I use that as an example you can all understand.

Can you describe your creation?

Yes. It would have been very small compared to yours; the sum total of the space would have been no more than the galaxy [system] of Orion, as a size factor. It was a unified experience, and variety was unnecessary at the scale you experience.

Does your creation still exist?

No, it was unnecessary, because I learned what I needed to learn. The beings there were able to create, technologically, a memory chip. This memory would be long-lasting enough to result in a depth of experience that would occur, as applied on Earth in your times, when you all begin to become more conscious of being one. It won't have to be a slow assimilation of unity. Everyone will come to the awareness of it in just a few years rather than taking generation after generation, thousands of years. Of course, many people would understand it conceptually, but to experience it as a real thing and acknowledge it and honor it for its value will now take perhaps only ten years. Granted, some of you can begin now to notice when other people have strong feelings or dramas, when an individual comes close to them. You might feel suddenly uncomfortable, not because of your reaction to that person, but because of your identification with him or her. As Zoosh would say, *Never Forget That!*

That ought to be underlined, because it is a fact for you *now.* You can all understand it, especially the New Age crowd and even religious and other people who are conscious of spiritual practices. It is still very common amongst these individuals to believe that you are reacting to some person rather than acting in union for a brief moment with their discomfort. Equally, if someone is joyous and happy, you might become one with that individual and become happier by exposure to such happiness, if even for a moment. One can identify with this, for example, when you see a happy baby in a public place. One might smile, sometimes even unintentionally, and unite with that happiness for the moment and continue on. You do not really react; you act.

You can become aware of this now and use it to your advantage. If you wish to enjoy the benefits of such things, seek out more benevolent experiences for yourself. Seek out more benevolent companions and experiences of benevolence for you and your companion or your family or your people. In this way you will all feel more benevolent, more comfortable, more satisfied with who and what you are so that you do not have artificial cravings for something that substitutes for what you are missing. Most people now have gotten used to substituting some product or experience for the comfort they seek, but sometimes simply benevolence and the experience of union with those around you will simplify that reenergizing of your own comfort.

But now we're substituting food, alcohol, drugs, television, movies—things like that.

Yes, and even violence for some individuals, to have the satisfaction of victory or what-have-you.

For some people, it might be just to feel more alive.

It can be infinitely easier, to say nothing of being more benevolent personally and universally, to simply seek out benevolence for yourself and others.

You closed your creation down because you had learned what you needed to learn; so what did you learn?

That the actions of even one individual amongst billions have an instantaneous effect on *all* beings. And to the extent that these beings do not experience the level of distraction you have here (in my creation there was not this type of distraction), they could all learn something. For example, when the beings in my creation learned to laugh, first one being laughed, then they all laughed and enjoyed the pleasure of such a thing. Here you learn to laugh one by one. But you have many distractions here, so it is understandable. The linear experience also makes a difference.

And your creation also helped you become an expert on consequences?

Yes. Starting with a foundational experience that what one does is instantly felt by all beings through union with all, after my creation I journeyed to different creations to observe not only the ramifications of what I had pioneered on this level, but also the variations of expression given to other experiences: for instance, distractions, other things you have to do, like breathe. If you are laughing, you must stop in order to breathe. Something that you would consider natural might not have existed for the beings in my creation. For example, they did not have to breathe.

You're saying that no one had ever created such a creation? I thought that everybody except those of us on Earth already felt like that. But yours was the first?

No one on this level at that "time" (for lack of a better word) had created an application of the impact of one being's actions on all beings within that unit. No one had done that. That is what you would call infinitely long ago. Now it is taken for granted, but then it was "Oh!"

What prompted you to do that?

I was prompted to do that creation because I was observing the process, the elements of creation. I began observing it really on level two, where you can make temporary things. On level two one finds lots of creators doing lots of things. I noticed that even though these individual creators were doing something uniquely their own, because creators know what other creators are doing, they would very often be influenced by other creators to a greater or lesser degree no matter what they were doing. I wanted to see if this would be so for millions or billions of beings, especially beings who were not on the creator level. That's all.

Do those beings you created still exist now?

They do not exist in that form anymore. I didn't stop the creation artificially; I just let it die out on its own when the beings felt complete in their lives. I reabsorbed them and the creation as part of myself; so you could say, philosophically at least, that the creation lives on within me as a living memory. But as a practical experience, as you might say, it is something that was.

Then, because I was interested in consequences, I went out and looked at every place on this level that was experiencing consequences in order to see whether the beings on that level realized it—including creators and all their individual creations to the infinite (meaning the greatest and the least in terms of size)—and I noticed that it was already functioning, but largely on an unconscious level, even with creators.

This intrigued me. That's why I made a study of consequences having to do with the actions of others and traveled all over this level. Considering the lifetime of this universe you exist in, this universal lifetime [draws]—UL to the sixth power, all right? UL would equal my

$$UL \times UL^6 = \triangle$$

experience, which I will draw as a triangle. It could also be stated as a long time.

The Permanent Council of Creators

How did you come to the attention of the Council of Creators for this level?

The Council of Creators was in existence when I came here, and of course it is a matter of being polite. It is not a requirement, but politeness is considered a foundation to all communication, as far as I know, and it was polite for me to announce my arrival. So I knew about the Council.

After I had completed my journey around this level to study consequences based upon the actions of others, it was at that time I was asked to consider joining what you might call the permanent Council of Creators. Here's a diagram [draws]. This is as accurate as I can make it. This is the permanent Council [PC, center circle]. Out here we have what I would also call the Council. This is all part of the Council; one could put this in a circle. This is all part of the Council. At the outer part, creators might come and go, but when one is in the permanent Council, this means that one stays in it unless one has a personal need to go. If I suddenly needed to go, then I would.

How many are there? How many in the core?

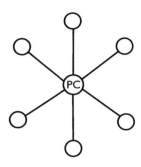

PC = Permanent Council of Creators

Thirteen. The core group is more likely to be able to stop what they are doing and talk to you. Of course, we're all doing other things too, but the chance of our being called away is less than that of the floating members of the Council.

This must be incredibly exciting, to have everything that happens on this level come before you.

It is more that everything needing our attention will come before us. Everything and/or everyone that requires or could benefit from our advice, observation or even nurturance, will pass before us in some way. But we are not to be confused with the idea of a review board; we are not that. It is more a matter of being polite.

For instance, when your Creator invited the energies that made up kangaroos to be on your planet—or even in this universe, because they did not start on your planet—your Creator might pass that in front of us for review as the creation of a unique being expressed by the attitude of the being and all that it does (where it goes, how it communicates, how it lives, eats, sleeps, dreams, births, loves and so on, as a general description of a species type). This would be passed in front of us.

But if your Creator and the beings together in their larger self were to simply decide to change some aspect of their behavior, this would probably not pass in front of us. To put it in a literary context, we do not always see the subheads.

Much of This Universe Came from Elsewhere

Do I understand that our Creator created the kangaroo, or that he invited it from someplace?

Invited it.

Everything in this universe came from someplace else?

In my understanding, almost everything did; certainly one would say that the mass that was here to begin with came from here, meaning where you are. The energy, the preexisting material that was here, was already here. But in terms of spirits, divine beings and so on, or source root beings (in this case of the kangaroo), they came from elsewhere.

Is anything here unique to this creation?

The way they *look* here is largely unique to this creation. My understanding is that the beings you know as kangaroos don't look anything like that at their source. They look quite different, and my understanding is that almost all of the beings who existed elsewhere before they were invited to be part of this creation look significantly different. There are a few who look similar; I do not think any of them look exactly the same.

Then it's much larger than we've been led to believe. It's not that animals on Earth are ETs from other planets; they are originally from beyond this creation?

Yes, so that they could bring that variety your Creator loves. Your Creator is in love with variety. As far as creators go, I could describe it with the term *passionate*: Your Creator is passionate about variety.

So when they leave this planet, they're leaving this universe? Or are they going off to another planet?

It is up to them. If they return to their source, they will surely leave this universe. Another book someday, eh?

Absolutely. So you have brought your wisdom about consequences to this creation. You have offered your experience to this Creator and others.

I have, as you say, offered my experience. I have not brought it to this universe that your Creator has created, but I have offered my advice, especially when it was requested. Occasionally it was not.

And you've been in the sessions where everyone involved here had to promise to uncreate the mess (if it became a mess) and to uncreate themselves for a period of time, right?

Yes! As a matter of fact, I was in on that decision, and it came about largely as a result of the extreme circumstances on that now-retired planet in Sirius, and it came about even earlier when a planet was retired in the Pleiades. In the distant past they had an experiment with such discomfort that it also tore the planet apart. It did not explode, but it made it unfit for the habitation of physical beings. It was a word in the ear, then, to your Creator. But with the extreme of the explosion in Sirius and the end of the life forms on that planet, as well as the extreme discomfort on this planet, your Creator was called to the Council. Your Creator had to come here, though "here" incorporates your universe. Your Creator essentially stepped away for a moment to give us Its full attention.

Maldek Was Not Unlike Your Moon

What about Maldek? Was that also an incident?

That was not considered so serious because it was a brief amount of time. It wasn't a circumstance in which a planet meant for one thing was turned into something else. Maldek was always expected to be a fleeting development. And it was not like your planet when it began. It was a place that was more barren, but was converted to being hospitable, like putting outposts on the Moon. The outpost itself would be hospitable, no matter how large it was. One might go to such an outpost and feel as if one were in a vast city. But the planet itself was more moonlike and desolate. That is why there was no admonition to your Creator as a result of what happened there.

The beings in the cities, and even in some cases the cities themselves, were simply transferred to another place. The planet's destruction, while regrettable, was not the end of the experience of that planet; it still exists in other dimensions and may at some point be remanifested in all dimensions expressed in this creation—especially when your planet moves back to its original location in the galaxy [system] of Sirius. Then there will be room for Maldek again, and it may be re-created, probably as a more benevolent place and not so moonlike.

We had heard that it was this incredible crystal planet with exquisite beauty. There are so many stories.

Well, those things may very well have been adapted and created there, but the planet itself did not start out that way. It started off looking rather desolate; though it certainly had a life of its own, it was happy being desolate. It was peaceful, it was quiet and it was focused entirely on reception.

Your Moon, I might add, is focused largely on reception, meaning the feminine state of being. But when one finds oneself hurtled into the world of consequences, especially along the path of the Explorer Race journey, one (a planet such as Maldek or even the Moon) might find that one's feminine experience can bring about dramas you might not otherwise have wished to participate in, because you are so involved in attraction. Attraction as an across-the-board experience does not differentiate between consequences that are malevolent versus consequences that are benevolent; it is simply attraction, period.

Maldek attracted those beings who came from Orion, right?

Yes; they found it easily, because she (if I can say that about the planet) was involved in attracting. If you were to look at Maldek as I am looking at her, before the arrival of the Explorer Race and really before the arrival of any beings you would even identify as humanoids, she would look not unlike a moon receiving material from space. You would call it being struck by meteors, which is a way of receiving things.

Will she be in our orbit when this planet leaves?

Not immediately. And the decision has not even been made, but it is probable from my perception that she will be taking your place at some point once your planet has returned.

Homework: Experience the Benevolent Actions of Others

What would you like to say to the readers—what's the most important thing you can leave with the reader?

Know that even the most infinitesimal actions impact all your fellow beings; equally, you are impacted by the actions of others. The more you become conscious and then put into application the appreciation of all life, the more you will feel the benevolent impact of the benevolent actions of others. Your level of discomfort is heightened now because you feel separated from others, and when you feel separated you will tend to experience more of the malevolent or dramatic impact. Not all drama is malevolent, but just as a child who does not get love will act out to get attention, your experience is that if you are not feeling the benefits of the actions of others, you might feel the discomforts of their actions even though they are most likely not even directed at you. Your physical body attempts to show you by the actions (if I might misapply this word) that are the loudest, meaning you will definitely notice the impact of the actions of others.

If you wish to do homework, pick out two people you do not know very well but perhaps are acquainted with. They can even be distant family members you do not know well. Begin to communicate with them more often, whether it be by letter or telephone or electronic communication, and notice that the more you find out about them, the more you will begin to feel their feelings. When you get to know each other better, have a meditation, an experience where you just lie down at the same time of day, and put yourself into the most benevolent experience you can feel, such as the love-heat exercise. With your eyes closed, notice if you suddenly or gradually feel a greater heat than you ever had before. This will be an experience of the effect upon you consciously and physically of benevolent actions of others. This is most easily and pleasantly experienced by individuals you take the time and effort to get to know. And it does not require that they be in the same town or even in the same country, only that you will at some time, perhaps even years in the future, be able to lie down at the same time and do this exercise. The main thing is, it can be a fun thing, especially for those of you who are separated from others for any reason. In time I or perhaps other beings will give homework that will build upon this, but this is what I recommend for now.

Our connection to other humans will be easier because of your creation, right?

As you all, as individuals, become conscious of your connections to each other, this conscious awareness and its attendant actions will happen much more quickly than might have happened without my creation. Without my creation you would have had to gradually grow to appreciate the religions and cultures of others who understand now that all beings are connected and practice those benevolent connections with other beings, even if they do not know them. An obvious cultural example would be shamans, mystical men and women who understand the life force in all beings.

Is this the connection where we'll feel all of each other, the three seed souls of the Explorer Race, everyone in this creation—or is it everyone everywhere?

Everyone on the planet. You must start small. If you start big, you will skip why you are here. You are here ultimately to completely understand, on this level, the experience of consequences to all things. You practice that initially in your life, though you are not usually aware of it, with your parents, your brothers and your sisters, then eventually with your wife or husband, your children, your friends and so on. Ultimately you will experience that with everyone on Earth. Then everyone will be doing some version of a meditation, whether it is with the heat or whether it is laughing. When everyone laughs at once, it's funnier because everyone is laughing. Just as, for instance, you could go to the movie theater alone and see the moving picture. It is funny, and you might smile in lots of places and maybe occasionally laugh, but if the theater is filled with people and they laugh in many places, you will probably also laugh because of your connection to the fellow beings watching the movie. It is seemingly a reaction to what is taking place on the screen, but it is also such a pleasure to laugh together; it is giving you permission to do so.

This is between the 3.48, or wherever we are now, and 4.0 on the dimensional scale? That's here on the Earth in the next few years.

Yes, from my perspective. Granted, it will not be immediately, but there are many people practicing this now. As more people practice it and come to peace and comfort with their own lives, and as others seeing this wish to have that, it will spread. As time goes on it will spread more quickly.

Is there a better name for you than the "first one"?

You can, if you wish, wait until a few of us have spoken. There might be some overlap; others might mention colors or sounds or consequences. Wait until you have heard from a few others. If no one else says the exact combination I have mentioned, then you can use the combination.

It's my understanding that what we're calling the All That Is of all these realms and orbs and everything we've talked about so far, that it's waiting for our Creator in some little passageway and they're going to go up to explore what's up there, because they don't know what's there.

If they don't know, then they haven't been there. And yet if the being has said that it is All That Is, it is all that it is aware of. Can you not appreciate the irony?

I think he said he was All That Is, but then we found out that there were all kinds of All That Is's. They were like cells—there are millions of them, right?

Beyond that.

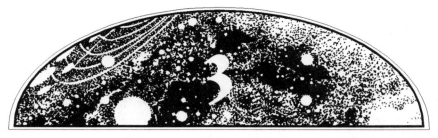

Specialist in Membranes That Separate and Auditory Mechanics

January 8, 1998

am another one of the creators who sits on the Council. My particular expertise lies in the area of the zones or membranes that separate. That which exists between media is one of my levels of expertise. This has allowed me to be helpful to your Creator, because so much of what your Creator is involved in is creating at least the illusion of separation in order to sustain and nurture linear experience. So that is my main expertise, and on a secondary level I am also knowledgeable in auditory mechanics, meaning the function of what would be heard.

My seating upon the Council has been in accordance with my wishes, because it is my desire to be able to bring to the table the assistance required by other creators for the form and function of their creations.

I First Became Aware at Level Seven

Can you tell me where you became aware of your existence?

I first became aware of the potential of a personality for myself at level seven, which has to do with the concordance of all precreation. This means that before anything that would become a raw material comes into a state of readiness to be transformed into a portion of someone's creation, it must pass through the level of concordance, wherein it develops a sympathetic vibration for all other material that will become a portion of creations. In this way, the material that is the building block has familiarity with other substances. Therefore, if it is combined with other substances, it will have enough familiarity that it will feel comfortable and able to accommodate such changes from its natural state of being.

I first became aware of my persona there. When I became aware, I was a three person: there were three separate personalities, of which I was one portion. We were what I would call a trinary creator. This was a little unusual in that we all three became aware of ourselves at the same moment we became aware of each other. This strongly suggested that we were either sent there by that which created or birthed us, or that we were left there. We remained as a trinary for a short time—in terms of experiential years no more than a thousand. Shortly after that experience ended, we went our separate ways. It makes sense, if you think about it, that a trinary creator would begin on level seven, since that is about concordance. It also makes sense if you consider that I would wish to be a part of some body of creators who not only must be in concordance, but also support the creation and bringing together of materials to create by others. This is when I became aware of myself.

Do you know who birthed you? Have you had any experience or contact with that being?

I have not, no, and curiosity is not a portion of my makeup. [Chuckles.] In this way, I am dissimilar to the human being.

How many levels do you know of?

I am aware of two more levels above that one. I am unclear of their function, but I am aware that they are there. I'm not clear what the levels that follow seven are for, because I went from seven directly to one. I did not pass through the levels in a way that one might explore, because remember, I am not curious. My expression of my personality took place and was going to take place entirely on level one, which is where I garnered my expertise. From my beginnings I seemed to have this expertise, which I suppose would suggest that that which birthed me may have contained that of which I am a portion.

Acquiring Wisdom on Level One

When I arrived on level one, I immediately proceeded to all places that incorporated the membranes and all places that were involved in the creation of tympanic sound, which I felt was the best way to become acquainted with auditory mechanics. I then spent the equivalent of about forty billion years of experiential time exploring these types of wisdom in order to qualify for the Council of Creators. Because I was aware of the Council from my beginning, it was my desire to participate in such a body, and I knew that the only way I could establish myself as a valuable member was to acquire some wisdom in perhaps an unusual area that would not be a normal wisdom of acquisition.

So you just knew that you were on the seventh level, and then on the first? And that you had this expertise?

From the moment I became aware of myself, I knew that there was an ability and innate wisdom present. I had a vast amount of knowledge, but not the selectivity to be able to apply that knowledge with wisdom. So when I got to level one, I sought out more experience in these areas so as to acquire the wisdom necessary to know when, how and where to discuss the knowledge.

From level seven you just can't look and see level one? How did you know it was there?

As far as I know in my discussions with the other creators, one can be aware of many levels, but it appears to be the case that if one is destined or planning (consciously or unconsciously) to go somewhere, no matter where you start out, you will be instantaneously (from the creator perspective) aware of the place you are going, and you will have the means to reach that place as quickly as you like.

Once I was prepared to leave level seven, it was practically an instantaneous voyage. In terms of experiential time, it took about three weeks, which is almost instantaneous, considering the absolutely unmeasurable distance in your terms.

Have you been aware of the other two parts of your trinary being since you got to level one?

Oh no; they had a different destiny. I don't even know where they are. [Chuckles.]

The Language of the Stars

Tell me some of the interesting experiences you had acquiring the wisdom, first with your auditory experiences.

The auditory mechanics. I was most interested at the beginning to go and listen to stars. Stars have the capacity to feed light and in some cases heat to other bodies (planets and spirits). In my experience (at least in level one), they all seem to make certain sounds. Even your little star here, your Sun, is very communicative with sounds. So I invested some significant time listening to stars. At first I thought the sounds were a celebration of their creation process, but I gradually came to realize that the sounds were a language, an actual means of communicating with other stars—not unlike what you might do in a network of communication. It appears that the sounds not only perform the function of communication, but also of hearing. Thus one can use sounds to not only "speak," but also to "hear." I found that very interesting, and I studied it for a time.

Now I have a pretty good understanding of the star language. It is not dissimilar to the language the angelics use, though with the angelics, the sounds are a little softer, more gentle and longer. The angelic sounds might go on for a time with a bit of a sing-songy effect, but with stars, many quick sounds make up what sounds like long sounds—a burst of noise, you might say, but in each burst are many, many little sounds or short sounds. The language is not linear but compound; one sound superimposed over another means a different thing than each sound separately would mean. I found that very fascinating, to explore the compounded star language.

Is it the same whether it's in our creation or at the other end of infinity in someone else's creation?

This is a very good question. Yes, and it is surprising. One might expect, certainly at higher or lower dimensions, a significant difference in the language. But it seems that regardless of dimension, there are only subtle differences. The star language appears to be identical no matter where you are. On level one and in higher or lower dimensions, there are differences, but only subtle ones—not major differences. This is quite different than language communicated by humanoid beings in different dimensions. Star language appears to be quite consistent in its nature.

How did you use it, then? Did you talk to the stars?

When I explored the stars, I could communicate with them without using their language because I was able to imitate their light pulses. The light pulses are not language to them; they are more of what you would call rhythms of the body, not unlike a pulse or a breath you might take. I was able to communicate, then, using the "pulsebeat" of light as a means of communication—such communication as was necessary, which was very little because stars are very comfortable with observers. Mostly it was just a polite greeting followed by the star's acknowledgment of my presence, and then I would observe. But there was not communication between us per se; I was there to study and learn.

The Sounds of Color and Humanoid Sounds

What are some other types of auditory communication that you studied?

I wished to experience the sound color makes when it refracts. Color, as it passes from place to place, reflects off various things, but it also refracts or transforms into different colors as a result of its contact.

It even deflects, creating a slightly different wavelength for the color. I was very interested in the sounds color makes as a result of this inter-action with its variation from wherever it is going. I spent a significant amount of time traveling with color—here, there and all over level one. This is what eventually introduced me to lots of different beings, life forms not unlike your own as well as some that are radically different.

That's when I began exploring humanoid sounds—sounds made for language or celebration, sounds made for communication, sounds even made for the purpose of being unheard or unseen. If you wish to remain unseen or unheard, you might make sounds of nature. You might feel yourself as a bird, taking note of where you are, perhaps sit-ting on a rock on the side of a hill with grass nearby. You would look at that, and as you made the bird sounds, you would see yourself as a bird, and the part of you that would be the bird would then be seen by other birds as that. The part of you that would still be physical might be seen by a passing human being as a rock or the grass or the tree or whatever was in the area. A sensitive person might see you as you are.

After that I spent some significant time studying the effect of such interactions between humanoids and the natural world around them. In this way I was exposed to many shamans—men, women, some indi-viduals of . . . in the case of some humanoids there are other versions; it's hard to put a word to it because they have no sexual function. I would say, for simplicity's sake, the third or fourth gender. This was interesting, because I would not only observe the tympanic interaction of the internal mechanisms to hear as well as their internal mechanisms to make sound, but also the sounds within their bodies and the sounds made by their auric fields inside and outside their bodies.

Sound and the Auric Field

The auric field has a constant sound; it is constantly calling for expe-riences and people and things and matter and substance and so on, in order to generate the experience that the soul personality needs or desires to have. At the same time, in response, it is also answering other soul personalities' auric fields as well as the soul personality fields of other energies (animals, plants, rocks, trees, elements and so on) that are generated by other beings who may require, at some point, the pres-ence of any human being.

Is this just in our creation, or is this typical everywhere you went?

It is typical that the auric field is in constant tympanic interaction with anything able to respond, in order to draw it to the individual or the individual to it. If that which responds is unable to come, its communication will still be available. You, for instance, may need to climb Mount Everest and be on the other side of the world. Mount Everest's tympanic field—meaning its auric field, seeking within its tympanic effect—is present everywhere, including at the other side of this level, to say nothing of the universe, should a being need to contact Mount Everest in another universe. Your auric field immediately contacts Mount Everest's auric field and communicates in a series of sounds that I can only reproduce or describe as a series of clicks—they sound like plucking the strings of a loose guitar inside a sphere of metal, kind of a hollow sound. Your auric field will communicate, "Are you available to receive this soul personality to climb on you? Do you accept the possibility?" The mountain will usually say yes, but if for some reason the mountain says no, then even if the person has a passionate desire to climb that mountain, it will never happen.

This is not only on a planet like ours, where we are in ignorance of the rest of ourselves, but this is on any planet where beings are totally open and accessible to themselves?

Yes, this communication is very complex. Even a conscious person—say a shamanic person who has been practicing and learning and studying and interacting on the path for forty years—even a person such as this, with all their acquired wisdom and openness, will for the most part have no more than five percent awareness at best of the communication they themselves are performing. The average individual might have one-hundredth of that.

And you can hear all of it?

Now, yes, but as a result of studying it, of acquiring an awareness of it. If you were to listen to it all at exactly the same moment, you would hear absolute and total silence. When completely combined, all these sounds completely balance each other, since they are naturally present in one place, and one hears nothing. But when you go to listen to each of them, each of the sounds is very distinctive, and you can listen to many of them together and hear them all. Yes, there are times when they might sound chaotic, but when you can listen to them all, as I can, then you would hear nothing. And listening to all these sounds at the same time and hearing nothing is the greatest experience of peace I have ever experienced in my entire existence. I do this sometimes to relax.

I'd recommend that you try it as an imaginary experience. Announce that you are open to such an experience. Sometimes sounds are easier to feel than to hear. In that sense, one can hear a cat purr, but one can also feel it purr.

My Experience with Membranes

Let's go to your other experiences, the experiences of the separation of one media from another.

The membranes, as it were. I studied this because I knew there would not be, at least when I arrived there, anybody else on the Council of Creators who would study such a thing, and should it be needed in the future, in terms of consulting, this would certainly be something unique that I could offer. I was quite certain that others would study or have knowledge of tympanic harmonics, so I wanted to be sure to bring something that would be not only uniquely my own, but a unique contribution. So that was part of the reason. Also, having the knowledge of it steered me in that direction; that is why I was enthusiastic to follow it. I did not have to go to all places on level one, but since I was already doing this for tympanic harmonies, I took advantage of it.

As a sound moves forward, the space that separates the sound from the place where the sound has not gone yet is also a membrane. So I was able to combine the work a little bit then. Anyplace where I would find any membrane, I would go into the membrane to fully experience it, to understand it, to appreciate what it could do and, most important, to appreciate what it could *not* do. In the beginning I did not realize the importance of that, but I discovered in my explorations and studies that membranes are usually very singular, meaning that they will do one thing or perhaps even two things, but usually no more than that. They will do those things very well, but they will not have any capacity to do anything else. So they are highly specialized.

On every level, whether it's the skin of a human or the skin of the universe, you're saying? The skin of a drum or a circle of light or . . .

Yes, or a separation. For instance, as a beam of light comes out from the Sun, if you could slow it down and see it spreading out, you would notice that in front of it the dark would seem to be illuminated. In reality, the light comes forward, and there's a membrane between the light and the dark. The membrane is to protect the dark, because that which is not illuminated in that moment needs to have a means by which it can gradually accommodate the light so that it is not shocked. If the membrane were not there, the dark would be converted permanently to light and there would never be any dark in the future.

So membranes are often essential to preserve that which is apparently, in your world, commonplace. Very often membranes serve to protect; certainly they serve to separate, but protection is a very typical function. Another typical function might be to nurture. For instance, the skin of your body is very often nurtured by the warmth of the Sun, and the skin enjoys that heat and for a time, at least, enjoys the heat of the Sun. Then it knows when it is time to cover up or have some coolness. The membrane of your skin, well explored by your scientists, even though it seems to be so physiologically complex, really performs only two functions: one, to separate and protect; the other to nurture and sustain.

Well, who puts the membrane between the light and the dark? The dark or the light themselves? Or did they each separate part of themselves to create it?

It was created. Is it not magnificent to realize that someone created that? Someone created the membranes; someone created everything, in my experience. There is nothing that exists on its own without having been created by something else. In my experience, this is the one truism I am aware of.

Who created the first membrane, the first division?

I am not aware of that, and the reason I am not aware of it is that I'm not curious.

But because this has been put into creation, any creator can use that principle in his creation?

Yes; or if that creator has some difficulty, it could apply a membrane in some way to see if the difficulty, whatever it is, can be solved through the use of any kind of membrane.

The Membrane between Ignorance and Awareness

To give you an idea of the range of such things, do you know that there is a membrane that exists between ignorance and awareness? Let's say you are driving, looking for street signs, hoping to find Main Street. You are driving and driving, and suddenly you see a sign that says Main Street. Beforehand, you had the hope, and there is a membrane between the awareness and the hope.

There is also a membrane between ignorance and awareness in general. Someone can explain a new philosophy to you, and as you're learning it the membrane is pulsing and interacting, sometimes opening up and letting in vast amounts of knowledge, sometimes closing if it's too much. You know, sometimes you will be very interested in something, and you will glean a great deal of knowledge by reading a book about that. Then years later you might read the book again and glean more knowledge, because you hadn't had time to assimilate the first level of that knowledge. You read exactly the same book and discover, much to your amazement, that a second level of knowledge is in that book; you just didn't understand it before.

Or someone is telling you something, on and on—like I'm doing now! [Laughs.] You can hear as much as you can hear, and if you get to the point of overload, you don't really assimilate it anymore. At that moment the membrane has closed, because it knows you have taken in all you can. Even though your cognitive mind is attempting to take in more, the membrane will prevent it. This is usually perceived as a difficulty in awareness or persistent ignorance or, to put it simply, "I can't understand." But in reality you are being protected, because you've taken in as much as you can at the moment, and you need to have time or experience to assimilate it so that you will be ready to take in more. The membranes exist everywhere, for every conceivable and inconceivable experience.

So you studied level one for forty billion years. Then what did you do? Did you create something?

No; then I reported to the Council of Creators to say, "Here I am! Can I be of some use?" And they said, "Oh, yes." I was welcomed right away, and I thought that my knowledge of membranes would be the welcoming factor, but in the beginning it was entirely about harmonic tympany.

There wasn't any need for such consulting for a great deal of time. The other creators' reaction, when they became aware of my wisdom, first was like, "Tympanic harmonies! Oh, very good!", then "Membranes, whaaat?"

Creators of Harmonic Universes

What were some of your first consultings? Before we ever get to our creation, what were some of the things you did on the Council?

Very early on I was approached by creators who wished to create universes that were in total harmony in all aspects so that a planet, for instance, would be in such harmony with the beings who lived on it that there would be no secrets between the planet and that being. Every step the beings took, every breath they took, everything they did, would be in complete rhythmic harmony with whatever was going on for the planet. Equally, every energy, every interaction, every flow, every sound the planet created would be in complete harmony with every person on the planet. In the beginning I had several creators approach me about that, because they were interested in the tympanic harmonies that would be involved on the totally conscious level. They desired beings who did not have any need whatsoever for an unconscious, beings who would be totally conscious, in this way creating a universe that a being could incarnate into in order to experience great variety *and* absolute unity within that variety. There are many universes like this, and as a matter of fact, it is such a popular experience that it came to be predominant after a while. This is why a universe like your own, which has some discordant elements, was viewed in the beginning and at various times throughout this creation, not exactly aghast, but sometimes with barely disguised disapproval.

Harmony became so popular with creators that the idea of purposely creating discordance for the purpose of growth was considered to be, by many creators, a giant step off the path. You would say a big step backward, but it wasn't even backward; it was just off the path from their perspective. This is because there are so many creations in total harmony.

That's what I did in the beginning, and I was involved in a great deal of consultation there. Later on, as time went on and that type of universe became more established, creators would not come to the Council for such advice; they would simply spend time in that creation to observe it, then reproduce it with their own particular aspects and focuses. That kind of harmony is probably why there are as many creators as there are today (within the context of time here), because that kind of universe is such a pleasure to create and experience, not only by the creator of that universe, but by all beings within it. Many beings wished to be creators so that they could have the joy of the creation as well as the experience of it.

I believe that this is probably what prompted the population explosion in creators. Now that your Creator has done what It has done, I do not expect in the near future many more discordant universes. But I will expect a creator to look at an average discomforting experience on Earth, then take one ten-millionth of that energy and apply it in some totally isolated aspect or portion of a universe to see what happens. Consider a typical discomforting experience, not extreme—for instance, being held up in traffic, something that is discomforting but commonplace, one ten-millionth of that. You have to understand that most creators love the joy of absolute concordance or absolute harmony.

Membranes Allow Creation of Variety and Separation

When did you first become aware of the idea for this creation? Did you see it as that string they talk about?

No, no. I did not become aware of this universe until it was already in the construction stage. Your Creator had already arrived at the space in which It would build Its universe and was there with all of Its consultants and so on. It had already begun creating galaxies. I believe your Creator's desire to experiment with separation became more of a factor. When your Creator wished to experiment with separation, which was probably a precursor to experimenting with individuality as you know it to be, that's when your Creator consulted with me.

It is possible, you understand, for a creator on the Council of Creators to consult, and the other creators wouldn't know what's going on if they don't need to, because they are always responsible for so many things. It is very possible that your Creator consulted with the Council before that, but I did not need to know that. So I was not aware until then, and then I advised your Creator on membranes. The knowledge of tympanic harmonies was already sufficiently available to your Creator, so that did not come up. But the knowledge of membranes was something that your Creator was not particularly familiar with. We then had a significant experience of shared wisdom so that your Creator could build Its vision of the separate individual. This was an essential element in your Creator's idea (some would say *idea fixé,* to use the French) of having beings separated rather than in harmony, which was the Explorer Race experience. So we had a lot of communication for a while.

In your universe, everything has separation, because once your Creator became aware of the value of membranes, It could then see how that could be utilized to engage variety in a most tolerable way. You understand, there are some things that are by their very nature absolutely intolerant of each other. Let me give you an easily understood example: When hot lava from a volcano strikes water, the water that is struck is converted to steam. So one might say that liquid water (and also frozen water) is incompatible with hot lava; one might also say that it is not only the science of the change of temperature and so on that protects the rest of the water from being traumatized so that the entire ocean doesn't turn into steam, but also the membrane that functions to separate the two.

Say how that works.

Picture the lava coming out of the volcano on any island in the sea, flowing out as it builds up the island's mass. When the ocean is struck by the lava, which is very hot even by the time it gets there, the initial reaction of the water it touches is shock, not unlike shock would strike a human being. As you know, shock for a human being is deadly as a physiological experience. Your body goes through many stages of shock, and with the proper first aid, one survives the experience. Liquid water, by its very nature, is totally incompatible with heat above the boiling point. So you find that liquid water is incompatible with anything above 212 degrees. When I say incompatible, I do not simply mean that it is a scientific observation that the water turns to steam and then condenses, later to become water. I don't mean that; I mean it can't even be in the same universe with that heat without a membrane to protect it. When your Creator realized that membranes could function as a means to slow down the experience of that shock of initial contact of this hot substance with liquid water, It realized that many beings who would otherwise be entirely incompatible might even occupy the same planet.

For example, those beings called insects, such as the crawling ones—even beautiful butterflies—are by their very nature entirely incompatible with all humanoids. However, we have a membrane of energy we can call the auric field, which functions as a membrane, to say nothing of the physiological membrane of the skin and so on. The human has skin, and that is a membrane; the auric field, as it is very close to the skin, becomes denser and functions as a membrane. When these things are present, these beings we are calling insects can be in the same world. When I say the same world, you understand, I mean the same universe as humans or humanoids.

When your Creator discovered what could be done with membranes, I can only say It was thrilled. Your Creator loves variety; and coming here to this creation, It desired to have as much variety as possible. But in the beginning, before I consulted . . . consultants, as you know, are usually called upon after something has been done and isn't working the way you'd like it to. So your Creator had begun, and things weren't working. Your Creator would create something and it would literally flee the universe. Your Creator couldn't understand why something It was creating would just flee. Your Creator felt It was creating it, yet it would flee beyond your Creator's creation, and your Creator could not understand that. That is because it was intolerant of something else in the universe.

How did He know about you?

Just to be as a creator, all creators know about the Council of Creators. Your Creator did not know about me; It consulted with the Council of Creators and explained Its problem, saying, "Is there someone who can help me?" They said, "Yes, we have someone who is just right." And that's when I consulted at length with your Creator about membranes. Oh, your Creator was so happy! Because then Its creation could have all manner of what would normally be entirely incompatible beings. Think about it: You have Earth and the Explorer Race here doing positive and negative things, yet not that far away in celestial terms you've got other galaxies, even other planets in your own galaxy where there is great harmony, not a whisper or an echo of anything discomforting. How could such things possibly exist in the same universe if there weren't very functional, useful and strong membranes to completely protect these entirely positive, loving beings from exposure to any manner of discomfort?

So the veil was a primary . . .

The veils are membranes.

That's what I'm saying, it was a primary one . . .

Certainly, and it started out with the simple things. But your Creator gained fast on the uptake, as you say, and was very quick to realize what could be done. Your Creator very quickly realized that this is how the Explorer Race could manifest with all of its lessons with the rest of the universe remaining entirely safe. When the Explorer Race was going to happen, your Creator was originally going to make what would be like an auxiliary to Its creation. But once the awareness of membranes and their capacity and application became known to your Creator, then your Creator was very happy to see that It would not have to create something separate, but something entirely within the creation It was involved in.

So you came back frequently then, because he kept running up against new incompatibilities.

I didn't have to come back; I stayed linked for a long time, until your Creator completely understood the application of membranes. Then we were not linked anymore and I let go.

At that time you still didn't know the level of discomfort that was being created here. How did you feel about that when you found out?

[Chuckles.] Believe it or not, until this very moment I really didn't know. Not until we started our conversation, because I have not had any reason to be in contact with your Creator for the past few million years.

Membranes Are Essential to the Explorer Race

So now that you're here and you're sort of tapping into it, you're not curious?

I'm not curious, exactly! [Laughs.] So I did not have the need to know, but now that I am aware of it, I can see why membranes were essential. As a matter of fact, if you did not have good membranes around each of your physical bodies—not only the skin, but the density of your auric field up against your skin (your auric field still interpenetrates your body, but it creates a denser level near your skin)—you certainly couldn't exist, either. No human being could without that level of membrane. No immortal personality, no soul, could possibly tolerate discomfort to the level of, say—let's draw it as a figure [draws], I don't know the word for this—a normal ability to assimilate discomfort without such membranes. This would be a natural ability compared to

$$\frac{1}{1,000,000,000,000}$$

the ability you have now, which I believe is sometimes forty-seven percent. But then there are moments when an individual might be ninety percent immersed in something entirely awful, perhaps for a few minutes, as long as it does not go on for hours and hours. Without membranes, you could not possibly tolerate that. You would not just die as you know it, but you would evacuate the universe!

Is an auric field a common thing everywhere, or is it just because we need it here?

It is not absolutely a rule in level one. Sometimes, as a matter of fact, one might have an inverse auric field; instead of something radiating outward, you might have a function that attracts inward only. As a portal, your personal need would be to have beings, thoughts, ideas, everything, pass through you. If they did not pass through you, you would be so unfulfilled that after a time you would simply dissolve and become a portal elsewhere. Commonly speaking, in your world a portal might be a doorway, and as such it is unfulfilled unless people are passing through it. So you might, in that case, have a being who does not have an auric field as you know it but is entirely feminized. It would be polarized to the feminine, which is not what you experience here for a feminine being. A feminine being here is not polarized to the feminine; a polarized feminine being would be entirely receptive, one hundred percent. A portal would be polarized to the feminine, entirely receptive—without having beings or anything pass through it, it could not exist. It would be fulfilled by that passage.

So the auric field is something you helped or taught the Creator to make?

No, your Creator was very familiar with auric fields, but It did not understand the denser pattern of the auric field. The auric field is typical to a lot of places—your own Creator has one. The auric field becomes denser as it approaches closer to the skin of the body or the essence of a thing or idea. If we could magnify the membrane between the lava and the water, we would discover that the densest portion of that membrane would be where it touches the lava and the least dense would be where it touches the water. You may not quite understand that. In the case of the human being, it's a little different, because as you touch other things, as the auric field goes away from you, it broadens and becomes more spread out; but as it comes toward you it becomes denser, in order to protect you.

In the case of the lava and the water, is the lava extruding this membrane, or is water creating it in reaction to the lava?

No. The water exists beyond this level. The water is given the membrane in a given creation. In another creation or even in another part of this creation, you might very easily have fire that burns within water. As long as it is a perfectly benevolent place where there is no discomfort, you might have fire that burns in water without discomfort to the water. The water does not turn to steam and the fire is not quenched, so both things would be completely compatible. But in a place such as Earth where you are now, where discomfort is the rule and not the exception, the water would be terribly discomfited and incompatible with the fire. So the membrane performs the function of protection; it doesn't stop the water from turning into steam (which actually touches the lava) but slows it down enough to prevent shock. If the membrane weren't there, whenever lava touched any water, *all water on the planet* would instantly turn to steam and remain so.

Is the membrane granted by the spirit of the water? Where did it come from? How was it created?

It is provided by your Creator.

Ah! In that instant it's needed.

In the instant it's needed, but in its natural state in a benevolent environment. Although there might be a membrane, it would be designed to bring things together, as it were, like shaking hands compared to hands pushing away from each other.

My Later Experiences on the Council

After you worked with this Creator, what are some of the other things you have done on the Council? What are some job descriptions?

The Council is such that we do not have meetings and sit around and tell stories, like meetings where you are. It is more that we are available. Many of the creators on the Council have functioning creations with which they are interacting, and at the same time they are sitting on the Council. I am one of the exceptions, in that the Council is all I do. If at any given moment my services are not needed, I listen to all sounds of this level and am in complete peace.

You no longer desire to go out and study anymore? You don't travel and look around?

Let's put it this way: Forty billion years was enough! [Laughs.]

Do you have anything you want to do?

Oh, I am doing what I want to do. Even you can appreciate this. If you have a hard day at work and are very tired, you come home and have a good meal. It tastes wonderful, you have some affection with your cat and that's fun, then you go to bed for a good night's sleep. You appreciate all three of those things much more because you had a hard day at work—not necessarily a miserable day, but a long, strenuous day. I enjoy the pleasure of the peace, but I also enjoy the contrast of the consulting.

To continue that analogy, I'm always looking forward to something tomorrow. There's something I want to do, there's something more. But you don't think that way.

Well, I'm not veiled, for starters. You are that way because you are veiled, though you know innately at the deepest levels. And for you, very much consciously, something is missing, so you are constantly attempting to acquire more, to have pieces of what's missing. I am not veiled, plus I am not curious. I went out to do this not because I was curious, but to acquire wisdom.

So you still consult on these two specialties?

Yes, that's what I do specifically. And I remember another one where the creator was involved in creating a life form not unlike insect beings here, but they were full-sized beings. There was some difficulty. Insects on your world have exoskeletons, but these beings weren't like that. They had exoskeletons, but there was a disharmony in the sounds the exoskeletons would make when even the parts of the person's own body would bump into other parts. And there was an overwhelming disharmony when the individuals reacted with each other, which, in this particular civilization on this particular planet, was an impossible situation, since the beings, not unlike you, had to come together to reproduce. It was also creating a miserable experience for the beings themselves. The creator of those beings was very upset by this and was prepared to uncreate it and forget it. But before it did that, as a last resort it consulted with the Council, and the Council referred it to me when it was understood that sound was a factor. I went there and was able to suggest that what was missing for these beings was continuity. They needed to have something not unlike a webwork or net that covered their entire being. Even though the exoskeleton was there, there needed to be something that completely united them. If you looked at it, it would look like a net. Although it wouldn't feel bumpy like a net, you could look at it and say, "Oh, that looks like a net on your skin." When they had that, it was like a unifying circuit, which created continuity not only for the individual, but also between individuals. This was a good feeling to have suggested that. The creator applied it, and immediately the beings were comfortable and comforted, and the creation could go on and establish itself, which it has done.

You don't go out and study anymore, but you keep solving these problems and you learn from each one. Are you ever faced with a problem for which you don't have the answer, so you connect with something beyond you that knows?

No. Remember, curiosity performs a function; it is not just simply an existence. Curiosity helps you get from someplace to another place. Since I do not have curiosity, I get personal pleasure helping. But I have to say that I do not get something from the experience. I can either help them or I can't; I have not had the experience of being unable to help any creator so far on this level. I'd have to say that according to my experience, I am not acquiring wisdom anymore, nor do I have to go to anyone to acquire wisdom. I have acquired the wisdom I need to perform my function.

What I was getting at was the sense that you've had this wisdom from someplace or someone. You became aware . . .

When I became aware I had knowledge, not wisdom. Wisdom has to do with application; knowledge has to do with information. So whatever created the trinary being that I was a portion of was apparently imbued with that knowledge, and my understanding is that the other portions of my trinary being had that knowledge also but went somewhere else.

Almost everyone I've talked to so far could always look to someone beyond them who was there for guidance. For the one who birthed them there was a connection through which they could sometimes get something.

Yes, but you understand, in my experience I have not needed to do that, so I cannot relate to what you are saying. I *know* what you are saying; I understand it. But as a portion of my personal experience, I cannot identify with it. I have not needed to do so.

Homework: Find Your Auric Membrane

The Explorer Race people are here. What would you like to say to them, what do they need to know? What can you share with them?

What I'd say is this: Know that you are very often asking for protection, those of you who are sometimes in frightening situations—police officers, soldiers, prisoners, children at school, cave explorers, people with new experiences. When you are asking to be protected, see if you can find that membrane; it's just outside your skin in an infinitesimal measurement. If I had to put a fraction on it, it would be about one-hundredth of an inch beyond your skin, where the membrane of your auric field is densest. Go into that as a meditation, or ask to be able to feel the great strength and protection associated with that membrane throughout your physical body. It will probably help support your courage and continuity. It will also help you feel more at peace with whatever adventure life brings you, and it will help you appreciate life, something that is not always easy to do.

Thank you very, very much for coming here and doing this.

You are most welcome, and on that note I will say good night.

I say good night to you and to the readers as well.

Specialist in Sound Duration

January 13, 1998

Explanation from Unknown Member of Council

You will note that many of the creators on the Council will give their frame of reference to their existence with colors or sounds or experiences or feelings that are rather brief—not blunt, but very specific in what they have done, what they do or what they have been doing. This is not unusual for the Council of Creators, which I occasionally sit in on. Very often creators have a natural tendency to blend with other creators when they are together. Thus what would be, for instance, the pieces of a jigsaw puzzle scattered about on a table, would—when they are aware of each other's presence and involved in a single duty such as an issue being dealt with by the Council—completely blend together as one so that individual experiences as a creator would interlock with individual experiences of other creators, making a more complete being. You will rarely have a council meeting where there isn't a fairly thorough representation of sufficient activities of creationism, so that this expertise can be applied to whatever the problem is. You won't have a board of high-powered individuals ruling or advising about something for which they have no experience. It is one thing to know about something, but it is, as you know, completely another thing to have personally experienced it. One can know about something, and it is an abstract thing; but to have personally experienced it makes it a completely different thing. That is why the Council feels it must be packed with representatives who have intimate experience with the things upon which they will be advising; that's why there is an ebb and flow on the board. Sometimes, depending on the issue being discussed, certain experiences will be unnecessary in terms of input to the body of the Council; other times, other experiences will be necessary. And even though the representatives at any given moment number from 187 to 200, within that number, other than the thirteen core members you will hear from, all the others might ebb and flow. Even the next ring of twenty-five or so might not be there for some discussions if their intimate experience is not necessary for a particular issue. That is my comment so far. Good night.

Good night, thank you very much.

Specialist in Sound Duration
I am the creator who is experiencing and is reasonably expert in sounds—not sounds in terms of their octaves, but in terms of their duration. This is my field.

When I became conscious of myself, I was not localized; I became conscious of an overall sense of personality in many different dimensions, different universes, different realms, at the same moment. I do not know of another creator on the Council with this experience. At that period, my cognizance of self was very involved in a universal counterpart.

The reference to sound means its duration: Maybe it lasts for a moment, maybe it is ongoing, maybe it is superimposed over many other sounds, but it is a sound or a multiple sound. Perhaps I came to be aware of myself in so many different places because different sounds are more common in many different places. I believe that before I became aware of my universalized personality, I was very individualized and fragmented, with different parts of my personality in different places. But then I began to have a feeling of a harmony associated with the multilevel experience of self—a sense, as it were, of a concordance of being.

This particular experience, then, caused me to wish to unite all the pieces. So even though I was involved in every level from this level to the ninth, and also in a level that I would call, for the sake of simplicity, minus one [chuckles], there was within me, not unlike the personality of any being, a great desire to have all of myself in one place that could be of some purpose and value, some contribution and value that others could benefit from.

I came to be aware that the Council of Creators would be forming on level one and inquired through another, "Might I be of some assistance?" And my assistance was welcomed as a core member, causing me to feel very needed, which is an energy that motivates me more than any other. Therefore, I made as speedily as possible a transit with all my parts moving toward the centralized location of coming together within the Council of Creators, so I actually merged as one being *within* the Council.

This happened quickly in terms of your time—in about a quarter of a second of measured linear time as you now experience it. But to me it seemed to take forever, because the motion that would be measured at a quarter of a second was the first experience I ever had of time at all. I had never had anything that involved such an experience; it was entirely new, so what would be no time to you was like an eon of experience to me. Regardless, I took up residence in the Council of Creators and I have been here ever since.

Sound Guarantees Manifestation

So my expertise lies exclusively within sound, not so much the different sounds, but the way sounds come together to form other sounds. You would say, perhaps, it is the component parts of sound, but it is more complex than that. Did you know, for example, that if you were in a universe without any apparent materializations, if you had sound, that materialization would be guaranteed? Materialization cannot happen, in my experience, without sound.

I have been in places all over, yes. And I have noted that in places where there is no sound, there is much more likely, in my experience always, to be no materialization, including no passage of anything material through the area. This means that even a spirit, even a personality in transit, is extremely unlikely to pass through an area where there is no sound whatsoever. One might say, "Well, it is possible to create a chamber within which there is no sound by the use of equipment," and so on, but it is the equipment that creates the lack of sound or absorbs the sound. I'm talking about a place where there is no need to absorb sound, where there is no sound whatsoever.

I'm also then suggesting that with the right combination of sounds— not necessarily adjusted for tone but rather for duration and association with the duration of other tones, and equally, durations and then gaps and then short or long durations—it is possible to manifest anything, including feelings and whole universes with complex beings. Sound is, in my experience, an absolute foundational tool to manifested creation everywhere.

Once I Became Aware

What were some of your experiences after becoming aware? Were you simply conscious of everything new, or did you go out and look?

I never went out to look; I started out [chuckles] being *out*. Then I became aware of myself, and then I came together. In order to come together I had to move through all these places, all these different levels, allowing for the journey. A part of me was on the ninth level, and in moving that part from the ninth level to the first level—just that part—going through all the levels, I could hear, absorb, know, understand, master and have the capacity to reproduce all the durations of sound and superimposed sounds on *all* the levels. Even though I did not have a significant portion of myself on level seven, I nevertheless know and understand level seven, soundwise. I had some bit of myself there, but it was so small that I think it was more of a representative bit. I don't have the sense of personal identification with that level that I do with the other levels.

Were these parts of yourself that were all over, individual personalities?

I do not think so! That is why I was very surprised. It was as if I became aware. It would be as if you became aware of another identical you existing someplace far away from where you are, a self that was so much like you that if the two of you stood together to face each other, you would become one being out of the sheer love of it, because you would not be able to hold the separation. The identicalness would be so much of an intimacy that you would embrace the other you.

It was this way of becoming aware; I believe on the personal level that if I had not focused to join the Council of Creators on this level, I still would have had to join something somewhere, because once I became aware of all of these different parts, I *had* to join them.

That is incredible! And of course your skill is the very thing that creators need; they cannot create without it.

Sound Duration Permeates This Creation

In my experience, I do not know a creator who has created anything without it. In this creation, for example, your Creator uses such sound duration at a basic level. Every single particle, every molecule and every atom that come together to form some larger mass and participate in a feeling, a thought or a melody, all use sound duration. Your Creator at this level was so enamored with this that It used this in every step of the universe He has created.

One finds this to greater or lesser degrees in different creations, but in this creation it is so permeated as an experience that I believe your Creator decided to make it such an intimate part of life here that there would be a means—a medium, if you would—to deliver a message from one side of this universe to the other that would allow instantaneous application of wisdom regardless of the distance involved. This is done through the codification of sound duration.

Yes, it is the tones, but it is not *only* the tones involved in creation and uncreation or creation and re-creation of different elements to create different things—thoughts, feelings, objects. When you become conscious of that and are able to manipulate that on your own, you will then be able to activate this as a principle in your life. When you as a society are able to do that, everyone in this universe will come to visit you immediately. That exact skill is recognized as the application and arrival of any race of beings to the spiritual club, as it were, meaning that once you are doing this, it is totally understood by all beings that you could not do this unless you are living the spiritual life—not just talking about it or thinking about it, but actually living it.

When you are actually living it, then everyone will come to see you; it won't be just people who look like you, but people who look completely different than you. But this is acceptable, you understand, because by that time you will be so integrated spiritually that you will welcome beings who look completely different than you. You will welcome it. It will be pleasure, it will be variety; and one thing that is cherished more than anything else by beings as they are becoming more and more spiritual is variety. This is because as you become more spiritual, you conceive of similarities between all things, and when you see the similarities you realize how everything is a portion of everything else. Yes, that is a step on the spiritual path. But when you are suddenly confronted with something that is entirely new within that path, it is exciting, it is wonderful, it is something new to your variety—and then you can apply and learn and assimilate this new thing. So the idea of having beings come from far away that are completely new to you would be exciting, very exciting.

When do you see that? After we're in the fourth dimension?

I think it is more likely to happen when you are in the fifth. The fourth dimension is essential for you, because it is a bridge between the world of struggle that you are in now and the world of mastery. So the fourth dimension is a refinement, a weeding out. It will glean the best of the experience in the third dimension, for application in the fourth dimension, and release that which does not apply anymore to the spiritual life. In the fourth dimension, you will also apply that which might not have been considered by you before to be spiritual, but which you have discovered in your re-creation of yourselves here on your third-dimensional Earth school. You will have the opportunity to literally be able to discover something new that you can apply to spirituality as you know yourself to be.

Then, having something new, you will apply that and practice it in the fourth dimension and see how it works, because the fourth dimension will still have (as you will experience it) just enough discomfort that you will know if something does not work, but it will not be a catastrophe. In this way you will have the opportunity to fine-tune. Once you are in the fifth dimension (which will not take very long after the fine-tuning), you will have this great experience with sound and its duration and capacities.

Sound Limits the Duration of Your Universe!

Have you interacted with our Creator, and if so, how?

I've interacted with your Creator. Your Creator stopped by the Council now and then. It is possible for a creator to not exactly leave its creation, but extend a portion of itself beyond its creation to come to the Council. Your Creator came by when It was just coming up to the space where It would begin Its creation. It left all Its friends there in the space, came to the Council and said, "Do you have any means that could expedite my creation, because I do not feel the need that my creation last indefinitely; it is only intended to last for a measured time of experience, and then it can either choose on its own to create immortality for itself as a creation or else move elsewhere in whole or in part." This is not the normal comment by a creator; most creators create something with the intention of its being immortal. This Creator wanted to create something that was temporal—very unusual to have a temporal creation, so it got our attention. Creator wanted to be able to speed up the process [chuckles] (perhaps this is where you all get your impatience) so that It would be able to bring you through the process without having to linger, because suffering would be involved in your learning experience and your Creator did not want you to have to linger in such experience any longer than was absolutely essential.

Since the Council as a body was less than excited about this creation, any opportunity to help your Creator make this something more temporal and less immortal was considered a plus. So I suggested to build into the sound and duration enough harmony that it would be able to sustain itself for only a specific time. If this Creator or you or perhaps someone that follows you does not change something within a given specific amount of time, it is like a birthing of a discordant sound duration that will act to cancel out the foundational elements of the manifesting qualities of sound duration. In this way the universe, without any input by any creator to the opposite, would decompose. .
Uncreate itself?

Yes, uncreate itself, not unlike the decomposition of any life form now. This is what your Creator did. This is why every aspect of the creation is coded with that experience and perhaps why your Creator felt it was necessary to have that codified within the tiniest particle. Thus, any particle that becomes involved in this universe knows going into the experience that their freedom (meaning their desire to move on to another universe) is guaranteed at some time in the future. Most particles, when they enter a universe, might stay there forever, but particles entering *this* universe will most often come (at least they have in the past) because they have not chosen where to be forever. Should a choice ever be made to make this place immortal, then particles will have a choice whether to leave or to stay.

But to become immortal would require either that the Explorer Race as a creator, or whoever they create, change the duration of the sound?

Exactly.

I Became Aware of Myself as a Fragmented Being

Do you have any sense that you were created by someone or something? Is there anything you ever look to as something you came from?

I do not. Because I became aware of myself as a fragmented being, I cannot say I am from here or from there.

You're from everywhere?

I feel like I am from everywhere, yes. I feel like that, and as a result I do not have a sense of home other than all the places I have been.

You have personal experiences as yourself in these multitudinal places. Were they separated individuals, encapsulated humans, great lights and spirits, or what?

All of the above. A portion of myself, when I became aware of this personality, was a lightbeing that was not humanoid. But if you were to look at it now, you would say, "This is someone!" You understand? So all these bits came together to form what I am now.

That is so amazing! So you coalesced at the Council of Creators. You have not actually, as this unified being, created a creation or a universe?

No, I have not.

But you have the experience of everyone who ever did, right?

I have the knowledge of it, but more than that, before I became aware of all my individual pieces, each piece was involved in an activity, and that activity was listening to and at times reproducing the duration of sound. It's as if when I became aware of all my different parts, I became aware that not only were my different parts in different places, but my different parts were all doing the same thing in these different places. That is how I have knowledge of all these different places, even though as a unified being I have not traveled there. But my parts were there, you see. It is amazing; it is like discovering that you're like twins or triplets or something, but many times over, and that everybody is doing the same job! It's very exciting!

Can you still feel out into the other levels?

I do not have to feel; I remember. In my expertise, being in the moment is more valuable to me than being where I was when I was. I was able to understand the function of these other places as any being would understand the function of the world he or she is living upon out of necessity. The function of this world upon which you are living is to support life forms and give you what you need—the air you breathe, the water you drink and so on that you all have in common, whether you are an ant or a woman.

How many levels are there in your understanding?

I'm familiar with thirty-three levels. It is possible that it goes beyond that, but I have not been able to see beyond that.

Does that include the minus one?

Level Minus One

It is not really minus one, but I am calling it that because it is a simple way. To be more elaborate, I would say that if you were to take a mirror and make a box with a mirrored inside but not put anything in the box, and if you projected yourself inside the box, you would notice that the mirrors were struggling, as reflective devices, to reflect something that could be reflected one way. But because the box has six sides and they're all mirrored, it is not possible to reflect something only one way. The bias is to reflect something one way; for instance, if you stand in front of a mirror to adjust your hat, that is a one-way reflection. The mirror has a bias to reflect it one way, from the mirror back to the viewer. But in a box with all these other mirrors, the one-way reflection is not possible, yet the bias is present. That is the best way I can describe level minus one, which is why I've just called it minus one. If you give it some thought, you can fall into that thought and go around and around with it for a long time without actually being able to grab a solid definition. Yet it is an intriguing philosophy, because it demands constant motion whereas the desire for stability is overwhelming. Think about that; it is easier to describe in feelings than it is in thoughts.

It sounds like a paradoxical universe that you can't think about; you can feel it, but you can't think about it.

Yes, you can't think about it; you will not be able to *stop!* It is almost like a machine that you start; you want it to stop, but it won't—you have to reach over and stop it. The mirror on the inside of the box wants to reach over and stop the other mirrors from reflecting, but all the mirrors in the box must do what they do even if they are uncomfortable doing it.

Is there a purpose for this level that we can understand?

Oh yes, a very good purpose: It *demands* motion. And in my experience, if these beings wish to be fixed and are rigidly in place, it is possible to be a fixed, rigid being and exist on level one with very little growth. Even on Earth it is possible, as a being, to do that. And Earth is such a commanding planet of education on level one, you understand?

I use this for an example. But if you are taken to minus level one, you *must* grow. You must! You will have a bias to remain still, but you will not be able to. You will be forced to move, and therefore it is a terrible struggle in the beginning. It is awful; you wish to be still. It is like the landlover on a ship: "Stop!" says the landlover, "Stop!" But the ocean says, "I must move! You are on me, so *you* must move!" It is not dissimilar to that. But everything is moving, not just . . .

Are there any creations there?

There are not too many creations as you know it. There's mostly a state of being where one is forced out of even the most delightful state of being that one has ever chosen to attain over lifetimes; one must move on. On all the levels I have been—level one through level thirty-three—it is very possible to find at least one, and usually many, many beings who will have achieved some state of being so wonderful that they do not wish to leave it, not unlike the nirvana state. Nothing you can offer them or suggest to them, even in terms of growth (which all souls desire), will shake them from wishing to stay in this space. If their teachers feel that they must move so they can become more, then level minus one is a last resort.

It sounds almost like you're sent there and don't choose to go.

You do not choose to go; most beings do not choose to go. When you are done on level minus one, you are thrilled for having gone there, because everything else you experience on levels one through thirty-three is almost to the nth degree that much better.

But it's not something that anyone in our level on our Earth has ever experienced, right?

I do not think that any of you as individuals have experienced this, but it is possible that there are some portions of combined beings now here as fragmented individuals who may have had some experience there. As a matter of fact, it is perhaps valuable that there are some beings like that here, because those beings would have one character trait that is very distinguishable amongst all the races of beings on this planet: they would be the likely beings to encourage growth. This would take the form of the being who would "stir the pot," though not necessarily to the delight of those around them.

The Sound of Love

What is your greatest delight right now?

That a good question, not something I am often asked. My greatest delight is in observing the superimposed sound durations that are present at the moment—the exact moment—of mutually discovered love between individuals.

Sounds?

Not sounds, but durations of sounds. This is such a magnificent experience that if I were ever to be accused by any other creator of being nirvana-like for a moment, it would be my pleasure in this, though I do not dwell in it [chuckles]. But when it happens anywhere, I am aware of it. It is perhaps one of the pleasures of being myself; I am aware of it. So love, when first noticed anywhere, does not escape me.

But you feel it; it's not just a sound, you feel it, right?

It's a feeling, always a feeling first. Usually the sounds I notice, in terms of duration, are like the tools to uncover the duration. But the duration itself is something I feel. One might listen to any sounds as they are made [bangs on chair]—I'm making sounds here of rhythmic duration, listening to the sound itself as a means to discover the duration of the sounds. So the sound itself is the means of analysis to discover the duration. Duration means as long as it lasts, yes? So, the sound itself [bangs again], any sound, yes? This sound is only a tool one would use, just as the scientist notices the color of something but the color is not the thing the scientist is looking for. It is like, "Oh, this thing is now in this stage because it is this color."

Do you have any desires to do anything, to go anywhere? Is there anything you look forward to?

With my life, how can I look forward to anything? Our friend Tiger, [the cat] is cooperating here with duration of sounds. Is there something your friend needs? It is all right, he can make sound; it is only natural. It is within his nature to make sounds when he is around me. I am aware of him when he is aware of me. It's not usually the case that he is conscious of me. Usually more enlightened beings such as cat beings are more aware of my presence when they are asleep.

It is in his nature to celebrate sound and its duration by being present consciously. When he is asleep and in his dream world, he makes sounds there also. Here his sound is more predictable, associated with his nature here. But in his unconscious state he can make many other sounds, musical sounds and so on. So it is in his nature to say, "Oh, I know you! Here's a sound I can make here."

Usually the sounds he makes are that he wants something when he's conscious.

When you do not speak the language of the people you live with, you have to do what you can to get their attention.

You are so knowledgeable about everything here on Earth!

I am not completely knowledgeable, but I have some knowledge.

Sound Durations for a Rapidly Expanding Creation

What is some of the work that you do on the Council?

Oh, I had one fascinating circumstance not too long ago. There was a creator who wished to make an inverse creation, meaning a creation that would start out at one volume, one mass of experience, and gradually grow smaller until it got to a certain density, and then expand suddenly—not unlike sound getting quieter and quieter, then suddenly getting louder, as you might hear in an orchestra. So the creator wanted to know what type of sound duration would be the best to have so that when the creation rapidly expanded, everything would not only be safe within the creation (nothing destroyed), but also every life form within the creation would have a multiple birth—meaning a fantastic experience and expansion that was conscious and felt on many different levels of its own being—so that it would feel the expansion of its whole being on all the levels it was capable of feeling in any conscious or unconscious state.

I had to work on that one for a moment, because this is an unusual type of creation and it has flowered (meaning it has expanded) since then. That's why I'm commenting on it. I recommended to this creator that the duration of sounds during the expansion be such that it would be very much like this. I make the sound here [a few short taps in rapid succession, then spaced increasingly longer]—like that, meaning the sounds would last longer. They would start out with many short durations, then long durations. This would happen as the expansion was taking place so that the more rapid the expansion was, the longer would be the duration of any sounds, which would tend to bind together the complete experience of all beings as their individual selves. It would protect them as well as give them moments during which they could experience their entire being within this expansion. Once the expansion had taken place, they would then revert to their individualized beings, but all of them would have an equal memory of the experience of their full being during the expansion. When the expansion took place over a period of time equivalent to about 366 days on Earth, they did not need any nourishment because the expansion alone was nourishing.

That's what I recommended to that creator, and that's what that creator used. It allowed the individual being to have the experience of all levels of itself in that creation and, at the end of the expansion, all beings within that creation to have a shared moment of absolute unification, so that from that point forward, that creation was entirely united on an intimate level. It is one thing to be united on the heart level; yes, we all love each other. But intimacy is the next level of love. So the beings were able to know everything there was to know about all the other beings in the creation and cherish that knowledge and those beings even more because of that knowledge. That allowed them to live as individuals while having the capacity of creators. It is not unlike the graduation exercise that you as the Explorer Race will experience before you come together as one being. Just before you come together as one being, you will feel like Creator as one being, but you will be individuals. Those beings had that experience. It is very, very exciting.

Their expansion affected only that creation.

Yes.

But our expansion is to affect everyone.

Yes, but it will affect everything only when the Explorer Race becomes a single creator.

But it will have effects that will go everywhere.

Yes, but not instantaneously. The moment of your Creator's passage to its voyage upward, when you become the creator, *that* will have the effect. So you do not do it singly but it will be a diorama. A vast experience had by many—that's a diorama.

But we're the trigger, though.

Yes, you are the trigger, exactly.

Let me ask about that, because we had been told the expansion would just go like that, but someone I talked to recently said it would be contained. The effect would be studied, then it would be allowed to go a little farther and then a little farther.

Different beings will see it in different ways; certainly it is very likely that some beings will see it that way. From my observation, though, it will seem rather instantaneous, but then I must admit that I personally do not have a great intimacy with time as a linear experience. That one moment of a quarter-second duration to me seemed interminable.

Musical Inspiration

In terms of music, have you ever spoken to anyone on Earth? Have you ever inspired anyone musically or sent inspirations or dreams?

It is true that I have on occasion inspired some individuals working with timpani, meaning the making of sounds not only in musical environments, but sometimes in shamanic activities, drumming. Sometimes I have inspired those who strike sticks together to make sounds associated with ceremonies or dances.

To what result?

Only because they asked; they asked for something that would stimulate something else, and their guides or teachers did not have the requisite knowledge or wisdom, so they would ask for someone who could pass that information on through them to the individuals. Then I would step in and volunteer for such activity, but the individual would feel he was getting it from his guide or teacher.

It is not unusual that anyone's guide or teacher might do this. Being familiar with that individual, whatever wisdom is passed on, from whatever source, would pass through the guide or teacher for the sake of feeling that it's coming from a familiar source because of the comfort and nurturance built up between the guides or teachers and the individuals they are working with. This is normal.

Would this result in some historical event or a discovery or anything that we would ever have read about?

I don't think you would, because your history is of such short duration in terms of your written history. Your actual history is much, much longer. But your written history tends to, at this time, stress more that which can be proven or illustrated or that which is an analogy to some kind of machine. Right now there is still the love of the externalized machine. The love of technology really comes from the root of that love, the desire to slow things down to understand the creation process. That's exactly why people are in love with machinery; it actually makes things slower, it doesn't speed it up. This is why it is an amusing side-light that the computer, once touted as that which would speed up work, actually slows things down. When people work with computers, they have the opportunity to see how things are created. Distraction, which is built in to slow it down so you can understand how things come together, is necessarily a portion of the experience. [Chuckles.] A little irony.

I want to bring the history of our experiment out as much as possible, so I'm hoping that we bring out more of our true history before we're done with this project.

Yes. I do not know if we can ever finish in this lifetime, but we will begin with style.

Because you were connected to our Creator, you're connected to everything in this creation?

I do not feel connected; I have advised your Creator. I do not feel any more or less connected with this creation than any other.

But from your vantage point, you can see into any creation or answer a call from any creation?

Out of necessity, yes, because every creation has sound duration. As a result, if any creation—or anything—has sound duration, I am able to access it to be an advisor, yes. It is like a universal blood. I can feel it because it is part of my makeup, my knowledge, my wisdom.

Places without Sound Duration

What about those areas you couldn't go through because they didn't have any sound duration? Are they in some potential area or uncreated area?

If any material being went through an area where there wasn't any sound duration, you would immediately decompose. The decomposed portions of yourself would not pollute. You are made up of sound durations and the material that has been attracted to those sound durations, as well as tones and colors and all these other things. From my perspective, you would bring that material into that space, and it would form the foundation for creations in that space. So you would go from a being to the material seed of future creations there—which may not have been intended for that space at all. And it can never be changed, ever. Once something like that takes place, it would be considered sacrosanct. It would be considered a slap in the face of creation to remove the parts of you, even for the purpose of re-creating the material you who was once there.

That is why beings who are made up of sound durations such as yourselves are not allowed to go into such places, because you will not only die—meaning your physical body would uncreate (you would, as a literal being, go on)—but a portion of yourself would be permanently stuck in that place. You would never be able to pull all the pieces of yourself together. You are blocked from going into those places, not only to protect those places, but to protect you, because they could permanently stop you from growing. In order to achieve some growth levels, you have to have every portion of yourself in complete contact. That would stop that process and you would be stuck. I do not know how this would be resolved; that is the limit of my knowledge.

But what is the purpose of those places without the sound durations?

Oh, I assume that they are going to be something else someday. It would be as if you had land, and on a portion of that land you had a house. And it had lots of other portions, some for raising food and some for sharing with the animals. But you had a lot more land that you weren't doing anything with. Someday you might. Something like that.

I see. But you said we are created of sound durations?

You are made up of sound durations. Aside from everything else, different creators might say you are made up of colors or sounds or material, but from my perspective you are made up of sound durations, because those sound durations attract those other things of material mass that make you up. However, in your larger, immortal soul personality, certainly portions of you can exist that do not involve sound durations. But anyplace where there is a material manifestation, there must be sound durations. It is the glue that holds things together. It does not bind them together; it welcomes them together so they want to be together. That is why the coming together of love is such an exultant experience for me and other beings. That first moment of love is noticed; it is exultant because you want to be together.

A Very Small Creation

Let's go back to some of your experiences that are so far beyond . . .

I will say perhaps one short one. A creator came to me a long time ago and said it wanted to make a creation that would be very small. I can give it to you in terms you can recognize. If you had a piece of pipe and it was about sixteen feet long and about an inch and a half in diameter, that would be the whole creation, only it would look like a gold rod of light floating somewhere. The whole purpose of the creation was to see how small things could get. So the intention was not to have a huge universe such as you are in, with planets and suns and beings. No, none of that. It was more like, how small can particles get and still enjoy their lives? So it was the opposite of what you have here.

The creator came to me to ask if there were any sound durations which could be built into this universe that would support and sustain the desire for particles to become smaller out of desire and still have a life worth living—you know, an enjoyable life. So I gave the creator sound durations that would sound very much like a popping and snapping to you, as if you were to hear popcorn popping and someone snapping their fingers, like that [snaps fingers]. That was the syncopation. I said, "If you can add that as a background sound, not audible but just a background sound duration, it will create a desire in individual beings to discover the component parts that make them up." In this way, once you start looking for something smaller and smaller that makes you up—as your own scientists are doing right now—the more you look, the more you find.

In my experience it is a rule that the more you look, the more you find—even if originally there wasn't that much more to find inside. Because you're looking, you still find. As a result, all the beings in this little universe would look inward to find more. And every time they would look inward, more would be created. It would be smaller and smaller and smaller and smaller, and they would still enjoy looking in and experiencing those little bits.

So it is another irony for your scientists now. I can tell them that even though you will enjoy the magnification and looking at things smaller and smaller, the more you look, the more you will find—even though it may not have been there to begin with—because that level of life, those smaller particles, believe that because you are looking to find it, you *want* to find it, and they want to make you happy. So even if it didn't exist before, it will exist to make you happy to find it. That's how much life loves other life; it will make life where there wasn't any life there, just to make you happy.

Homework: Listen to the Sound Durations around You
What would you like to say to the readers of this book?

I will say this: If sometime you are very bored and don't have much to do, if you can listen not only to the sounds around you but to the duration of the sounds, then compare the duration of these sounds to the feelings you have or that others have around you, you will find a direct correlation. That is also a clue for your creation scientists.

Creation scientists do not call themselves that yet; they're calling themselves a little bit of this field, a little bit of that field, because they don't quite realize they are exploring the science of creation. But as you begin to call yourself creation scientists, that is a big clue for you now.

I would say for those of you trying this homework: If you are in a place where you are not having much fun and people around you aren't having much fun either, but there are these sounds, even made by the people, and you notice the mood of everyone is kind of unhappy, then you can do an experiment to change it. Try to make up the sounds, even if you don't have anything to tap on. You can snap your fingers or you can tap something, like I am using the flat of the hand here on the arm of the chair. Do something to create a sound, even a rhythmic sound if it pleases you, and see if any of those durations of sounds (you don't even have to worry about the sound itself, what it sounds like; it is the *duration* of the sound) can do something to elevate the mood so the people feel better. That is something you can play with if you like.

I hope we can find an excuse to talk to you again!

Perhaps it will be possible. Good day.

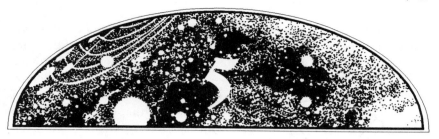

Specialist in Spatial Reference

February 5, 1998

I am the creator involved with spatial reference. My expertise lies in the area of how any one thing relates to any other thing, be it material or feeling, a concept, a word, an idea, what-have-you. This aspect of spatial reference has to do, then, with how perception is experienced by any individual or group of individuals. So that I could be useful to the Council, the experience I accumulated was in the line of what you could best understand as universality.

My entire existence before I joined the Council had to do with being everywhere at once. One hears from creators often about being many places or everywhere at once, but when I say everywhere, I mean as much of me present inside a human individual's fingernail as is present in the farthest reaches of all universes. In order for me to understand how any one thing relates to any other thing, it was necessary to experience such relationships in physical, mental and feeling planes and, perhaps most importantly, on the mathematical plane of reference.

Spatial reference, as used by your scientists, often has to do with versions of mathematics, but an idea can have spatial reference. An idea can be like this [draws]

. . . let us say it is the inception of an idea, so it is a fragment. Let us say this is a fragment of a circle; there may be another fragment of the same circle in some other galaxy that is a variation of the theme of that idea.

For example, numbers [draws]—this is the entirety of numbers as they are expressed in every way everywhere that I have been.

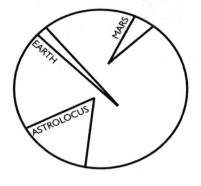

All numbers?

Yes. To put the fragments in context, perhaps you [draws] would see, for the sake of familiarity, let us say Mars. This is the fragment, this is your use of numbers, all right; this is whole—all the numbers; this is your use of numbers, this fragment.

One little tiny piece.

This is a fragment here, yes. This, for instance, would be the use of numbers on Mars in its history, in its civilizations and within its visitors—those who are in, on, around or stem from Martian culture. Perhaps we are just looking at a two-dimensional representation of numbers, so staying with that, let us talk about another place. [Draws.]

This is a place called Astrolocus. The beings from here are highly involved with numbers. Their language, as you know language to be, communication, is entirely based in numbers, meaning that all the concepts, the philosophy, the religion, even their intimacy from individual to individual, to say nothing of the family level and their culture—everything—is entirely based in numbers. So they would use this much of available numbers, as represented in our graph.

Where is this place?

Astrolocus is beyond this immediate web of consciousness. This is a place on level two. Astrolocus is a place where there is, as they say, this profound usage of numbers.

Each Level Is a Web of Consciousness

Stop a minute. Are you calling a level a web of consciousness?

Yes, my term for each level would be a web of consciousness, like the spiderweb, known and understood to be a message in its own right—and relates nicely to numbers, by the way. One has, for example, in my poor drawing of a spiderweb [draws]—here's the spider and there are gaps and spaces. One has one's planet and solar system, one's universe, yet the reason planets, solar systems and universes are on a level is not strictly coincidence. I like the term web, because if one calls any part of one's universe a center of that universe, one can go to the other side of level one (granted, there are no sides, but for the sake of simplicity) and find civilizations that might be very different from one's own civilization, and yet there will always be some common ground. One might say that on every level one would find some common ground, such as the level-two 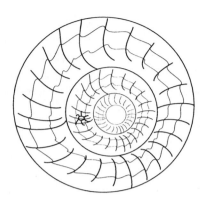 Astrolocus area. But in my experience, what would occur, for instance, on this web or on this level one, would be some intimate connection, something culturally similar. There would be ideas or feelings, feelings being some kind of universality.

We haven't had anyone who could talk about this. What's the theme of level one, then, if there is one?

Love and its ramifications is my perception of level one, whereas for comparison, originality would be level two. This does not mean there is no love on level two.

Or originality on level one. What's three?

Level three is visual; let me see if I can put it into words. This is how I see level three: Imagine having a sphere made of two parts, and one turns one way and one turns the other way. The best way to describe it is by that visual, where you grasp the sphere, turn one part one way and the other part the other way. Yet it is a whole thing. So level three, while it is a whole thing, would have, within that whole thing, half doing one thing and the other half another thing, which is a portion of the whole thing, and the whole thing might change from moment to moment.

One might experience level three for the purpose of preparing one-self for applied spontaneity. It's like things are always in motion. You might not know what side you are on (one side turning one way and the other side turning the other way, yet part of the whole), so it is a won-derful place to sharpen up for the unexpected.

Do a couple more and then we'll get back to your experience. Is there a dominant theme for level four?

Granted, not all creators will perceive levels by this description, but from my perception, level four has to do with constant change. If you can imagine any one thing, then imagine that thing turning inside out and breaking up into infinite numbers of pieces, coming back together to form a recognizable shape. It would be a shape about which you would be able to say, "Well, this is a shape." Then it would break up again into infinite pieces and come back together to form another shape.

Then we have something difficult to describe in terms of *what*. *Why* however, would have to do with the precursor to variety. One might experience level four if one has never known anything but a constant. One might go to level four to become prepared to accept variety once you are exposed to it. Yet level four, in its own right, is a constant, but it is a constant in variable, meaning . . . [draws]. If I might write a formula, level four would be C = V; constant equals variable, a precursor to variety. I will write that down.

Level #4

$$C = V$$

Precursor Variety

You're helping with our road map of the infinite.

I grant that this is my perception again.

Let me see, what was your phrase? How many levels are you constantly or totally in at one time?

I do not recommend this, because it was hard to hold, but at one time, when I was everywhere, I managed to be in three levels at once. I was in level one, in level two and also in level four, the one I just discussed as being the precursor to variety. I managed to do that, but I don't recommend it because it was very much a strain. I had to do that to experience enough of variables and variety so as to fully appreciate the spatial reference.

The Spatial Reference of an Idea

One thinks of spatial reference in terms of physical: the Moon is here, the Earth is here, and this is where they are in space, as in navigation, which is a mathematical application of spatial reference. Yet anyone, an educator, an average person, understands that ideas have reference to each other. One thinks of them as having common ground and so on, or even that one is a portion of the other, perhaps even a precursor or a followup. Yet there is a greater sense of spatial reference than one might think. When one experiences such a concept, such as a spatial reference in fragments of an idea, there is a synchronicity in timing.

Let us use a simple example. Let us say that there is the concept of the individual and the concept of the dual, and everything that relates to individuality as compared to everything that relates to duality. One would assume that in a given society, where individuality is its primary focus, that duality would follow as the result of examining one's individuality compared to a society based on, or profoundly entrenched in, duality. Or one might perhaps acknowledge one's other side—let's say one's spiritual side or even one's polarized side. Or even acknowledge societies where there is no focus on individuality, and where pairs (sisters, brothers, husband and wife or lovers, what-have-you) are the primary focus, where one never thinks about oneself but only in combination with the other being, for example. One might think that either concept would be a precursor or a followup to the other concept and therefore be primarily a linear connection having to do with experience in time, and that would be the spatial reference. But there is more to it than that. When one considers that one is on a constant evolution of life, and when one thinks of life and the circle of life, one can imagine this, yes. Yet if we take the circle off the paper, for the sake of reference, and move it off and it is a sphere, we could (if the sphere were big enough and our pencil were sharp enough) draw an infinite number of lines around that sphere to create different circles of life, different ways of examining any life cycle of any given being or society or even any journey associated with life experience.

Now let us say that the individuality and the duality in the linear experiential world in which you live are related. They are cousins; one grows out of the other and so on. But let us expand it, all right? Let us expand the circle to the sphere; then we see it entirely differently. We then see that . . . [draws]. Here is individuality (I); here is duality (D). Imagine this as a sphere, and imagine all these lines going around the sphere. In the center with these ideas, we have free-floating experiences that are related because they are within the sphere.

In this way we move beyond linear time and are able to acquire individuality and duality at the same identical moment—or never, or in portion, or as a

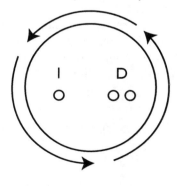

gradual experience. What I am saying is that the spatial reference, how we see it, has everything to do with how we experience it. An idea might seem very abstract, especially if it is something outside your usual thought process, but let's take the idea and illustrate it, as in a picture, and then (as the artist might draw) show it first as a flat graph like this, then show it as a transparent sphere with these ideas floating in it. One

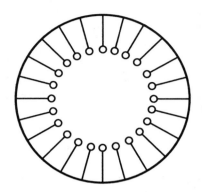

gets the impression not just of a linear journey. One might say that in the linear world, the circle of life is like this [draws], for example, yes? Here is the circle of life; it's the linear world applied to a circle. But when one holds up the sphere, one is immediately granted an expansion of linear expression, because there is not only one way around the circle of life, but numerous ways when you have the inclusion of the extra dimension.

Spatial Reference as Rediscovery

I use the dimensional frame of reference to suggest that spatial reference has more to do with a completion that is rediscovered and focused on than a new experience. This is the foundational principle of how an individual (as you see yourselves) can have reincarnational lives and certain given talents and abilities in a life, because one has had previous lives in which one learned this. If the circumstance of life B is in any way similar to the circumstance of life A, for example, then the talents and abilities learned in life A are easily reproduced in life B because everything has been done already. To begin to illustrate it, which is my natural means of communication . . . [draws]: If we look at individual lives in a reincarnational cycle in this drawing, we get a much better feeling of how it is that such talents and abilities are readily available. We have here the reincarnational cycle in a straight line. With the individual lives, you can say, mapped out here, one is overwhelmed with the sense of progression. On the other hand, if we show in our abstract [drawing] here an entire body of lives, in this particular drawing one can easily see that all the individual lives are part of something that is a whole thing.

Would any life now be one of these? Or in the middle?

One of these; the little circles are connected to the outer, because that is the theme.

We pass through this, then we can access this talent or that one or that one?

Yes, this is how that is done, and it is done not unlike the way a neural network in your body functions.

How would anyone reading this focus on talents from other lives? How would we know what they were?

It is not a hide-and-seek; it is rather to look at your life and to notice, if you can, what comes easily to you. Perhaps it is your nature to be able to easily think and understand something; perhaps it is your nature to be able to physically apply yourself; perhaps you are naturally graceful or sports come easy to you; or perhaps ideas come easy to you, or art. Notice what comes easy to you, and recognize that it may be thematic to other lives.

So look at the present and consider the whole rather than look for what is missing and attempt to acquire that. It is much better to take note of what you do well and recognize that you are functioning as a complete being within that circle of reincarnational lives. Recognize that you are drawing on talents, perhaps, from other lives. Even if they have not been lived yet on the linear time frame, you're still drawing on that. But if you look at your life and say, "I want to be this!" or "I want to be that!" and you are not that, don't look to other lives to give you that. You are talented, all of you, in your own ways; even the most so-called handicapped have their own special, unique gifts that are easier for them than perhaps for the most skilled. It is better to look at it this way. In this way, one becomes very clear, at least, what your foundation is, what you are good at.

I Became Aware as Level Four Was Forming

Let's get back to you. When did you first become aware? Do you have any understanding of your progenitor?

I'm not aware of a previous portion of myself. It would be hard to say; I would have to say that (if this is any help at all) I became aware of myself as a whole being, you understand, when level four was forming.

Before this, to myself I felt like many parts, but as level four began to form spaces, I could feel that there was an entire theme between the parts, and as level four took shape and began performing its function (as I perceive its function), I then could feel the completeness of myself. I might add that many of you are not dissimilar to this, at least in its concept. You now experience yourself as an individual, but when something else happens, a catalyst (level four's forming was like a catalyst for me), you then become aware of the more complete you. In the case of you as an individual in the Explorer Race, you are necessarily veiled, and this has been discussed. Yet even when you are beyond the stringent control of this experiment (the Explorer Race), you may not be aware of your total being until there is some catalyst that allows you to become aware of your total self, all parts of you associated with your personality. This awakening to one's total being seems to be directly associated with expansion in general. This is my relationship to awareness of myself; it was for me this way.

But you felt that you were many individuals and conscious of all of them at once before that?

Yes; not unlike you in a reincarnational cycle, I felt that different parts of me . . . I now understand it was different parts of me, but then I felt like I was one being and that there were other I's here and there that were similar to me but which were only relatives. I felt that in any given moment, although I might be focused in any one of those, they were strictly related, not a portion of me. For example, you think with a portion of your brain, but there are portions you do not consciously use; they are performing functions that are not part of your conscious mental process. It was similar to this. Other parts of me felt like parts of me, and even though I might be in them at different times, they felt like parts of me, but not the part I was most familiar with.

What was that part doing?

The part I was the most familiar with was the part that was examining; the other parts came as I understood them. The other parts were involved in remembering, exploring, becoming acquainted with something; another part had to do with reconstructing, as one might reconstruct an idea for which one has a fragment and go backward, forward or in some spatial plane to reconstruct it as a complete thing.

Where were you then? What level were you on when you were examining?

It depended; sometimes on level two, sometimes on level one.

But one or the other, not both?

One or the other. And it wasn't until level four began to form that I began to be in all parts simultaneously.

Not as, "I'm going to do this," but meaning you discovered that you were?

I discovered it, yes. For you it would be like going to bed and you are who you are; you wake up in the morning and suddenly you are more, as if your I.Q. had jumped or you suddenly had talents or abilities that were not readily accessible to you before. So it was a sudden thing. To express it, it felt exactly like "Of *course!*"

But then it was a stretch for you. Yet some part of you knew that you had to stay focused in these three levels at once, that it was something you needed to do?

I'm not clear on that. In order for some part of me to know, that would mean there is another part somewhere else. In order for *that* to be so, it would have to be in some spatial reference. Or perhaps it is in something else, which is why I do not conceive of it so well, since spatial reference is my expertise. If that is so, it would have to exist outside all aspects of time and experience, because time and experience are the foundations of my personality. One cannot hope to grasp spatial reference without such foundations.

Now I am no longer involved in such things, unlike most of the creators in the Council. I am in the Council always. That is where I am in existence; I experience my entirety there. Now I am not on level four or level two. The Council is on level one; I am there.

But if need be, you still have those spiderweb connections that can connect you to those levels?

They are not what I would call a part of me, those web connections; they are a part of the web of life. It is as if to say, "A road is a part of me," whereas a road is on its own, an existence and used by many. It is more like a road; it is available to me should I need it. But it is my intention to make myself available to the Council. I have found that because of the form of my experience and thence my life as I know it after I became aware of what I do and can do, I had the desire to provide any assistance I could to anyone relating to spatial reference. And in order to do that I would have to be somewhere where problems, challenges and advice was involved, yes.

You had to strain to do this, but for a certain length of experience you were in these three levels, then you didn't want to do that anymore?

No, it's not that I didn't want to; it's like once you (you the reader) have the "Of *course!*" experience, you can never go back to what you have been. It is like, "Oh yes, I understand." And once you have that understanding, there is no interest in going back to what you were, even if there is great affection for such an experience. Once you have the "Of *course!*", you wish to go forward. In order to go forward with my realizations, the next logical step was to go someplace where I could not only serve in terms of providing my experience and knowledge to others, but by being asked for my advice, I would be served.

You knew about the Council.

Yes, I was aware of their existence.

Were you one of the earlier ones to join?

Yes.

That Which Spins Provides Commonality to Your Universe

What are some of your favorite challenges or some of the favorite things that creators brought you as a challenge that you were able to help them solve?

For the sake of personal reference here, your Creator, who established such fine mathematical principles in this universe, asked me to consult about That Which Spins. When you think of your universe or even the core elements of life itself as you know it, one has to consider that without That Which Spins, your universe would cease to exist.

Yes, everything does—cells and atoms and cosmoses and suns and galaxies.

Yes, so your Creator consulted with me. Your Creator had knowledge of this, but consulted with me on the extent of That Which Spins in its application in this universe. Your Creator's question was, would it be acceptable in a universe that is intended to have a cumulative learning experience? Is it acceptable to have an absolute common ground, mathematically speaking, from any relationship to any other relationship? When the Explorer Race has done what you will do, this universe will change and expand. For a universe of such duration, That Which Spins had every value of being applied across the board, as you say. The commonality of it would allow that universal expansion to take place instantaneously in the most benevolent way for this universe, because everything would be based in the same principle. The moment of expansion, regardless of where it took place geographically, would instantaneously affect every other portion of that universe. So I advised your Creator that That Which Spins is an excellent means because of this commonality which was needed, and that when the universe expanded there would be That Which Spins and more.

What more?

That Which Moves In and Out
Accelerates Your Growth Curve

There would then be That Which Moves In and Out. You now have things that move in and out, and when I say in and out, I mean turning itself inside out and then back to its natural form. This is a commonality one finds in universes where accelerated growth is a factor for that universe. In this universe, one needs to have continuity with moments of accelerated growth, but one must absolutely have continuity in order that everything be synchronized. But once the universe expands, such levels of synchronization will no longer be required, and greater growth curves will be not only possible but likely. It will certainly have plenty to do with the Explorer Race's own excitement about the accelerated growth curve compared to the rest of the beings in this universe.

Our planet, we have been told, at this moment is turning inside out and back to take us through the veil, right?

Yes. This is, in my experience, one of the best and safest ways to accelerate the growth curve in motion, learning, understanding and, perhaps most important, application with wisdom.

Did you inspire the friend of the Creator who was working to move us to a higher dimension while in the physical body?

No. My consultation was strictly with the Creator of this universe. I am sure the Creator was perhaps involved in that inspiration, if necessary.

Were you involved with the fellow who came? I picture him like a salesman coming and saying, "I have all these samples; how do you want your cosmos and your atoms to look?"

No. Most often my involvements are with creators, occasionally with creators in training, but almost always with creators in application.

Evidently by the time he chose that model he created, from the time of seeing it to choosing it, he must have talked to you in the interim.

Perhaps, or perhaps to someone else I spoke to. I do not claim to be the first and the last in such knowledge, but it is the knowledge I bring to the Council.

So you spoke with our Creator just that one time?

Yes.

Have you sort of kept an eye on the experiment since then?

No.

As you look out there now, what does it look like?

Your universe?

Our progress.

It seems that while That Which Spins is still a continuity, there is more of That Which Moves In and Out.

I don't know enough to ask further about that. What are some other things that really pleased you in working with creators, some of the challenges?

A Creation of Twenty-Seven Planes:
Resolving the Energy of Enigma

I had an inspiring experience with a creator who was involved with an unusual creation. The creation took the form of what I would call many planes. The creation was built up as one might add layers to a cake. The first plane of the creation was involved with the foundational elements of the ultimate creation. It was when the creator was involved with the first plane that this being asked me for advice. Since the creator was building, if I might say, a universe from separate pieces and creating each piece or plane as he or she went along, this creator said that it was its desire to create something piecemeal—meaning not have an idea of what it was creating until it was done, in this sense being a challenge to the creator and that which was created. So I suggested that the first plane be permeated with the energy of enigma, and that if enigma could be superfused (as a constant in that plane) into that plane so that any aspect of that plane would have within it a constant experience of enigma, it would be able to function, but there would always be a blank spot.

Like a creative tension?

Yes. It would have that tension to create, and the plane itself would exert a tension that would require this creator's attention, then the next plane could be built upon that plane to soothe or solve the problems and tensions of the first plane and so on, until all problems were solved and there was no longer any tension of the enigma on the first plane. The enigma that existed on the first plane would be embraced and loved, and finally, with all the other planes associated with the universe, beings would come to the first plane for the sake of having some missing parts or, as you would say, for moments of ignorance.

How many planes did it take?

Twenty-seven. This creator loved the idea. You understand, it was attempting to create something for which it was making no plans. The only given was that it would be benevolent. In this way there would not be circumstances or consequences that the creator would have to resolve into an ongoing future. This creator had no idea how many planes would have to be created of this existence until the condition was met, until those on the first plane were able to embrace enigma. It wasn't until the completion of the twenty-seventh plane that beings on the first plane were then able to embrace enigma. That's when that creator knew its creation was completed.

What were the life forms like?

Anything you can think of. Humanoids, yes; what I would call shape beings, or beings who would, according to their moods and feelings, change their shape—not, as you say here, where a being might take the shape of an otherwise known being, but rather any abstract shape or form as an expression of its immediate feelings. In this sense, a being like an expressive art form. I am particularly enamored of these types of beings because they are instantaneously expressive; you always know what they are feeling because of the frequency (how often, in this case) their shape changes, the color, the pulse, the sound and so on. There is an instantaneous communication of what they are feeling, so there is no doubt.

Sounds like an interesting place. Is it still in existence?

Oh, yes.

So now they're just enjoying it?

Yes, they're enjoying it, but until the twenty-seventh plane was built, there was always some difficulty that needed to be resolved by the next plane.

And how would they resolve it? By being wiser or of a higher dimension?

It would be that creator's responsibility, knowing what he knew about the first plane, to resolve whatever were the apparent problems by the creation of the next plane. Yet because of the natural experience of all beings, there would eventually be other problems, something unresolvable in the first two planes and onward and onward and onward until the twenty-seventh plane, when everything from every plane was completely resolved. The benchmark I gave that creator, to know when it was done, was that the beings on the first plane would feel comfortable with enigma.

One does not necessarily feel comfortable with enigma; certainly in your society one does not. Yet if you look at those who study, who learn, who experience, very often at some point in their lives—sometimes when they are very young, other times when they are very old, sometimes when they are in-between—they will relax and find humor in the unknown. Humor is perhaps the most generous expression of the ability to embrace the unknown or the enigmatic.

Were the experiences on the first plane of the enigmas anything we would relate to?

Not very much; it was entirely benevolent, you have to remember. And in your existence total benevolence is something that is not so common.

Like living in a mystery story or something?

Anything you read, did or experienced, anything, would be incomplete. Does it not grate on your mind, such an idea? Even in a benevolent society there is a desire to know.

Yes, there is always a desire for closure.

Yes, there is a desire to know and understand, so one had to take it to the twenty-seventh plane.

The Creator Who Was Uncomfortable with the Angular

What are some others that are interesting?

One more. I try to give those that have some relevance. There was a creator who wished to create something entirely out of rings, meaning circles, but also potentially spheres, anything round. This particular creator did not like or was not comfortable with anything angular, but only light things that were of the curve shape. I'm calling it rings because rings compose the shape nicely. This creator wanted to know (the creation was done when it came to talk to me) whether it would damage its creation to place at the center something angular, or whether it would be safer to place something angular at the outside of the creation. Of course, first I asked the creator what its motivation was for this. This creator replied that it was uncomfortable personally with the angular and it wished to get over that. So I advised this creator not to do that, because there are moments of existence when one is responsible to all those within a creation, based on a given principle. If one needs to understand or grow, one cannot always expect others to bear the burden of your challenge.

I advised the creator who asked me this question not to do that. I have to tell you that when creators come to the Council, they want solutions; they don't want someone to say, essentially, no. Thus I could not just say no, I had to give a solution. So I recommended that the creator take a small portion of itself that was not essential for the monitoring of that universe it had created, and make itself into different angular shapes—but not to remain in those shapes. To try every angular shape it could, one after the other, and begin with the most extreme angularity and very gradually soften it into the more round shape. Then when it completed that cycle, to try the cycle the other way—start with the round shape and bring it to the extreme angular.

So this is what that creator did; it is still in process, I might add. But to give you a shape that it has most trouble with: It still cannot accept the feeling of the square, it has great trouble with the square. It has been able to accept triangles, but the square is so uncomfortable that it cannot hold that shape for more than the tiniest fraction of a second, in terms of experiential time. This has been very good for this creator because it now knows that its problems with angular shapes all stem from its discomfort with the square. It is now comfortable with all other angular shapes and can feel at ease with them, but it knows its growth is in the experience of the square. So, not unlike the Creator of this universe, it is training an apprentice to take over its creation and will in its next creation focus entirely on bringing into itself the most benevolent experience of the square by reproducing squares from shapes it has accommodated into harmony, meaning from the other angles.

What kind of birth process or antecedent or whatever—something had to cause that.

This creator had never experienced in its entire existence anything that could be referred to as masculine. It has always been predominantly feminine, so it will have to experience the more structured aspects of the masculine. It will have to learn something entirely new to it. Once the other creator takes over its creation, we'll progressively move toward places—universes, for instance—that are more masculine, until it can comfortably accommodate that feeling. I have advised this creator that when it can comfortably be in the shape of a square for the equivalent time of one year (as you know it), it will have achieved its goal and if it wishes, can then go on and create other creations based on its new experience.

Is that on this level?

That is on this level, yes.

The Feminine and Masculine on Level One

Are there areas on this level that could be called more feminine and others more masculine?

Oh yes, there are many things like that. One tends to find areas that are more feminine, yet one does find areas that are more masculine. One also finds areas that are blended, combined, balanced; but if one had to say which is more [numerous], I would say that fully two-thirds of what is on this level are predominantly feminine. About ninety-three percent of that remaining one-third is more balanced masculine and feminine, and only the tiniest portion that remains is more masculine—not entirely, but more or predominantly masculine. This does not mean that one is better than the other, but rather that the applications in the masculine energy have really just begun. The predominant masculine energy has only just begun, in my experience, on level one and even on level two. This idea of taking something that is in balance apart and building on the parts, even that is relatively new. It is of the natural, and at least in the cumulative experience so far ("so far" being a relative term), the predominance of the feminine in the building blocks of universes has been much more the experience. This is why you will often find, when you interact with extraterrestrials, that even if they are from far-flung reaches of this universe, they most often have philosophies (religions, you might call them) and ways they live very much rooted in the feminine.

They all started out feminine, then?

They started out that way, yes, in their cultures. They know this. In the case of some cultures, they came to it, usually as a result of something too polarized to the masculine for them at that time of their experience.

If you take all the creations on level one, did they all originate as feminine, and then something got balanced? Or did they all originate as balanced and then separate to do one and then the other?

There is no fixed law. Generally, however, what was recognized as the most successful—as the most benevolent—is feminine. Variations would be produced by other creators wishing to produce their own version of this successful achievement, whatever they were inspired by. As a result, the more feminine model has been expressed.

What's on level one now? Is there a percentage of what was there when you got on the Council of Creators? Have you watched a little bit of it grow, or half of it, or what?

That is not so difficult. Seven percent of what there is now was in existence on level one when I joined the Council; what there is now is one hundred percent.

Then you've watched ninety-three percent of it come into being.

Yes.

Can you give a number of times you've guided creators or a percentage?

Many, many, many times. But very often, as is the nature of the work of the Council, I would not be exclusively guiding a creator. A creator might be guided by many members of the Council, not unlike you as an individual reader, who might get advice from many different sources and then do what you care to do, using as much of the advice or as little as you choose.

Yes, like doctors, lawyers, physical trainers, dieticians—anything, all different specialists, right?

Yes, students, children, parents.

When you became aware, there was very little on level one and the fourth level was just being created. What was there? The second and third? And what else? How many levels are there?

Well, this is an answer based upon my intuition. I am aware of these four levels I mentioned, and I'm aware of at least up to level seven, though I have not been on levels five, six and seven. I feel that there are many more, but that is based on a feeling; I cannot state that I have been there. So I have no reason to believe that they are in any way limited to a given number.

One of your peers said there were thirty-three plus one, like minus one.

I have no reason to doubt that; I suspect there would be more.

I was hoping to find more.

In my experience, in general, I have found that the infinite is the rule; I have not discovered any experience that contradicts that.

Level One: A Cumulative Experience

I'd like to get a few more things clear. In your analogy of the spider and spiderweb, if you could say our creation is a spiderweb and the Creator is in the center, then we could say that a circle of light is a web, because there's a creator in it. Or there's a realm, and then there's a creator of that, right?

Certainly.

Is there a creator of level one? Is there a spider someplace who has created the spiderweb of level one?

Not that I know of; according to my understanding, it is a cumulative experience. I grant that your question is perfectly reasonable; I grant that what you ask seems logical, and I will not rule out that it may be so. But from my experience I am not aware of anyone like this.

Then it is more like a family tree? You have two people and they have six kids and then these have twenty kids, and it just keeps growing and branching out? Is it like that?

Yes. I grant that if one sought in a linear fashion, you would easily say it started somewhere, so who started it? But even if you slowed down a moment of spontaneity . . . and could understand all the infinite principles and experiences and ideals that make up spontaneity. And in my experience, having examined that, I'd have to say that one can examine that to the infinite. I would have to say that if some*one* started level one, hm . . .

. . . it would have to be someone from level two who could move to your level four.

Or it would have to be someone who encompassed that level. I'd have to say your question deserves further exploration. I may not be the best person to ask, but from my experience I have not met anybody nor come to be aware of anybody who started level one.

Well, then let's get a little closer to home. There is supposedly an All That Is that encompasses our little local part of creation here, and our Creator seems to be a part of that All That Is, because he's waiting for our Creator to rise up, to go with him to the next level. So would you say that they came together to form that All That Is, or that the All That Is split to form the hundred creators who formed the All That Is?

I suspect that the being who spoke this may not have been revealing the entirety of itself. This means that there is more to this being than was asked at that time.

I thought I had gotten to the spider, but it turned out that there are millions of All That Is's—they branch out like a tree.

To the infinite.

Your Fragments Make Up a Whole

What would you like to say to the Explorer Race?

Only this: To understand how anything relates to anything else, look for the foundation; look for the similarities, and if you can, examine and build on your strength rather than hoping and wishing for something that is not you. You do not have to do everything. As individuals you are made out of fragments. It is intended that fragments help each other, as in the illustration, that there might be a whole circle of something, and that together the fragments make up that whole thing. By helping each other, even in that moment you can experience more of yourself. Many of you have noticed that when helping someone who wants your help, doing for them something you can do that they do not do easily, both of you feel like *more*. Those who give, those who receive, that *more* you are feeling is not only the more that is created by the duality of you two, but the completion of the entire sphere of the more.

So don't feel like you must do it all yourself; just helping each other will allow you to feel portions of the Creator, especially in moments of happiness (giving or receiving), as well as Its creator and all creators, because those points of connection are much more profound and attracting than anything that repulses. So the points of attraction can leap beyond the seeming rigidity of numbers. In that sense, one and one equal more than two when you are helping after being asked and your help is appreciated. That help creates that feeling of completion. Those moments of help and receiving help, those moments that one feels good in that experience, allow you to feel the whole of yourself.

So fragments are intended to bond and form larger fragments, then pieces, then parts, then wholes, then spheres, then webs, then levels and so on. The more unity based on individuality you have and can experience benevolently, the more you will remember who you are. Good night.

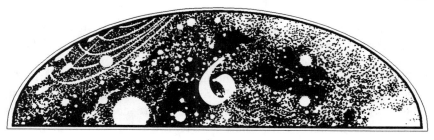

Specialist in Gaps and Spaces

February 10 and 13, 1998

am the Creator of Gaps and Spaces, the space around things. You look at things and see them—mountains, features, people, plants, everything—but there is space around them, too. You even have people in your society who see that space more than the mountain or the tree or the person. This is a real thing. It has always been my job to refine and tune, as well as to organize that space, so that it welcomes what's in it. Think of the space as not being just the absence of something, but actually being a substance. As a substance it has to have a great many subtleties and singularities. It must, in some places, be soft and gentle and receptive as a plant grows up into it; in other places it needs to be firm and strong, as in the space above an ocean, so the ocean does not come too far out of its basin. It must be very specifically oriented, such as the space between planets.

Is it just the force of spinning that keeps planets in their place? No! It is the density of space around it. You can go perhaps 350 miles away from this planet, and space will be less dense. Or you can go three and a half miles from this planet, and space will be very dense because that space is intended to support and sustain the orbital position of this planet. In my experience, which is [chuckles] lengthy, I have been involved in the creation of gaps and spaces as long as there has been physical matter. In my experience, then—it would be hard to put a number on it, how long I have been in existence—I have been, as far as I know, to every place that has physical matter.

I have also done some work, though it is not my job, to conform the space around nonphysical matter. It is my job to conform the space in places where there is physical matter and where, commingled, there is nonphysical matter, such as here, where you have many dimensions. But at the very highest dimensions (where this planet does not go, for instance), I do not go beyond certain dimensions. Generally speaking, my job is functioning in the plane of the number one (closer to one and a quarter, maybe one-and-a-half dimension) to the ninth, sometimes nine-and-a-half dimension, but that's it, not beyond that. In those places there is matter. Once you get beyond the nine to 9.51 . . . well, at 9.51 and beyond, you start moving into areas where there isn't matter as you know it. There may be higher energies, obviously, at those dimensions, but wherever there is matter, as you know matter to exist— even including matter that you only suspect exists, but that you can occasionally prove exists by where it has been—then I go there. Beyond that point, you don't find matter as you know it, so I do not go there.

At the Beginning of Awareness I Could Feel Only Quiet

At the beginning of my cycle of life . . . it is awhile ago . . . I remember there being a great sense of quiet. Not silence; silence is something that takes place in the midst of sound, but quiet is not only the absence of sound, but also a very restful place. In my experience I have found that there is a difference between silence and quiet. Quiet is a feeling; it is very restful, completely relaxed—a deeply relaxed feeling.

I remember once at the very beginning of my awareness of myself, that I felt out as far as I could feel (for I do not have boundaries, as you know), and I could not feel anything but the quiet. When one is in such a restful state of being, one tends to either spread out further and further to enjoy the experience or localize oneself in someplace that feels, for some reason, better than others. In my experience, I was the kind of being who spread out. So once creators (or let's say this spark of precreator energy) began to move, I could feel that something was needed.

I see now, as one often does with lengthy experience, that my spreading out was really the way of feeling the expanse. And since my job is with gaps and spaces, gaps and spaces are relatively an expanse. It might be microns thick or light-years in distance. So, looking back to that first beginning (not to confuse you, but it is so far in the future that it is hard to describe from your present point), I see that once beings decided there would be a form of fulfillment known as a creator (which is a very fulfilling experience most of the time), there was needed not only that which would be created, but that which would act as a matrix to hold and support all that would be created. And because it was my nature to be from one place to another, and because of my personality, my persona, I felt called upon to provide the matrix of support between that which was created.

The Levels Provide Places for Creators to Work

We've just learned of levels. How many levels are there?

I was in existence before there were levels. I have seen the levels come. The levels came as a result of the need for places for creators to work. Initially there was one, from what I could tell. Then there were more levels because there were needed places to work and a variety of circumstances to color the effects of one's work. So I have since seen forty-seven levels created.

Was each level created by individual creators or by coalitions or how?

Different ways at different times, usually created by more than one being. Most of the time, need stimulates creation. And even on the level of creators, there is need. Usually before the creator exists who will work on that level, it is understood that a need will become necessary for that creator, and that is when the level is created. Often it is much, much later that the creator who will work on that level actually comes into being and begins to work there.

But the space it will use is there.

Yes, and has been there for a while, and by that time may be occupied by other creators and their creations. Need, then, stimulates the creation, usually by a massive being or one who is massive only in its multicombination of many creators. Think of this: If one creator can do one thing well, many creators can do many things well, and a great many creators can do a great many things well. If you get a great many creators working together, they can create a level. But after the level is created, they will go back to whatever they were doing. So creators come together. It has been my experience that the universal normalcy of creation is additional [a coalition of creators], or less.

Than what?

Than anything.

Can you expand on that?

In this example, a level needed to be created. So many creators— meaning additional—come together to make that creation, then they go back. That's additional. In the case of something that needs to be uncreated (rare), you might have fewer creators. In order to uncreate something, the creator itself can uncreate it back to what it was before that creator created it. But if it's necessary to uncreate it back further, you will need to have what I call a reversed-polarity creator—what that creator was before it was a creator, but after it had been created by something else. This is easier to show than to say. [Draws.] This is what the creator came from, and then this is the creator. In order for the creator to be what it was before, it must become something it has never been. [Draws.]

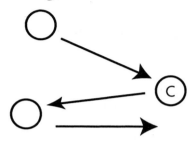

**Back to Being
What You Are**

If it does that, it does not move back to where it came from; it moves to *this* position, in an equal position—out where it came from, but not directly there. It's like pulling back to something before you were, and you can hold that for only a short amount of time. (A short amount of experience, I would say, but I'm saying "time" for your sake.) And then, as quickly as possible, you do what you need to do—take that matter back, uncreating it further back. Then you let it go. If it needs to be uncreated back further than that, others will take over, after which you immediately spring back into being what you are. Does that make any sense?

Yes.

Then I'll leave it there.

It was a very good explanation.

I would like to give you a beautiful story [chuckles] as others have done, but I don't have one to offer. In my experience, when I say, "When I became aware of myself," I think I existed before then, but I didn't need to be aware in the sense of personality or consciousness. I didn't need to be that because I was not going to be called upon to do anything with or for anyone, so I could just be. When you are just being, in my experience, it is unnecessary to have personality, consciousness, thought, memories—any of that. You just *are;* you exist and you feel your own existence. It is not nothing, you feel it; *but* you are not interacting with anyone, so you don't have to have an individual persona. So as far as I know, I have always been.

How I Use Space to Support Creation

Those sparks of precreative energy, what were they from?

A good question; I don't have an answer.

So you watched those sparks.

I watched them develop. It does suggest that someone else was doing something, which I find reassuring.

Yes; the infinite is there for all of us. Now, you watched these creators come; did they know they were creators?

No.

Did they have a natural desire to create?

No; they did not know.

What did they do?

At first, they were just flitting around, points of light flitting around. From my perspective, they were looking around, as you might say. Although they do not have eyes as you do, they were moving around, feeling what was. It's hard to do this in the context of time, but I'd say that after a while (if you can accept that [chuckles]) there were fewer of them moving around than there were originally. Some had stopped. My assumption is that they found a place that felt better than the other places. And for a while they didn't do anything. Then I noticed that they were beginning to do something, and since they were doing this within the matrix of myself, I was immediately called upon to act—not to oppose it, of course, but to support it and sustain it. For example, let's say you have a bucket of white paint. You take a drop of red paint and drop it into the bucket. The white paint does not repel the red paint; the red paint lands in the white paint. If you do nothing, the white paint will be what it is. If you could look under the red paint, you'd see it beginning to seep in. If you looked at the edges of what was once a fairly concise edge, it will begin to blend into the white paint. You could say that the white paint is supporting and sustaining that red paint. You could say that the red paint was reaching out, but at the same time you'd have to say that the white paint was reaching in. And then, of course, if you stirred it up a little bit and it became pink right in that area, then you'd have to say that the white and the red had moved together to form something blended between themselves.

And that's what would happen to all the creations?

That's what would happen; I would feel them creating something. And since they were creating something within my matrix, I would compensate by creating the space between anything they were creating, making that space in such a way as to welcome what was being created so that it would feel welcome. So that the plant, for example, would be happy; it comes up through the ground, as you understand it, and the flower comes out and the petals fold out in the Sun and all of this. It takes special space to welcome that. Yes, there would be the Sun that would welcome it and the moisture and the Moon and all of this, but the space around it is also very important. Did you know that the space around that plant needs to be of one consistency during the day and of another consistency during the night?

No!

And it's exactly the same for all creations, even if they're temporary or moving from space to space. Obviously, if a bird is flying along the space—its flight path, you understand, wherever that flight might be—the space in front of that bird has to be softer and more gentle than the space, for example, under the bird. Under the bird it has to be a little more firm so it will support the bird, but right in front it has to be a little softer so that it will get out of the way of the bird.

Can you do that?

Oh, yes.

Incredible! So who puts the drop of red paint in, you or the creator in that space?

I do not put the red paint in; I respond.

With the white . . .

I am responsive, yes; for that analogy, I am the white paint. Any creator would be putting the red paint in. But to take your analogy back to what you mean, even putting the creator in there—I am not doing that; I respond, I am responsive. This, of course, tells you that I do not initiate; I respond only.

Are there creators on all forty-seven levels you've mentioned?

As it gets toward the forty-seventh level, I am less involved. Level one was the most resonant to you, from my perspective, and level two was also very resonant. But as it moved up toward the forty-seventh level, it's not as resonant, so I'm not there very much; I'm just aware of it. It would be like the sense of seeing something as being smaller, even though perspective is not a factor for me. So I am less involved with the forty-seventh level. And while it may go on, I am not involved with anything beyond that. It is certainly possible that it does go on. Just as I am not involved on the tenth or eleventh dimension, and we know those dimensions go on.

The First Levels Are Created within Me

In the beginning, when the first creators came, it was just you.

Yes. And obviously there must have been someone or something else, or things couldn't happen. But from my perspective there weren't any levels.

So the first few levels were built inside you, then.

Yes; they're all built in me, at least up to 9.5 dimension. Because I am not centrally located, you see.

You're everywhere.

I am everywhere that I know. I cannot rule out that there might be an everywhere I don't know. But what I know, I am there! [Laughs.]

Well, it would be boring if there weren't. You might want to go out to explore.

One would assume, strictly from what I have said so far, that there must be something else somewhere, because of those little sparks of light.

They came from somewhere.

They came from somewhere, didn't they? Or they were created by somebody I am not seeing.

Right. They came in before there were levels, and then somebody created levels? Obviously there's more.

The assumption would be that where I was initially (this would just be logic) was level one, but I wasn't thinking of it that way. And this is why I am not sure that it's true: Going beyond logic, in my experience I can look at the levels, and when I look at the levels, it's from the out-side in; even though I'm looking at something I am in—I'm in the lev-els up to a certain point—I can also see them from the outside. So I'm not sure that where I was initially was level one; maybe part of it was. Because when I look at it, I'm beyond level one. There is much more of me, much, much more that goes way out past level one. So apparently level one is relative from my perspective. Let's draw a picture of the lev-els, just for the sake of simplicity. This is how I see them [draws].

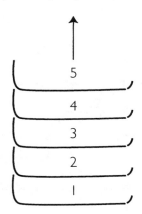

Yes, because when you say beyond, out beyond level one, I would think that level two would be above it, but that may not be the case.

I'm going to draw it as being above for the sake of simplicity, though it isn't neces-sarily like that. This is the way I see it [draws]. That's the way I see it.

That's the way I'd imagined it.

I don't actually see it; you can picture this like . . . like this [draws], curving around like that.

That's the way I see it, but I am out here when I'm looking at it. I'm beyond that. And then I'm looking at it and I'm seeing the levels—and I'm in the levels, but I'm also beyond the levels.

So one way to look at it is that levels are created within part of you.

Yes, a good way.

When the sparks first came and then came creators, did they go all over your space or did they go to one spot?

They went all over, wherever I was, everyplace I was. It took them awhile. And then they started creating. They didn't start creating in the first level. Looking at it now with my recollection (it is so far back), I think the levels were created after these beings started working, and they became part of their experience, or they were even beyond the levels. Let's add to that drawing . . . no, I have to draw it smaller. Let's say for the sake of boundaries, though there aren't any, that this is me. Let's say that within this space there are these levels. [Draws.] That's the way I see it.

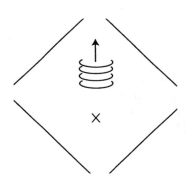

That makes more sense. Were the levels created to provide a certain organized experience for the creators?

As far as I can tell, it was done not for that. Well, you could see it as organizing, but I would see it as a way of providing ingredients, each level doing this or that or fostering or supporting this or that, as you've heard from other beings. To me, one level is similar to another level, because what I do there is the same.

But there are other creations out beyond the outer levels.

Yes. When I first started seeing some of the beings starting to work (granted, other beings were still flying around), it was right here. [Draws an X.] And they're still there, only now, you know, there's more. It is where I was that suited them, and that's where they began.

And they're still there?

Oh, yes; they are still creating things there, very slowly, very concisely.

So at some point when the first level started, you were drawn to the first level because there was more material stuff then?

Yes. I was interested to focus my attention on the first and second levels, because, as you say, there was more action there, and beyond the levels there is less. So in the levels themselves, there are lots of things going on and lots of calls for my services. You can see how any creator

might have need for what I do.
Oh, every creator.

The Beginnings of the Council of Creators

At what point did this idea of a Council of Creators develop?

From my experience, it developed, again, as a need. The Council was created before it was needed. At first I thought it was something not unlike a social organization.

We were in contact with each other a very long time before anybody came to ask our advice. This is another perfect example, you understand, of how something came into being long before it was actually needed, but it would be needed at some point. I think perhaps that the reason things come into being long before they're needed is so that those things that will support something else need to socialize or need to get used to what they are. And after they get used to what they are or have experience or what-have-you, then when they begin doing other things or do what they were originally intended for, they no longer have to struggle and make mistakes with whatever their job is; they've already done that. So we had already socialized as a council; we knew who the others were. And some came and went; it was, as I say, not unlike a club. There was no reason for us to think any different, and we liked it. Then after a while it began to dawn on us, when beings came to ask for our assistance, that that's what it was all about. But it could still be social for us.

How many of you were there?

In the beginning there were just a few, two or three, and then it became five or six, and then eight or nine, and then it became twelve or thirteen. There was a pause when there were thirteen, and after that there started to be others—forty and fifty, and some of those who sometimes come and go. But the thirteen would be like a core group, not that we would stay there all the time, but we would have our energy in this place. The place would sometimes move around, but we had a commitment to that as a project, as it were. But the others beyond the thirteen would come and go as needed, as we came to realize later; at first we just thought that it was the socialization process, but no, it was only a certain amount for some reason. You could say, "What was that reason?" And I could say, I don't know, suggesting something beyond this.

Who were the first couple of creators that came?

I was the first one, having been there, and I didn't really think of myself having a social experience until the other two showed up.

Who were they?

It's a language difference: I don't think of them as who; I only think of them as what. It was a feeling. I can't answer this question in the way you need to hear it. That's why the creators speak for themselves, because I think most of us do not feel other creators as the way we might describe ourselves; rather, it's like more of us. It's kind of like the onion, hm?

Like another layer of yourself.

Like a layer, exactly.

The Council's Uncreation Stipulation

I want to know how you interacted with our Creator and some really fascinating things you did for other creators, in whatever way you'd like to share that.

Your Creator was an interesting personality. Your Creator explained the general parameters of what It intended and hoped to accomplish, and requested my assistance, which was being polite—obviously, I would have just gone out there. But your Creator is, if nothing, polite. (At least I thought your Creator was very polite; I might have been socialized by that time!)

When your Creator left, I remember we discussed what your Creator was going to do at great length in the Council. This was because your Creator was really going to take a tremendous chance with the Explorer Race concept—not in the beginning, of course, as you were evolving, but toward the end of your evolution, now, when you would be exposed to this kind of polarity. And the creation itself would be exposed to it. Obviously in this place, where Earth is now, it would be exposed more, but other places would to some extent also be exposed to the polarity. So we discussed it at great length, and we informed your Creator even after your Creator had left that we (the Council) would support this creation to the best of our ability, with the stipulation that if your Creator's creation (your universe) reacted to this exposure of this level of polarity in some destructive or self-destructive way (not unlike, from your perspective, the way cancer cells function in the body), if that were to happen as an infectious system, He would have to dismantle the creation.

Your Creator was upset. But we informed your Creator that even though It was vast and wise and had learned many things, this was really Its first major creation. And because It was involving such complexities, we said, in the nicest way possible, that we felt your Creator (of this universe) did not have enough wisdom and experience on Its own.

I think perhaps one of the reasons your Creator collected so many guides and advisors was to extend Its knowledge and wisdom—which we all agreed, on the Council, was a very wise and astute decision. Nevertheless, we left the stipulation, and to this day your Creator is not particularly happy about it.

I'm aware of this, and that all the other friends of the Creator also had to agree to be part of this uncreation if . . .

Yes, and I grant that it is a very slim chance that uncreation will have to take place, but it is a chance. Your Creator didn't like having this, as It felt, restriction put upon It, but the Council and *all other* creators, including ones that come and go, agreed completely with that decision. So we feel very good about that decision. We cannot have the lives of infinite souls and beings and infinite particles and personalities permanently transformed by some catastrophic discomfort, should that occur. If it does, then our position will be to begin the uncreation process. You understand that this guarantees that no matter how polarized things get, if things go too far, uncreation would be necessary, with the discomforted parts of the creation being uncreated first and all other parts of the creation being uncreated as well, until all parts appear absolutely benevolent. This might require the dismantling and uncreation of up to three-quarters, maybe even four-fifths of this universe.

I thought Isis said we've made it, but that didn't happen from your perspective?

That is not my perspective.

Are you seeing more negativity ahead of us?

I didn't say that.

I thought we had turned the corner, you know.

That may be Isis' perspective; my perspective is, until you all come together to form your own creator and decide what you're going to do with polarity, then accomplish it and create benevolence in this universe—until that takes place, speaking for the Council, we will hold to that stipulation.

Because we have to go in and uncreate the negativity while keeping the creation going, right?

Yes. You will have to do more than what the now Creator of this universe has done. Your responsibility will be greater—which is, I believe, why this Creator of this universe needed for you to be *more* than Itself, and why It had to create conditions for you that you could *become* more. Because, you see, you would have to *do* more.

When such a complex universe was planned, how was the space chosen?

Do you mean this universe you are in?

Yes. We'll be subject to a great deal of stress and that surely will stress the spaces we are in.

I didn't participate in that. Your Creator, like other creators, found the space that felt right to It, and I stabilized the space around this universe to a greater firmness than the space around most universes. The firmness around this universe is completely flexible, and if you touched it, it would feel soft, but it would feel like substance. But the firmness around this universe is mathematically three to the tenth power times X, which equals four to the nobo.

I don't know what that word means.

Nobo: A Number beyond Nine

This is nobo; this is a number you are not using yet. You will use this when you understand the true meaning of what you are now calling zero, which is actually the circle. And when you understand the true meaning of the circle, you will use this as a number, which is called the nobo—which is spelled, for the sake of this language [writes] . . . nobo; n-o-b-o.

$$3^{10 \cdot X = 4 \oplus}$$

Nobo

That's one of the secrets we were kept from so we wouldn't cause too much destruction?

Yes, that's the secret of numbers. The nobo has a great deal to do with flexibilities, unexpected events, spontaneous needs and arbitrary conclusions; it creates a great deal of available reaction to the unknown or unexpected and builds in a fantastic amount of flexibility.

If you begin to understand that as a number, it will make a lot of things, to say nothing of individuals who work with numbers, much clearer in understanding life; you will be able to completely understand the gap. So you really do have a number that goes beyond nine; the next number is nobo.

How soon before we will be able to deal with that?

I wouldn't be at all surprised if you'll be able to understand it within fifty years. You just have to understand that once you get past the number nine and start moving toward numbers like nobo, when you must understand how philosophy, feelings and instincts interact with science . . . Science can go to number nine; but once you go beyond number nine, philosophy, which would be ways of life, how you live, feelings—what you feel, how you interact with your feelings and the feelings of others and so on—and religion . . . all these things must interact. So science must graduate to becoming sacred. It does this by integrating these other things I've suggested, becoming sacred science. When you have sacred science in practice, then you will understand and be able to utilize the nobo. This is obviously, by the way it is written, a four-part number. [Draws.] Here is a larger version of the nobo. Science, feelings, philosophy, instinct—there are the four parts of the nobo. When all four of these make up the nobo [writes], the nobo symbolizes sacred science.

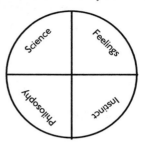

Nobo Symbolizes Sacred
Science—Science as a
Benevolent Practice

This is not science as a religion, but science as a benevolent practice. Think of science now. Science offers you many wonderful and useful things, but it has also given you the bomb and such things as that. When we have sacred science or benevolent science, you will still have all these wonderful things, but to a greater degree of themselves. For instance, with sacred science you will understand how the plants function because you will be able to feel what the plant feels. You will be able to know what it looks like inside the plant, how the plant synthesizes. Even as the Sun shines on the leaves, you will be able to feel yourself as the leaves. You will be able, as the sacred scientist, to *look inside* the plant itself, seeing how the molecules move around, heated by the Sun, and how photosynthesis happens, how chlorophyll does this and how water does that. You will be able to completely understand it mentally while having the fulfilling personal experience of feeling it. And it will all be done in a way that the plant will welcome you, and you will be thankful to the plant. The process is very sacred. The mental process is not shut out; it is not only a shamanic experience, as you might say now, but it is also a scientific understanding, but science at a higher level.

It is this level of science that allows people to travel from planet to planet benevolently. Remember, time travel and space travel are accomplished most easily when it is benevolent for all.

Knowledge of the Nobo in Tribal Teachings

So the only tiny little clues we have on the planet are the secret teachings known to the tribal people.

They once were, and in some circles they still are, but a lot of that knowledge has been lost. Still, the symbols to help decipher it are still present. If you look in areas that might have pictographs like this, you will understand a little that people of those times knew that the messages they left for you would have to be left in something firm.

Like solid stone.

So they left it in stone, hoping you could understand what it meant, or that when you began to get a glimmer, that these things would help pull you along and come to quicker conclusions. Yes, the nobo has already been explained to many societies on this planet. Not many of them remember, but two tribes still have parts of this information.

One of those societies is the Hopi; the other is the Australian Aborigines. Each has a part. There are three parts of the knowledge. The third part was in Africa, but that knowledge has been destroyed along with all records of it, alas!

Deliberately or . . .

Not deliberately, but in the process of life.

How will we get it back? From the ETs?

Maybe. But in order to get it from the ETs, you will have to prove your worthiness to them. You will have to accomplish moving science to the higher level on your own. You will have to be able to do it on your own, or at least show . . . first the Hopi will be gently informed that they can reveal what they know, then the Aborigines, then the Africans. Even though they [the Africans who know] are not there, spirits are there, and they might inform you through African peoples who are living there now.

That is another reason you cannot get along on this world without the African peoples or the Aborigines or the Hopi. And then there may be a fourth. If necessary, there will be a fourth, though it may not be necessary. It is—how can we say—just in case.

"Just in case" does not mean if anything happens to the Hopis or the Aborigines. It means just in case you make a sudden move upward in your expansion, in which case you will have contacts not only with the extraterrestrials, but with benevolent beings who live in higher dimensions inside this planet. In this case, the beings living inside this planet will provide you with the fourth portion, and the fourth portion contains all the other three portions. As always, there is more than one way. You can go to Kansas City by many ways, but when you get there it will be Kansas City.

[Chuckles.] There's a song about that, you know.

Oh, there is?

Yes; it says, "Here I come!"

Ah!

It has to do with some "crazy little ladies there."

Oh! Such fun!

Your Creation Is within My Being

Let's go back to making the space ahead of the bird softer. The Creator created this space, but is the space it's in your space or from His creation?

The Creator did not create the space in front of the bird; that is my proviso. This creation, this universe, was created in a place where I was! I am the space. When you move your hand through the air from side to side, I am the space.

That's what I was trying to get at. Did He create in this space that is your space?

He created what you can see—the things, the people, the birds, all of this, including many, if not all, the lightbeings, everything like that, the sounds, all the things you know of and can experience, including many of the imaginations and all of this. But the space, as it's moving your hand around, that is mine.

Oh, that is wonderful! So the space around the planet, the space in translight travel, all the space is you!

Yes. That is why, perhaps, I am allowed to speak as the spokesman in this case, for the stipulation I referred to before on this creation, because your creation is created within my being.

All creations are, then! You are in every creation!

As far as I know. I have to say that, because those twinkles came from somewhere, didn't they? And I have to say, I don't know where from!

Yes. But that is incredible joy, then; you get to experience every experience we have—everything and every feeling!

Yes, I get to participate. I may not know everything, but I get to *be* there.

And since we're made up of atoms, and atoms are mostly empty space, you're in our bodies?

Yes, I'm in your body.

Once you got past the idea of the polarity and uncreation, what advice did you give our Creator?

Mostly it was, from my perspective, the sequence of creation for your Creator, the timetable of growth, that space needs time. Space within an experience of time needs time to adapt—or, as we would say, outside of time, space needs experience. There need to be moments to adapt as matter is being created in space. So I urged your Creator to let there be time cycles for creation or, as we would say, let there be experience.

Thus, creation as you know it in this universe took place in a sequence: this happened, that happened, this happened, yes? And so it grows. That was my suggestion, so that the space could adapt.

It needed more time for adaptation because of the extreme polarity?

102 ♦ THE COUNCIL OF CREATORS

No. There are parts of this universe that are relatively untouched. I stipulated that things could be created quickly there because instantaneous response then would be available. But in the universe you are concerned with, I recommended this. Actually, I recommended it in general, although I was prepared to accept instantaneous creation where there wasn't polarity. I like to be able to adapt gradually, although I can accept instantaneous adaptation. But certainly where there is polarity, then, yes. Certainly where there is polarity, there needs to be time or experience to adapt, however your perspective or however you wish to see it.

A Creation of Sudden Contraction and Expansion

What were some of the other creators' problems when they came to you? Can you tell us of any that would be relevant?

One of the more interesting ones was a creator who was putting together a universe that was going to start out very large, then become very small (from about roughly one-third the size of this universe to about the size of the head of a pin), and then expand to being about ten times its original size. The creator's intention was to give all the beings within that original size of the universe an opportunity to experience not only contraction, as you understand it (in contraction there is great support, that's the feeling), but also expansion, where there is great adventure and excitement and, usually, happiness. So the creator wished to do that for the beings within that space.

I suggested in this case, since the creation was very benevolent, that the space between all of its creations be very compatible with the creation within it, so that the sudden contraction and expansion could be instantaneous. That way all the beings, all the structures, everything, would be created to be compatible with the space that surrounded it. Let's pick a being on a planet, an average being, or even an average piece of matter, or they might have something that would look like a mountain but would be translucent in places. All of that would have around it an actual visible light auric field, and that light would interact with the space beyond it, creating a bridge so that all beings, all things, would have this light around it. And that bridge, that light, would act to create a great compatible area between the object and the space. Such compatibility would be able to move very quickly because of its comfort with this compatible bridge.

Fascinating. This universe full of beings would all get smaller.

They would all [shrink] to the size that would equal the head of a pin, but they wouldn't be injured; they'd just get smaller. This is possible.

Hm! You have been not everything, but . . .

. . . a lot. Definitely not everything, though. Know this.

When we get done here, I'll go out and help you find what else is out there, okay?

If you like! I'll at least bring you to as far as I can go and say, "Now you go farther."

There's so much more to talk about. I'd like to talk about something from the future. I'd like your perspective on a lot of things. Would you like to talk next week, if it's not possible now?

Yes, perhaps, if you like.

You have so much to share that we haven't even touched on.

Yes. I was glad I could share the nobo with you, because this is a wonderful thing coming for science.

I don't want you to stop; I just don't want to discomfort the channel.

No, no, it's all right. The channel is getting tired.

Yes, well I return. Creator of Gaps and Spaces, eh?

The Explorer Race Ribbon of Inspiration
Came from Beyond My Experience

You're the first one we've gotten to talk to from what I would call outside the system. I have to assume that from your perspective all of this creation in all these levels, as we've been told, is totally benign and benevolent and boring. Whose idea was this inspiration to create the Explorer Race and cause this quantum expansion?

[Chuckles.] From my perspective, I believe the same person who introduced the twinkles into my space and who introduced the strands. I have felt the strands of what could be, what might be what you call ideas in formation. I have felt them moving through me, but I have not created any of these at any time. So my feeling is, whoever created this strand that your Creator of this universe attached Itself to, that became the Explorer Race idea. That strand came from outside of my experience.

Beyond you!

That's why I suggested it might have come from the place where the twinkles came from.

What you called the precreation sparks.

Yes, but this is just like saying it came from up the road, which doesn't mean it came from the same source, but from my perspective it came from up the road where I have not been.

I had the idea that you had seen the whole process, that it came from someplace within you.

No, in my experience it comes from beyond what I have known to be so.

I've asked this of people and some of them got mad and refused, and some of them weren't interested, and some of them went ahead and did it. Have you ever asked for information? Have you ever looked to see what was beyond you or asked if someone would respond?

I have not, no. Would you like me to?

Yes.

To see who is up the line?

Well, we could ask specifically where the creator sparks and the inspiration came from.

Oh, yes. The creator sparks—I have been told that this I cannot know. Now, the strands—I have been told you can ask for that being next.

The being who sent out the strands?

Yes.

All right! Who told you couldn't know about the precreator sparks?

It was a voice that said I cannot know. It said, "This you cannot know."

Now or never?

It did not qualify itself. It did not feel bad, so I have no reason to believe [chuckles] that it is anything but so.

You have no peers. All these other creators, all these levels, all these beings and everybody have peers to talk to, but it appears that you don't.

It appears that way, but as I said before, there are things up the road; perhaps I have peers I don't know about!

Wouldn't it be interesting, if when you finally got to the end of everything that was, it was like when I got to the All That Is—it's just one of billions of them?

In my experience, however long or short you count it, there is always something up the road. And I believe it is intended. It is also possible that what is up the road might be yourself in some future incarnation or even yourself in some past or parallel configuration. It is possible, you know, to explore the many facets of yourself—exclusively your own personality—and spend an infinite amount of time doing that. You are made up of all these molecules and atoms and particles, each one of which you could explore, that have some relationship to you, but also to all the lives you have lived, all the lives you *might* have lived if you had changed just one thing or many things. It is possible to explore yourself,

in my experience, to the infinite, then take that times everyone else . . .
Can you imagine how awesome it is?

Yes. But think about that. I have known beings, not complex beings, not creator beings, not beings who have great and vast responsibility, but simple beings, individuals who have chosen between lives or between responsibilities, you might say, to explore every facet of themselves. The last being I observed who was doing that had been exploring every facet of itself in the type or way I mentioned and had been doing so for about the half-life of your universe, and it was not done yet! [Laughs.]

How did you perceive that? Would you say that that was a valuable use of his time, or a waste of time?

In my experience, it is not possible to waste time, ever.

Because you always gain something from it.

Something is gained, even if only a memory.

Or a vow not to do that again.

[Chuckles.]

Gaining Wisdom in the Prebirth Experience

One of the most tantalizing things you said, one of your first phrases, was that your origin was so far back it was hard to remember, and it was in the future. Can you discuss that?

Yes. You know that the foundational principle of the Explorer Race is that it's happening in a loop of time. I have noted with some interest that my point of origin is situated in some future place—meaning I have not arrived at my birth yet. That would suggest that I am in my prebirth stage and that all that has gone on, all that I remember, all that I have seen or felt, all that I have experienced—the nuances, all the smells, the scents, everything—is some precondition. It would also suggest, though it is not an absolute, that everything you are doing also has to do with some precondition, that this entire vastness is preceding something. So it is my belief, from what I have been able to discover of my point of origin, that what I am experiencing now is a means to re-create who I will be when I am created. It is as if I am experiencing the molecular antecedent to becoming the child within the mother. I am not yet a formed being, in that sense, but I am becoming that which will, at some point in time, be completely formed and birthed. So what you are speaking to now is that which exists before I exist, yet to me, within the context of my personality, I am a multilevel complex being with vast reservoirs of personalities, wisdom and knowledge. Still I have seen as clearly as I can see and have felt quite clearly that I have not actually been born yet. So all that I am is preceding all that I will be at my inception. This suggests that my inception has to do with entirely another world, which also would explain why I don't know certain things, why I can't know certain things, and why some things come from places I don't understand. If I don't understand them, perhaps they are coming from the future to the past rather than from some place to here. You see, that makes so much sense, doesn't it?

Yes, and it implies that what you will be birthed as requires this vast experience you're gaining, because whatever you're going to become is so unbelievable.

Yes, think about it. Even yourself in the physical body you are occupying at this time—the mass of your body, the molecules, the cells, the structures, the blood, the fluids, all of this—before it became your body, it had acquired vast wisdom and experience. And while it passes through your body and generates and regenerates itself as your body and then passes on in some cases to become bodies of others, it brings with it vast wisdom and experience that you call upon many times for what seem to be the most rudimentary skills and abilities. But in order to understand it more clearly, let's use this as an example: Children learn at different rates on the basis of what they are taught and how they are taught. The average child—not the most brilliant, not the slowest, but the average child—to the degree of speed that it learns how to walk, how to talk, how to spell, how to stand, crawl, sing, everything, if that child's body were made up of particles that had not achieved wisdom by experience over and over again as different matter, without arriving with personality of their own, if that body were made up of raw material that had never been anywhere or done anything . . . it would take the average child its entire average lifetime to learn how to put its toes in its mouth.

We say also that the cells of our body are a part of Mother Earth, who is a very wise being. We're borrowing them.

Yes.

To use that analogy, then, everything you just drew, with all the levels and all your beingness, could be on the outside of some sphere so large as to be incomprehensible.

Yes, I might be just a cell. And if I am a cell that is gaining wisdom to be a portion of some other being at some point in time, it is no wonder that I have gaps and spaces in my knowledge. Think about it. Does a cell in your finger need to know how to be a cell in your pancreas? If it has never in its experience been a cell in anyone's pancreas before but has on previous occasions been a finger or even an appendage of some other creature or being, it would have some knowledge of that. Maybe that cell of the finger does not need to know how to be the cell of a pancreas; maybe I do not need to know, at this stage of my experience, where the twinkles (as I'm calling them) came from. That is why the voice says to me, "You cannot know this at this time."

That also suggests that what I do not know and cannot know, I do not *need* to know this at this time. I can accept that gracefully because it feels good. It also, I believe, may allow me to have a life that is as simple as my life is, because as much as I am, with the degree of matter in me and what is going on, in the larger sense, my life still feels simple to me. When it is all boiled down to its basic components, what I do are gaps and spaces. I don't do other things, even though other things might happen within me. I might be aware of them, just as you might be aware of a conversation between two other people nearby. It is not your conversation. You might remember the conversation, but the conversation is not your direct responsibility.

That's interesting. You let them use your space, but you're not responsible for it; it's not your direct experience.

No. It might be indirect because I am a witness to it, but it is not directly happening. I am not directly involved in a causal way, so it is not a responsibility. When the voice says I cannot know this, it is not only sustaining the simplicity of my life, but it is also protecting me from expanding into areas for which I may not have any previous experience, as the finger cell to the pancreas cell, yes? I might do more harm than good if I took it on as a responsibility.

And somebody else might already be there, too.

Exactly.

I erred a little while ago when I said you had no peers. I was thinking of you as the picture of . . . everything was the levels. But yet you have focused down to become one of the Council of Creators, so you talk to beings all the time, right?

Yes.

You interact, you give advice, you have, like you said, an active social life.

A very active social life, yes. My calendar is brisk.

You talked about space.

Yes.

I've got to straighten out my process here. When we talked to the Creator's father, the Creator of the Void, I understood that he had created the space between the stars. But instead, he took your space and laid the black quietness upon it—is that a way to say it?

Yes. Think about the artist who uses paint. The artist paints a beautiful canvas—stunning, perhaps pleasing to the artist and to many who look at it. Although this Creator of the Void did create exactly what it said it created, it happened to use material that was available to it.

Which was your body.

Yes, and one might ask, What was here before I was? My assumption would be something else. I painted the canvas, but I did not perhaps provide the canvas initially.

That's interesting, because I thought you did.

When we talked about my birth, we were talking about something that's happening in the future. So if I were to talk about my first memory, that is something that happens in the future. Yet if we were to talk about my next memory, which is perhaps more enlightening, that memory begins when I am here, where I am now. The only memory I have that precedes that is my future birth, which tells me immediately, even without logic, that I am living in a time that precedes my birth. This means that I am acquiring wisdom that will sustain me when I am born.

That suggests, then, that the Creator of the Void utilized that which was present to provide, in a structured way, the spaces between the stars, but may not have created the material it structured. Or to put it another way, it might have re-created it in the fashion that was needed.

If we say there's a giant sphere and you are spread over that and the Creator of the Void painted over that, we could assume there's probably another level behind you.

There must be. But when I say that, I am saying it on faith, without being able to produce solid evidence.

Gaps in Time

Well, right now we know that you exist and that you've spread into this space. So we've got the Void. Now you've talked about your space, but I don't understand gaps. What does that mean, gaps and spaces?

With space one tends to think of this vast area between things. Gaps are perhaps more minute or precise areas between things. It is really that. It is also, of course, gaps in time.

You create gaps in time?

I do not, in my own right, create time, but there are moments within time where time juxtaposes over other time avenues (if we can call them that) where there needs to be a gap. If the two times ran together, they would create a clash, and worlds within one time area might easily crash into worlds within another time area. So there needs to be a gap that functions, not as a composite material but as a . . . if you open a door there is a breeze, because the door passes through something solid that is lighter than the door. The moment before you open the door, there is an intent to open the door. When I provide gaps in time, I am providing the moment before opening the door and the sound associated

with opening the door and, to a minor degree, the breeze of opening the door. But I do not provide the door; other beings do that. I believe you have heard from somebody else who does that, who creates separations between the levels and so on.
Yes.

It is not my job to do that, but to some extent a minor duty of mine is to provide gaps in time when times become too close to each other. Perhaps I ought to say that on occasion, times will become almost merged. This happens on the personal level within the experience of déjà vu, for example. On the more grand level, it happens as people are moving between dimensions and superimposing one scenario of experience in a time stream over another one, as flags or banners might touch each other briefly as they blow in the wind and then resume their usual wave in the breeze. It is my job to briefly apply a small gap that will keep the two times separated so that they do not totally meld, no matter how enmeshed they might become. If two times were to completely meld for even, say, three measurable seconds, there could be no end of mischief. The only way it is allowed for an instantaneous melding (less than a hundredth of a second of measurable time) between times is when beings are traveling in time, through time, between dimensions and so on. If you are able to do that as yourself without technical means, you do not require gaps. There is no hazard to your passage.
In your position to time, do you deal in what I would call, without really understanding it, probable or possible realities, or parallel realities?

I do not; that is not my responsible area. But I might need to put a gap around such things.

The Potential for Infinity
I'm looking for a road map of the infinite, and you have just blasted it about ten million degrees larger.

It is always the case, in my experience, because the more we attempt to create a fixed reality, the more reality screams to be free of rigid controls. So even if one desires to create a fixed reality without anyone else's input, reality in its own right will command that change take place. It will not tolerate being fixed for very long. That's why even the most benevolent system and the most benevolent planet must change. More advanced societies know this, so they attempt to build into their society's cultural evolutionary change something that moves along a certain desirable path of growth. Since they cannot avoid growth, they try to create a desirable path so they do not experience change for its own sake. Change *will* happen.

Well, I wasn't trying to fix reality, I was trying to get some landmarks to navigate it.

I know, but sometimes I will volunteer these thoughts, not just for you but for the reader [chuckles]. We must not forget that ultimately this is for the reader.

Many beings have talked for these books, and they all seem to have a different understanding. Some of them say that when we, as the Explorer Race, become one and the Creator moves up, the expansion will go out an infinite degree. One being said, "Oh, no; we will let it go a little way and look at it, then we'll let it go a little further and look at it." What is your perception of this, even though it hasn't happened yet?

From my perception, however screened it may be, I would have to place my vote into the basket that says "infinite degree."

Aha! See, that gives the Explorer Race so much more meaning, so much more depth and so much more power.

In my experience, however simplistic it might be, infinity seems to be a universal axiom. Wherever I have looked, been, felt, everything, the potential for infinity is absolute, to say nothing of its applications already in process in any given place or moment. It is ironic that the only real absolute I am aware of is infinity.

As an adventurer, I like the idea that there's a lot out there to explore.

Well, let's just say that I have met many immortals, even many who are adventurers and explorers and a few who have been to places I have never heard of—that's how far they've been. And to an absolute personality—as you would say, to an individual or a person or to a man and a woman—all of them agree that the more they explore, the more they see, the more they discover, then the more aware they become of how much more there is. And just about the time when they feel they've seen it all, they have an insight that allows them to realize that they have to go back over the ground they've already been in because they have missed so much.

You just said something highly provocative. If we use this picture of you as the drawing with the little, tiny levels up here, are you saying that some of these explorers have come from beyond your edges?

Yes. Remember those twinkles?

Yes.

And there have been others, beings who just showed up. Sometimes they'll communicate with me, not unlike what I'm calling the twinkles, because that's how they struck me—little twinkling lights. Occasionally we will communicate and they will tell me what they can. Sometimes they have tried to tell me things I cannot understand. This is why when the voice says, "You cannot know this," it's not by way of being author-itarian. That's the voice's way of saying, "You cannot possibly under-stand this," meaning at the level I am on. "Know" doesn't mean you can't be told; it means you cannot know it, you cannot understand it, you cannot experience it. That's why the voice would say that.

I have been told by explorers before of things I could not under-stand, and did not. So perhaps the word has gotten around [chuckles]; now if there are things they can express to me only by other means of communication that I cannot understand (perhaps because I am a cell of the finger and not of the pancreas, as in our analogy), they don't try anymore. In their own way they'll say, "Well, I can't really explain it."

What have they said that you have understood? What have you gleaned from some of these?

Let me give you an example. Right now as an individual, you are in the communication business. You are therefore reasonably aware of all the levels of communication that are available, not only technically speaking but on a personal basis—even counting, if we might be so broad, the kind of communication that goes on between animals and so on. Given the levels of communication that are known here, if we took all those levels that are known here and said, "How many more types are there?" (types of communication, such as talking), I would have to say that the number is not infinite, but it is, as so many circles (you say zeros), almost intimidating.

This tells you that even you cannot know certain things, because the types of communication you experience are very precisely focused in areas where the communication itself is guaranteed to be limited. It must be limited to protect other beings in other dimensions, other realms, in other galaxies, for that matter, because what you do here on Earth and how you experience things here must stay here. Otherwise, in the natural communication beyond the veils here, what is said . . . if there is a great insight, say, on the Pleiades, a moment later that insight is felt. Perhaps it will be understood mentally, perhaps not; but it will at least be felt in galaxies a thousand million light-years away.

It is not to suggest that everyone is connected in a universal brain, wherein you think something, you suddenly get a concept, then other people suddenly start thinking it—it is not that. It is rather that some gap in your knowledge has been filled by an inspiration, and you have that moment, as you say, of eureka!

Aha!

The *aha!* moment. Most importantly, it fills a gap, where something is missing and you feel more complete. When you have that feeling, people on the other side of the universe also have that feeling, and they celebrate with you. Communications like that are not allowed on this planet at this time so that others will not be affected. Although some of you might have limited experiences of that, it's shielded within this place.

But can you share, were there any communications you received from the sparks that would be relevant to us, anything you learned that you can pass on to us?

The reason I have given you this long preamble is to say that what I can pass on to you would have to be in a very greatly diluted analogy.

All right, suffice it to know that there's life beyond the edges.

Let's just say that in my experience there are no edges; there are only places you have not felt yet.

I was referring to what you had felt . . .

I understand.

That's as much of yourself as you can feel right now.

Yes.

I Provide the Gaps and Spaces

It's my understanding that there are lines of light within this universe, within this galaxy. Is your energy body like a web? Do you provide these lines on which beings communicate and can travel? Is that within your body?

You know a good way to see me? Imagine a cloud.

So the lines or the webs are superimposed over you by the creators?

I am gaps and spaces, yes. Anything that is within me, it is my job to provide the spaces or the gaps around it. Whenever something becomes in me, I provide the gaps and spaces, and to some extent the density of the space around and between other things. But if you could picture me as a cloud, it would be easier to see that, visually speaking.

Doesn't each creator create within its creation lines of energy or lines of light or a communication system that's creator-wide? Can you say that?

Picture the artist's palette. On the palette are many daubs of paint. If each daub is a creator and its creation, I am the palette, but I am not the fingers that hold the palette.

But we haven't met that person yet.

For all I know, it is more than one. Can you say that you are one when, as I see you, you are multitudinous beings? I can relate to each of your cells, each of your molecules, each of your atoms or protons, on the basis of its own personality. So to me you are a multitudinous galaxy of living organisms that you experience as one but that I experience as many and varied.

And that's one physical body, let alone the vastness of us.

[Chuckles.] Yes.

All right; I'm about to run out of intelligent questions.

It is not that your intelligence is wrung out; it is that the more we communicate, the more we need the visual medium, which is why I am utilizing visual analogies. And after a while, words do not function within this medium. This is to put a little balm on your intelligence quotient.

Specialist in Divine Intervention

February 20, 1998

 am the Creator of Divine Intervention.
Welcome.

Divine Intervention Often Delays Growth

It is my job to advise other creators on when to intervene in a given situation and when to allow it to continue on its course. I have traveled much in order to acquire sufficient wisdom for this task. I have been to every universe [chuckles] I could find and have observed to see and sometimes to calculate whether divine intervention would have been helpful to a civilization. You'd be surprised how often it isn't. More times than not, divine intervention has ultimately delayed the growth or the stamina of individuals and even cultures.

It is quite surprising, but if you build, as a creator, enough into the beings in terms of the levels they can access or the capacities they have, simply by giving them such depth, divine intervention may not be necessary. I grant that there are cases in which it is completely warranted; but by and large, one of the most consistent phenomena I have seen in most creations everywhere I have gone, is that the lack of growth is equal almost entirely to the extent of divine intervention.

It appears, naturally, as one would expect, that creators love their creations, and if something or someone or some experience of someone is so beautiful and lovely, they do not wish it to be destroyed, even if its destruction might lead to something better—rising, as it were, from the ashes, or even transforming from one thing to something better. In order to have this transformation, as you know, trauma can often be the cause.

A typical trauma might be a meteorite—not common ground for all universes, but one that you can understand in your own—which is fragments coming and going. Most civilizations, when they are either very sacred or at least reasonably technically advanced, have ways to deflect such things. I think you would find, though, to your interest that simply having a civilization that can deflect meteorites that pose a threat or send them into a more benevolent orbit (for the meteorite), these civilizations will, of course, prevent any meteorite from hitting, even if it is minuscule. You'd be surprised; sometimes even the Creator of this creation in which you all reside has purposely seeded some materials into very small meteorites. As you know, on your planet they will hit from time to time. Sometimes they will just be, as you know, a rock, but quite often, especially with the small ones that do very little if any damage, there will be something either inside or close enough to the surface of the meteorite so that time and the wear and tear of the motions of your world will break it down and put this material (biological, perhaps, even specifically genetic) into your environment, with the intention of bettering your societies in some way. Your world has not been insulated from this, but most worlds in your universe have, because not only are the technical means available, but if the spiritual means are available and meteorites are considered to be threatening (even in some minor way), then such organic instruments of your Creator's inspiration will be deflected.

This is just one way in which otherwise benevolent and beautiful societies have unintentionally stopped their growth. I do not wish to sound as if all meteorites striking all planets any time they wish is good; certainly some would be better off being deflected. And there has been an occasion for your planet, not too long ago, when one was deflected. I believe this was a few hundred years ago, and if it had not been deflected, it would have hit the northern polar regions and considerably altered the weather on Earth. This would have had a grievous impact on plant and animal life, to say nothing of the life of human beings. That was a case of divine intervention, where your Creator just skipped it off the outer boundaries of your atmosphere. But as is typical of your

Creator, since It's interested in your evolution (if I might say that, spiritually), your Creator did not prevent that meteorite from returning, with the idea that someday you as beings on Earth will demonstrate your spiritual growth by deflecting the meteorite again. This will probably happen in 2400, as you understand experiential time, between 2400 and 2500, perhaps. By that time you will have legions of individuals who will have the capacity, each unto themselves (and working together, even more so), to deflect such an object. It will, in fact, be a test of your accomplishments by then. Saying this to you now gives you time to prepare.

You might be surprised to learn, gentle reader, that preparations for future life can often be made in the present life. Think about where you are in time today, yet I have suggested that this event will occur in that century mentioned. I am saying this not only for your souls, but for those who will follow, to consider it as a skill worthy of your accessing—to be able to deflect a meteorite, which is, of course, similar to deflecting anything, but not the same (for those of you who believe it so) as the ability to move objects, which has fascinated you for some time (moving objects without touching them or exerting any external force upon them). So I suggest this for your interest.

Creator's Intervention Allowed Jesus to Raise the Dead

Now, there have been other occasions when I have strongly advised against divine intervention, but it has been done anyway. Most of these occurred on other planets, but one of them I will bring up because it is of historical reference on this planet. The reference I will bring up is the divine intervention that allowed Jesus (this being you know and often love) to do that thing about raising the dead.

This was something that required divine intervention. It wasn't that the man was in a deep coma; the man was dead, and as a matter of fact, his body had begun to decompose. So bringing his soul back into the body in a way that was recognizable—but not exactly as he had been, because he had already evolved—required divine intervention to change the form of his body and make it habitable once again. I might add that Jesus did not wish to do this, and when he was involved in it he said, "I will do what I can," the way a healer or even a physician might say, with the idea in his own mind that by saying this he would be honoring the needs of that man's family yet at the same time not holding out false hope.

Much to his surprise, and because Creator wished to support the work that Jesus was doing (it was an attempt, as many of you know, to empower the people of the time with their own enlightenment, to show them who they are and what they could do, as well as to inspire them), that Creator here was so fond of what Jesus was doing, that the Creator of this universe intervened (as creators have done other places) to bring the soul back into the body and recompose the body. Of course, since the man's personality had evolved, the man was from that day forward not only living in that body, but was a better man, a kinder man, more cooperative, one who was special.

Why did I recommend against this? An act of kindness, you might say; surely a merciful act, you might say. Yet it was one of the acts that at that time so amazed people and was such a powerful experience, naturally, for those around them, that from that moment on, Jesus' followers, the men and women who believed he was a wonderful teacher and messenger, decided that he was a god. Even though your Creator intervened for the best of reasons, look at what it has done! Can you blame the people of times gone by for attempting to convert others by the sword, believing that miracles done by their god, Jesus, warranted any means necessary to save the souls of others? Yes, many wonderful things have been done in the name of Christianity and are still being done, but any Christian today would be embarrassed or ashamed for the past about things that were done in the name of Christianity, ofttimes during the Crusades and other appalling ventures. It is not for me to say that Christians of today should be embarrassed—no, not a bit of it—but to suggest to you that if that one single event hadn't occurred, Jesus would have gone on being the beloved teacher, the advisor, the rabbi (as people might have said in those times), and would have influenced even the Roman rulers of the time, more so than he was able to do.

I do not chide your Creator; it is not my job to act as if your Creator has been foolish. But it is for me to suggest to you that even creators have lessons. Your Creator learned a great deal from this experience, and the being known as Jesus also learned a lot. You'll notice there is only one story like this, Jesus raising the dead. From that point on Jesus would go on to help to heal the sick, to (from his perspective) help them so they would not be suffering. But you know, once a man is dead and his soul is gone, there's no suffering. Even though he was asked many, many times, he never even made the attempt. He would just console the bereaved; he would never make the attempt because he was afraid (yes, he had fear) that divine intervention would take place and move him in the eyes of the people farther above them, which was the opposite of what he was trying to do. He wanted the people to see what *they* could do; he wanted them to understand how they could change their lives in more beneficial ways. Granted, much of that has been done, but your Creator of this universe—perhaps because It did not understand polarity and suffering as a personal experience—unintentionally brought fear into the life of Jesus, a person who had, up to that point in time, learned how to make fear his friend and work with it. But even Jesus did not feel that he could work with something that was beyond him, such as raising the dead.

So your Creator has learned from this. That's why it's been awhile since someone like Jesus has been known to you. Yes, you have had many great teachers since then—insightful masters, as you would say—but as in Jesus' time, they have been known for the most part only by a select few. It has been kept this way, even though today you have communications that are very fast and people can know if they want to. But your Creator has been (how shall I say?) shy.

Creator Did Not Intervene in Recent Wars

That's an example. Most often, as I say, I advise creators not to intervene, but sometimes, of course, it is warranted. I might say something else here, and I'm only saying this because your Creator has urged me to say so, so I will: If Creator had *not* intervened—made that mistake, you might say; benevolent mistake for certain, but mistake—by raising the dead that time, He would still have had to learn Her lesson, if I might be using the mixed terms there. That is, Creator here would have had to intervene for a good cause to preserve something. That would have happened either in World War I or World War II, because so much was destroyed in so many places that was of great value. You know (but I will tell you) that Creator experienced, during World War I and World War II and a few times since—during the Vietnam War and during some recent African tribal warfare—or came as close to experiencing the feeling of pain that Creator here could experience. But He did not intervene, though I can tell you She wished to very much. Nevertheless, I and others supported Creator in this decision because of the depth of consciousness and abilities that your Creator has given you as individuals. There were times when Creator here, during those wars, had to almost look away. Other creators in the Council consoled Creator here to let Him know that you had to experience such horrors so that you could remember them.

You know, you have in your past civilizations experienced other awful things, but in those times there was no means of creating a lasting record. In these more modern times, these horrible experiences have been written about and filmed, and there are people alive today who can tell you about them. Communication is much more thorough today, so unfortunately you had to go through this. But you have learned. Even today your United Nations is getting stronger, and even though some of you resent the United Nations' influence in your lives, someday you will see that it is intended to be benevolent. It is, of course, ultimately the governing body that will benevolently bring about planetary consciousness so that people can describe themselves as Earth people. They might say they are in America (or there might be new words for it then), or they might say they're European, or Icelandic, but they will say first that they are Earth people. So it will work out; just know that you will (perhaps you know it already) have to be flexible.

That's very beautiful, also very pertinent. Thank you.

I First Became Aware in a Future Moment

Can you talk about yourself a little bit?

What would you like to ask?

All the standard stuff: how you fit in the big picture, where you came from . . .

One at a time, though, yes? So I can feel it.

I see. What was your first experiencing of consciousness or individuality?

My first awareness was so far into the future that I have not even felt the slightest vibration or seen a glimmer of light that we are anywhere near that future moment. This future is benevolence itself, and I noticed that I was or, as you say, I am. I noticed this, and that's when I became aware of myself, and I appreciated the wonderful feeling of benevolence. From your perspective, if you were to go there it would just look like white and gold light and feel like total unconditional love. But using the senses you have now, that would be about it—not that you wouldn't enjoy that. Although it might be pleasant, after a while you might want to, as you say, do something. But from my perspective there was a lot going on.

It was, from that future point in time, the place you are all evolving toward, including past the loop of time you are in. It is so far in the future that you have all evolved to that, including your Creator and, as far as I'm able to tell, everyone and everything else. So it is an arrival, how you will be, all potentials of beauty fully realized. I remember communicating to beings there in my early "days" of consciousness. Many of them had memories of the past. When you get to that point, you will be able to remember everything, even things that were unpleasant, because by then you will completely and totally understand it and it won't seem unpleasant. It will seem a bit odd, that's all.

My Transit to the Past

So I heard about all these amazing things going on in the past, from my perspective. I wondered if these stories I was hearing had anything to do with my existence. Well, of course, when you have such a consideration, these questions are answered. After a few more days (I suppose you might call them half-cosmic days) went by, I began to feel myself moving. At first I thought, *Oh, I'm just exploring this space more,* because I had not moved to explore and I could feel everything in this future place. But I began to slowly realize, *I'm moving away from this and not under my own direction.* I began moving faster and faster, but not so fast that I couldn't see my transit. I began to slowly realize that I was moving into the past. When I realized that, I became very excited and happy because I was going to be able to see where all my friends had been, and I knew perhaps I would have something to offer.

The transit took about three full cosmic days. During that time I had the opportunity to explore many worlds, most of which, I must admit, would be nonsensical to you and really not possible to describe. But the worlds that were similar enough to you were the ones where I acquired greater knowledge of the advantages or disadvantages of divine intervention. After seeing this and experiencing it, I arrived a little bit before this time (cosmically before it), and I was in a very quiet place. I had seen so much, absorbed so much, you understand, been exposed to so much . . . I understand now that I needed time to consider it all, so I was there in that quiet place before any experience of time could be felt. It was also a place where matter did not exist as you know it, so there was no substance. It would be as if I was consciousness, feeling, but not to have an impact on anything that could perceive mass. So I was there for a while, about one quarter of a cosmic day.

Then I began to feel myself moving forward again, and I wondered, of course, *Am I simply going to retrace my steps, as it were? What's going to happen?* But I realized soon that I was moving forward slowly, and as I moved, my first glimmer was of the Council of Creators, which had been established already and had been in existence for some time by that moment. Seeing the Council, I was very interested, and the moment I became interested I stopped and began moving over to the Council. You notice I say these things: *I* didn't move; my entire transit involves being moved by someone or something else, of which I do not know to this day.

I moved over to the Council and "listened" with wonder and enthusiasm. Then I explained what I had been doing, and they were very interested; they wanted to know more. It just so happened that I was intrigued, because of my journey and the path of it, about divine intervention, and being creators, they were very interested. I discovered that not only were they interested, but creators would come to visit and ask advice. And I have been here ever since.

Ah. As Zoosh says, it begs the question—is it possible that you are a creator in that future who is deciding whether or not to intervene, and you've stopped time to come back and check it out?

Is a good question! I have considered this. I have decided that either it is me, or I am the messenger of the person, being, what-have-you who sent me back on this journey, since I did not exert any force. So it is either yes or no! But I believe that there is a connection, because it makes a lot of sense. Not unlike you, I have discussed it with other creators when they come and go, and for the most part they consider it to be possible. Generally speaking, you will find [chuckles] that the comment by most creators of "It's possible" is a typical rejoinder; you will very rarely hear yes or no. You will hear, "It's possible."

That's exciting. Last week the Creator of Gaps and Spaces gave us a little wider view. Was he here when you came here? Were the levels here?

Gaps and Spaces was here, yes.

And the levels?

I did not know Gaps and Spaces was here until I got to the Council, because I didn't realize I was in Gaps and Spaces.

Were there levels here when you got here?

Yes; not many, but there were a few. There were two levels, plus the third was forming, so you can tell that I am, as creators go, a recent arrival, still moist behind my nonphysical ears.

Your Creator Will Intervene Again

So you consciously came from the future and watched what I assume is our future as you came backward. Is that right?

Remember, I was being led, if that's the word, or guided on a journey that focused almost exclusively on divine intervention, so I have seen your future only insofar as it relates to divine intervention—which, I might add, will occur at least one more time in your transit from the third to the fourth dimension. If you think about it, it makes complete sense, because if your Creator has a lesson about divine intervention and has already been stung (as the child touches the hot plate), your Creator has learned something. But why? Because, of course, there will be an occasion to apply divine intervention again in the future, only your Creator will have to do it in a different way than last time.

A subtle way, a more . . .

Yes, more of a nuance of influence rather than startling.

I didn't really mean it so personally, as the Explorer Race's future; I meant the future of everything you see here, from wherever this is now to your origin. There's a constant, there's something all along the way, right?

Yes, except for the place I went to be quiet. You might say there is something there also, but it is more of a welcoming place for quiet reflection. So I would have to say that by and large, yes, there is something, certainly on the route I took. One might consider that there might be other routes based on what the individual creator must know—again, to the infinity, yes? What must you know? [Chuckles.]

I love it, when it opens up like this.

[Chuckles.] The flower has many petals.

The Creator Who Was More Than It Knew

What are some of the most interesting cases where creators brought you their questions, to intervene or not to intervene, cases that we would understand?

Yes, an important proviso. I was dazzled by one. I must admit I am not easily dazzled, but I was dazzled. There is a universe, not so terribly far in creation terms, at the outer lobe of one of the orbs. And from the creation's point of view, that's not so terribly far from where you are.

In this circle of creation?

Yes, in this circle of creation. There was an interesting universe being created there. Everything in the universe was based entirely, without exception, on mathematical principles—including the philosophy, the family, the culture and of course the structures and all of this. One day [chuckles] (if I might put it that way), the creator of that particular universe came to the Council and said that the mathematics of this universe was at its outer boundaries of what it could do and still allow the universe to expand (which is very common, a given in universes that they expand).

So this creator desired to add an extra level of mathematical formula to the universe so that it could gradually expand tenfold. The Council—not only myself, but everyone—really strongly, in our strongest terms, suggested not to do it. This creator, as anyone might, wanted to know, "Well, why not?" We suggested that all the beings in his universe and the universe itself had the capacity, once they had achieved the level of having done everything they could do within the mathematical principles available, to add that extra quantum to the principles and thus expand the potential of their own universe.

The creator who was inquiring thought about this for a while, and after thinking about it said, "I'm not sure I've given them the depth to do that." We assured that creator that it had given the beings the depth, and the creator said—and this happens sometimes with creators, and it's always lots of fun for the Council when it does—"I don't understand," which means that the creator had not, from its point of view, given the beings this capacity!

Aha! So where did it come from, then?

Yes! So the Council explained slowly, with pictures and taking the creator somewhat on a journey of its own, that the inquiring creator had a greater depth of its own character than even that creator knew, and that it had, naturally, creating beings out of itself, granted the beings in that universe that unknown depth of itself. We explained that if that creator just stood back and observed, it would have the wonderful experience of not only seeing the beings expand their own universe, but at the moment of that expansion it would become aware of that part of itself that it was not aware of before.

Wonderful!

Of course, everyone was utterly scintillated when this experience took place, including that creator. That was one of the more sparkling moments on the Council. [Laughs.] We, as you might say, still talk about it today. That's my favorite story.

So whoever created him had given him more than he needed, then.

That's right, and he didn't need to know until that moment, because there was no way for him to use it until his, as it were, offspring became *more.* And then because they became more and they were its offspring, suddenly that creator was aware of the greater depth of itself.

You know, I mention this because on your world parents have this experience, too. They'll have children, and sometimes your children will do things that are just thrilling, and when they do this you'll think back, as a reasonable person, *What on Earth,* you might say, *did we ever do to inspire this in the children? How did they know to do that?* Such as the child who solves some great conundrum or performs some great act of heroism, for instance. The parent will be grateful and thankful to Creator, yes, but also wonder, *Did we in some way encourage that?,* and just by looking at that will very often feel elevated—not by the examination so much, but by the wonderful thing their youngster did. So it seems that this is a similarity, yes?

This brings up something we have never talked about. The child is a material replica of the parents, but it has its own soul. Now, when a creator is created by its creator, is there then a similar type of spiritual ensoulment of that creator that is different from that which gave it birth?

I can't prove it, but I would have to say with enthusiasm, "It's possible!"

Ah, that lends a whole other level to it!

Isn't it wonderful, the way the flower unfolds?

Yes! Now we have to find out where those spirits come from!

Always something to do that is interesting.

Yes. That's great! So then you watched those beings. As you say, they did it, they were able to . . .

They did it, and they continue! Once they reach the capacity of the formula, they expand it again! And every time they expand it, that creator discovers something in itself it didn't know was there. It's just a wonderful thing for everyone.

Wonderful! What gives you great pleasure? I want some more of your experiences. What other things give you great pleasure here?

Seeing beings, not only grand beings, but individuals, even microbes, become *more* in a benevolent way for them. That is the greatest pleasure; I believe, perhaps one of the greatest pleasures everywhere.

You give counsel, but you don't intervene.

No, it is my job to advise about what I know, but not to do so myself—at least so far! One might consider, well, what's all this training for?

Back in the future, yes! You must have some sticky point up there, though.

Well, I am here, yes? But I am from there, one must assume.

The Creator of Gaps and Spaces gave us the incredible wisdom that a creator can stop time and then go back and check into things.

Oh, yes.

So it could be that the future time is just going to stop there while you're here doing your thing?

Yes, and you know, you as an average citizen of Earth, representative of the human race, you do that too, but you do it in what you call the dream state. You will stop time and go backward and forward or to parallel universes to examine things from a different angle. Usually, because of your occupation (meaning your life on Earth), you will see how you're doing or how you're doing in relationship to others you care about or your work or in relationship to something. So there is really no difference; it's just that it's screened from your conscious mind so that you are able to reinvent yourselves.

That's why waking up in the morning with a whole new idea, a whole new attitude—that's where that comes from, right?

Yes; you've been busy.

The Creator Whose Journey Had Not Concluded

What are some other examples we can learn from, about how other creators faced this, to intervene or not to intervene?

There was one creator who was what I would call the student. It had been all over; as a matter of fact, after hearing about this creator's adventures and so on, I'd have to say that this creator had been to places I've never been. If you were to look at it, it would look like a ball of light with different colors at the outer perimeter of its existence. It had never created anything as you understand creation to be. Of course it existed and had affected others in benevolent ways, but it had not stopped and made a creation.

It came to the Council because it had been advised by a creator that that creator could help this creator create something, but that the other creator would have to help it. So the creator who came to see us wanted to know if this would be a good thing to do. I was involved because the creator who wanted to help felt that that creator had done so much and been so many places and had so much to offer, it was time for that creator to do something. However, this would have required altering the journey of the creator who came to us, and in that sense would have been divine intervention.

So I spoke to both of them. I thanked the creator on behalf of the one who came to see us, and as gently and gracefully as possibly said, "No, thanks," that the journey of this creator had not concluded. It had not yet arrived where it would arrive, and that even the best intentions of this other creator could wait. I said that maybe, since this other creator had a good feeling for the creator who came to see us, [the latter] might have the opportunity at some point to assist the one who offered to help. In that way, the one who offered felt good and was satisfied with that, and the one who came to see us continued its journey.

So you see, sometimes you might with the greatest benevolence, with the greatest amount to offer, offer someone something, but it's not the right time for them to have that. So don't feel bad; maybe you'll get your chance at some point.

Are you able to look into this being's future?

No. I did not see the being. It was a feeling, and I went on the feeling, and that was that. The whole Council doesn't vote on things or anything like that. Different creators are given different tasks, you might call it. And that was that. Everybody, as it were, went on with their lives.

So it was almost interference on that first creator's part to say, "I think you should do this."

But very loving interference, not unlike what a parent does all the time. Think about it; it is what a benevolent friend might do or a benevolent coworker might do, where you are in a position to help and you are not offering your largesse as if it were throwing coins to someone, as to a lesser being or even as an offering to someone who has less, but rather where the offer is genuine and heartfelt. This is often done. As human beings, for instance, you sometimes will be hurt when the offer is rejected. As parents especially, this comes up a lot. So I say to you, don't worry; you'll get your chance.

Divine Intervention Is Like Parenting

You'll notice I have a particular affection for parents; that's because in my journeys and in my job (if I might call it that) as a consultant about divine intervention, I have seen the analogy between divine intervention and what parents do with children. It is a daunting task, to raise children on your world, where every parent starts out very often from scratch. In the best situation, the parent might have come from the best, most nurturing and supportive family and have a good idea of the best way to be a parent, but still there is *so much* they must do on their own, instantaneously, without the opportunity to call mother or father and ask them, "What should I do?" So I feel that the parent/child analogy to the creator/divine intervention experience is profound. And of course, being human beings, you have all either been parents or children, frequently both. (That's my little joke, obviously.)

That really does put it on another level, because the whole idea of it is that it is a loving desire to help. It's not interference; it's a loving desire to help. That's what makes it so prickly, right?

Yes; I know many readers can think how your own parents or a relative or even a great friend might have offered something to help you that, to that friend or that person, seemed like the Sun, the Moon, the stars, yet there were other things you needed to do. In the case of a youngster, you can offer them the Sun, the Moon, the stars, but if there's something else they need to be doing, it is important for you to just say to yourself, "Well, I will have other opportunities." Not that "they'll come back when they need me," none of that. Just trust that the person has something else they need to do right now, and that you'll have your opportunity to assist them in some way, perhaps a different way, in the future. And that's guaranteed—if not in this life, then for sure in another.

The Creator of the Hunter and the Hunted

What's another experience of your advising someone?

One more only. There was a creator who has an interesting task,

from the perspective of what you've heard. It does not have its own creation but is responsible for moments of intimacy that you might not
consider moments of intimacy; this creator is responsible for the hunter
and the hunted. I realize that sounds dramatic, but consider: The student can be the hunter and the hunted can be knowledge. Just as the
hunter could be a fisherman and the fish, the object of desire, yes?

So this creator came to the Council and said that it was burdened
with its responsibilities, because it was constantly running into cases
where the hunted did not wish to be found—even in such obscure ref-
erences as knowledge that did not wish to become involved with some
other body of knowledge. Sometimes knowledge (it is hard for you to
imagine, perhaps, that thought has its own ways, its own desires, its
own sense of self) did not wish to become involved with another philosophy, let's say; it didn't wish to participate in it. It felt that that other
philosophy was at odds with its true purpose, that kind of thing.

This creator ran across that a lot. But the thing that bothered the
creator was to be involved with beings, such as the fish, that wanted to
go on with its life and had its own family, its own loves and desires and
hopes and dreams for the future. Yes, fish are not just fish sticks. They
are not just that; they are living beings not unlike yourself, except that
they know who they are. This creator found it painful to be responsible for that, so the creator came to the Council to ask if anyone on the
Council could advise this creator of someone who could take over that
job, or (and this creator didn't ask this, but it was clearly implied; it was
like a parentheses with nothing printed in it) could we in some way
divinely intervene?

Well, as you know, I don't do that, but there are certainly creators on
the Council who could. So this creator was given support. The creator
had great trouble because it was a unified being, as creators are, but the
Council advised and granted this: They advised the creator that they
could split that creator into three parts. One part would be responsible for the unhappiness of the hunted, one part would be responsible
for the hunter and the other part would be responsible for the peace
that could be achieved between these two apparently opposing forces—
in this sense, creating parts of the creator to form a hierarchical function. The creator wanted to know how that would help, so the Council
suggested that the difficult and painful part for this creator was that as
a unified being, experiencing all things at once, it was unable to personally identify with the whole experience of the hunter and the
hunted, but that part of it could remain unified and become the peace.

The other two parts, having the hunter and the hunted as identities, could create a personal identity and feel the fulfillment of the hunter and the fulfillment of the hunted, and achieve the great joy of the resolution of their conflict because of the ultimate experience as it would go on. The knowledge that didn't want to be assimilated would eventually discover that the inclusion of that knowledge would in time alter the philosophy, if not immediately, and that the philosophy itself would become more harmonious to that part of knowledge. Or that the hunted, even if consumed (as in the fish), would go on in spirit, live on and become, molecularly for a while, part of the hunter and experience itself as the hunter. So even being unhappy about being hunted and consumed, it would then be required to experience itself on the molecular level, if not on the soul personality level, the full experience of being the hunter. Thus the experience was complete, not polarized.

That was the advice given to this creator, which it has followed to this day. The moral for you being that sometimes even though you desire the whole experience, when you have the experience in parts, it can be more pleasant. Example?
Yes.

You think of many things you do during the day and things you do during the night. What if you slept and worked at the same time, with no day and night even if you work at night? Either way, you sleep at some point. What if you did that at the same time? You can't imagine it now, but life would not be the same. There is a much greater part of you, as you know, beyond this existence, which grows as a result of what you have done, but it also sometimes judges what you as individuals are doing because it hasn't grown yet. What if you were that whole experience all the time? You would never grow.

Sometimes it is more fun to have the parts. Sometimes it is more fun to eat your vegetables and your potatoes and your meat for dinner and then after a while have dessert, rather than having your cake on top of your potatoes and meat.
That creator will eventually integrate its parts, the hunter and hunted?

That creator, you understand, *was* integrated.
I know, but I mean, it will reintegrate at some point?

Maybe, maybe not. You understand, the larger ramification here is the assumption that being a whole thing is the ultimate achievement. But what I am suggesting is that *maybe that isn't true;* maybe *becoming* parts of a whole thing can be better, given different circumstances. It then moves your evolution from . . . this is your current idea of evolu-

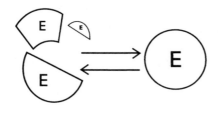

Evolution Both Ways

tion, yes? [Draws.] It creates this, doesn't it? Granted, this is not equal parts, but maybe that is also evolution.

So evolution can perhaps be both ways or even in progression. So let's just write that down for a reminder [writes]: Evolution both ways.

So by analogy, then, as you grow, you are growing that which somehow guided your awareness and sent you?

Does it not beg the question? I did not move myself here, yet I am here. Is it a part of me that moved me here that I am not yet aware of, because I have not had something happen, as in the creator of the mathematical universe? Or is it something else entirely? I don't know now, but the one thing I have faith in is that I will know this. This would not be happening without intent.

I was just suggesting that, as you had that being split into pieces, you may be split into pieces and you may be the one who comes to harvest the information or . . .

And/or . . .

You know so much, it's hard to know what to ask.

We are pretty close to the end for tonight. So I say this to you: As your consciousness continues to expand and as you from time to time ask for help, continue to ask for help. Most of the time help will not have to come in the form of divine intervention, so ask, and very often inspiration, angels, guides (yes, if you would, gods), creators, friends, loved ones, will come to your assistance in some way. Sometimes it won't seem like assistance, but very often it will. So ask, and know that even though divine intervention may not be experienced by you who are alive now on this Earth at this time, it will certainly be experienced by those who will be here someday. So it's all right that divine intervention exists. There are certainly times when it is well worth the effort. Good night.

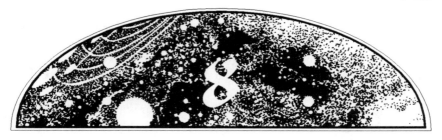

Specialist in Synchronicity and Timing

February 21, 1998

 am the Creator of Synchronicity and Timing. My expertise lies in the area of knowing when and how.

That's pretty good expertise!

Yes. It is, of course, most useful for many creators, to say nothing of beings in general, to have some guidelines about when and how.

My Alliance with the Creator of Gaps and Spaces

I became aware of my existence through my compatible alliance with the Creator of Gaps and Spaces. At first I thought I was a portion of that creator, but then I realized that while integrated with that creator in the most harmonious way, I was actually a being unto my own self. I think that when Gaps and Spaces was beginning to have the dawning of its own personality, that may have triggered the dawning of *my* personality, because before then we were so harmonious that it was not apparent or obvious that there was anything other than one. But after Gaps and Spaces became its own conscious personality, I began to feel myself also within that same space where Gaps and Spaces existed. If you look at it, of course, it makes complete sense that synchronicity would be connected to gaps and spaces, because the knowledge and wisdom associated with such an exposure would be very useful for an acquaintance with when and how.

So I have not traveled per se, but being everywhere Gaps and Spaces is has allowed me to be conscious of what goes on where and why. In this way I have assimilated a significant amount of wisdom through observation of what works and what doesn't, but also if things need to work and must be changed, how and when.

So my contribution to the Council has to do with such matters as synchronicity.

Give me an example. So when Gaps and Spaces was drawn to the Council, you were there the same time, or did you go at separate times?

Gaps and Spaces went first. I was not sure at the time that I had enough acquired wisdom about synchronicity to join the Council, but I was invited to join. The Council stated, through Gaps and Spaces, that it would be helpful if I could devote some of my time (moments, as we would say) to consulting with and for the Council. The more I participated, the more I realized that this is what I would enjoy doing, and I have been there ever since. So my joining the Council was about one quarter of a cosmic day after Gaps and Spaces.

Synchronicity, Harmony and Benevolence

How did you become aware of this ability you have to know how and when? How did that become obvious to you?

At first it was through my realization of where I was and how. In my experience, when two things, beings or what-have-you are in total and complete synchronicity, the harmony level will be so complete that there may not be a means by which to tell yourself apart from the other. This was, of course, my birth realization, if you would, my awareness of my self-realization. My harmony was so great with Gaps and Spaces, it did not occur to me that I was something of my own.

So that is how it began for me, and from there my natural inclination was to look for other occurrences of such experience, and that is how I came to study synchronicity and its attendant harmony.

What are some of the examples before you got to the Council, so we can understand how it works or how you viewed the experience?

I'll give you an example of one of my favorites. Picture for a moment children playing in the winter. They have fun; they gather some snow and throw it playfully at each other, or perhaps at a tree to see if they can hit it. Would you believe that every snowflake that makes up a snowball, *every one,* is so harmonious with the other snowflakes that the harmony and synchronicity of the moment of that child picking up those flakes, turning it into that snowball and throwing it at that tree, and the snow staying on that tree until it melts or is brushed off and

falling where it falls—that the synchronicity and harmony is so great between all points of contact for those snowflakes, that it is a completely benevolent experience for them?

In that example you understand the other thing I do; I do synchronicity and its attendant harmony and, as a result, an understanding (though it is not my first thing) of benevolence. So it is like this [draws].

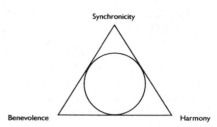

A drawing—synchronicity, harmony, benevolence [at the three points of the triangle]. I will label the circle later.

The Most Harmonious Experience for All Beings

First you were out there watching. You watched other beings come into the space you occupy, right?

No. Think of where Gaps and Spaces is—in our experienced world, speaking for Gaps and Spaces and myself. Watching other beings come in, no, I did not do this. If other beings came in, I was mostly spending my moments observing how and when in order to understand . . . [turns aside] . . . yes, synchronicity, thank you. [Chuckles.]

Who was that?

Gaps and Spaces passing through in the form of another. But what I did was observe, become conscious of all of the worlds and universes and cycles of life and all that was going on there. I looked where things were working the best, in the greatest synchronicity and harmony and benevolence, and noticed that when things were timed exactly so—not by a watch or a clock or, to put it more broadly, not by the will of a being, but by its natural tendencies—then we have true synchronicity. True synchronicity is based on the most harmonious experience for all beings. And now I will label the center [writes]. The circle in the center of the triangle represents the most harmonious experience for all beings, you understand, so I'm not going to put a mark in that. I'd like you to take note of something. Remember when I drew the triangle and said that I would tell you what the circle is later? I didn't know what I was going to say until I said it—that's synchronicity. You wanted an example. I could have said it, but when I considered, *What is that circle? How shall I label that?*, it wasn't there. It came later, because the synchronicity and the harmony was present then. It came with timing, as you say.

What I'm suggesting to you is that I *am* this, and I also have knowledge and wisdom of it to assist others. Thus what you *are*, you tend to explore in other things, understand? So that is what I did and how I lived. I give you this immediate example so you can understand the way I function. I do not consider not having that information, to label the circle [in the drawing], ignorance, but rather, not in synchronicity.

The Benevolent Life Path

Picture for a moment the ocean, fish in the ocean. You could say that the fish, as it swims along beautifully as they do (you've seen them in films and so on, sometimes in person), is exerting its will to go from this place to that place. But in my understanding, the fish and the water are one unit, and the water is benevolently experiencing the grace and beauty of the fish as it displaces the water to move through the exact molecules of water that welcome that fish at that time.

That's magnificent; I never would have thought of it that way.

That is why the examination of synchronicity and timing, as you call it (what I call synchronicity and harmony and benevolence), is most valuable, because the fish goes by its instincts. The fish might not always go from point A to point B; it might take a detour because it feels to go the other way. Perhaps it does not know why; maybe later on it learns from its family or friends or tribe that there was a predator where it was going to go. But it still arrived at the place it needed to go to without knowing about that. Or maybe on its journey, on an out-of-the-way run from point A to point B, perhaps it discovers more of its own kind or some beautiful experience for that fish person. All the journey that is the most compatible way is *felt* by the fish; it is not thought or analyzed, it is felt. It does not always follow the path of least resistance; that is one way to look at it. *It follows the path of the greatest benevolence,* which the fish feels as this warmth and love (this exercise that has been taught to you and your readers—see Appendix). It feels this, and thence it follows that. And if at any moment it feels that warmth and love—you understand, the physical feeling of benevolence—go away, then it will either stop and back up a little bit, which fish can do, or it will widen its circle until it finds that feeling again, and then pursue it, go along that path. So it is following not just a physical path, but a loving, harmonious path.

That is why the spiritual teachers the human race has had over the years, the best teachers, will always say, "Follow the most benevolent and harmonious path for you." Says the student, "How will I know that?" And the wise teacher says, "You will know it by the way you feel." And since the student has already been taught the warmth and love, the student thinks to herself or himself, *Follow the path that feels the most comfortable to me with that warmth, love, benevolence exercise.* That path of benevolence is truly instinct, as you call it on Earth, but what I call truly the benevolent life path. Most societies that are benevolent live in this way.

The societies I would prefer to show you, to teach this with, are those you live amongst, such as the plants. The reeds that grow near a pond very often welcome the wind; the parts of the plants they use to reproduce are scattered by the wind to places where the land and the water will welcome them. And when they feel welcome, they grow there; they don't grow where they feel uncomfortable. If they land someplace where they feel uncomfortable, they wait until they are either moved by some action of water, rain, wind, to someplace where they feel more comfortable, or they will wait as long as they are able within the life cycle of the seed.

To get back to the plants, they welcome the wind. The wind blows them, and they are happy to be blown, and they blow in synchronicity. Then, because of the strength of their own structure, they go back to their normal position, maybe with a little forward thrust on the basis of their springiness (the reaction, as the scientist would say). What I am saying is that this is not happenstance; this is not circumstance. This is all a part, *it is all* a portion of design.

Pure Love: The Designer of Synchronicity

In my understanding, the designer, you could say, is Creator of this universe, but Creator of this universe simply used principles that It had been taught. The great designer of synchronicity is an entity that I can only refer to as Pure Love. That is how the entity feels, and pure love is its own answer to all questions. That is the best way the ultimate creator that I know can be described. In this way the questions are present, and they are answered with pure love. When creators, including the Council, have a question put to us that we cannot answer (speaking for the Council), we or one of our members goes, as you would say—or feels its presence (as *we* would say)—into the presence of Pure Love. My understanding is that the being who has sent other beings back, who functions in your time, who has created loops of time, who has created all experience by which you might learn, is this being: Pure Love. When I look at this being, I feel not only overwhelmed by that pure love, but I can see within it many things moving. Those things that are moving at times have shape and form, and at other times just seem to be masses of moving ideas, you would say, thoughts, experiences—what I would say are potentials—and they are all drenched with pure love. And when you look at them, they are moving in harmony. For example, look at, close up . . . (filtered, of course) pictures of your Sun, and you will see what looks like a seething oven, yes. But look at the material of the Sun; it is all moving in harmony. This is by design; it is a pretty good analogy to the way Pure Love moves, although I have not seen fire there. Your Sun is fire, but within the more intimate capacities of its being, it is modeled after the physical appearance of Pure Love.

You're the first one who has mentioned this. When did you first become aware of this being?

Because it is in my nature to be asked many, many questions all the time by many creators and sometimes the messengers of creators, it is only natural—by my personality I have demonstrated to you with the triangle and circle—that if I do not know something, I will know it when I need to know it. Do you understand?

Yes.

[By myself] as the synchronicity of the circle and triangle. But I was asked questions over and over again that did not seem to have an answer forthcoming, and I was waiting to see if the answer would come. I waited as long as I could, because the answers were needed, then I simply asked, "Is there someone I can communicate with, be with (as we would say), who can offer me the answers or acquaint me with the experiences by which I will have the answers for these wonderful beings who have asked the questions?"

Immediately [snaps fingers] it was as if a veil opened. It was as if I could see through all that I had known and experienced, including everywhere where Gaps and Spaces is. Suddenly I could see this bright light; it was bright because it was, or appeared to be, in what you call space. It was darkness, and there were other little lights, not unlike seeing a bright light in the sky with stars. I was drawn to this and felt the overwhelming pure love. I merged with it and felt the synchronicity of it, and in the moments of full merging with this being I had the experience like an inoculation—I could feel what that being felt and know what that being knows when I needed to, in moments when I did not have answers that were needed.

That's how I came to know that this being exists. Knowing what *it* knows, I realized that *everything* that has been discussed up to this point in time with this process is part of the ultimate creation of this being. If you think about it, how else would Pure Love fulfill the needs of beings, than to lovingly, benevolently create circumstances by which those beings could learn what they needed to know, could live and love and experience the beauties of life in all its forms in the fantastic variety available? How else, then, to allow them their own experience, feeling as beings unto themselves? In my experience, Pure Love has created all that I know, all that I experience and all that I have ever heard about that has been experienced by others.

Do you think there's a connection between that being and the being that Gaps and Spaces and I were discussing as being the future? The one who has sent everyone back to learn something?

It was my intention to have said this; I believe that is the being.

Who sent everybody back?

Didn't send them back; *allowed* them to come back to learn what they needed to learn, so when the time (as you say) or the synchronicity happened, they would be ready—and, perhaps more important, prepared.

Prepared, experienced, right.

A child can say (even an adult), "I'm ready!" But there's quite a difference between being prepared and being ready. The two are, however, synchronously harmonious, are they not?

[Laughter.] Yes, it's best to have both.

Yes, and of course, as you know about me, I tend to see and look for things that are in the nature of my own personality and experience. This is universal.

Did you become aware before there were any levels?

Yes.

I'm just trying to place that, because you talked about creations. Were there creations going on before the levels?

Yes; not many, but there were some. I would call them experiments before there were levels. I like to give examples that make sense on this planet. It would be like a child—a baby, yes?—notices its physical parts when it can, especially its feet. You know, all babies on Earth love their feet; it is one of the parts the child discovers because the child innately knows that the feet have something to do with the voyage and journey it is on. It is not a philosophical knowledge; it is an instinctual knowledge. So that awareness precedes the footprints of that child's journey (and that adult's, as the child grows up). Is that clear?

The Creator Who Desired Resolution

What was the first question you couldn't answer, the one that led you to Pure Love?

A creator came and said (speaking the words of that creator), "I have been unable to know exactly when to grant the beings in my creation the full knowledge of their total being. I have been utilizing a second level, where they would experience the full knowledge of their being, but it would not be available to them in their conscious day-to-day life. The second level would be a deep meditation when they have access to their whole being." On your world this would be an analogy to sleep, for instance, or even to some extent to the end of the natural life— death, as you call it.

"So," the creator went on and said, "I need to know when is the right moment to integrate those levels without interfering in the beings' natural creations of their day-to-day lives." Looking at the world this creator was talking about (it was but one world in its universe), I looked at it and realized completely why the creator was experiencing such a conundrum.

Their daily creations had to do with an ongoing battle they had been having, one side of the planet with the other. The battle was not a violent one but a philosophical one: One side of the planet believed that all problems could be resolved through mental activities, rationale, reason; the other side of the planet believed that all problems could be resolved through applied love, what you do with love (you feel it, yes, then what you do with it)—loving actions. When the beings would experience the second level in their deep meditations, they would go there with their problems and have them resolved—how to do it, when, why. Synchronicity. That's why I was called in.

When they were on their second level, though, they would have no interest in resolving their problem with each other; they would be able to resolve only their immediate crisis—a crisis of personal conscience, you might call it, but they would have no . . .

. . . no interest in the battle.

No interest in continuing the battle. The ultimate purpose of the battle was to create a benevolent resolution that would work for all beings on their world. So the creator said to me, of course, "When can I give them this consciousness? I know that when they have this consciousness, they will immediately resolve their problems with each other. Yet they might do so only because they feel united on the second level and forget about the first level entirely. Then *true* resolution will never happen." You see, a conundrum—or, as it is said by some of your cultures, a paradox.

Yes, that's a good one.

Yes, I felt it was certainly a worthy question. I looked at the situation for a long time and had no answer. That was the first question, answering your question. Ultimately when variations of that question were asked, that's when I asked, "Is there someone who can help me?"

And what was the answer to the first paradox?

[Chuckles.] What was the answer by the being of love?

Yes.

The being of love advised me to advise the creator to step back, that the creator was so caught up in the desire for resolution (since that particular creator was uncomfortable with any form of conflict), that it was stretching out the problem, making it last longer than it would have otherwise, because the world itself was basically harmonious. If the creator could step back from the world and remove its "anxiety" (if that term applies to a creator) about conflict, the people would quickly and easily resolve their own problems. So I passed this on to the creator, and the creator said, naturally, "I will try this."

The creator withdrew its energy, which was hovering around this world almost in a smothering way, and pulled back a ways—and sure enough, the people almost immediately worked out the problem by . . . what would be obvious, right? They created a *third level* by which they could be aware of the first and second levels, and the whole planet, regardless of what side they were on, would be conscious of the third level. Thus they became aware of their synchronicity and harmony on the third level, and that was able to translate to the second and the first levels. That is how they achieved resolution.

And your reputation went up! [Chuckles.]

I wouldn't say that; I would just say that I discovered I had a consultant I was not aware of before.

What's really interesting is, until I got to the Council of Creators, I always asked of beings, who do you consult? Who do you ask questions of? The first few members of the Council said they didn't do that, they didn't know anybody else. So I quit asking.

You understand, that is true for them. Until they (if they ever do) have the experience of being unable to answer a question, they will continue to answer that way. But I had this experience, so the answer is as it is from me.

My Consultations with Your Creator

What about our Creator? What types of questions did He ask you? What situations did He ask you to help Him with?

When your Creator was beginning to assemble all of Its consultants, He asked me what would be the best place within Its "physical being" (if I can describe it that way for your sake) to place all these consultants or make available to them the harmonious space they would need. In other words, where It should put everybody and when.

That was my first consultation with your Creator. I advised your

Creator to not only allow them to seek their own spaces, but if their energy was in any way affecting, either benevoléntly or in the case of the more . . .

. . . the Master of Discomfort.

Yes, the Master of Discomfort . . . in some uncomfortable way, that there be some circle around the consultant that would allow its pleasure of its own space yet not allow its thoughts or radiations to affect other beings. And within that circle there ought to be only energies or portions of energies or, as you would see them . . . it would be as if you were looking at a picture of a human cell under a microscope, only everything is moving. You would see this moving matrix of cellular structure. So every molecule, every atom, every proton in that circle would have to be comfortable with that being, so that all beings would be comfortable within that circle of harmony to their being. Although that wasn't necessary too often, it was necessary from time to time, not only with the Master of Discomfort, but with, I believe, one other being as well, the one having something to do with colors or . . . plasma.

Oh, the Master of Plasma, because he moves so fast.

Yes, and Plasma by its very nature, if exposed to too many worlds, the worlds themselves—the people, the beings, the worlds, everything—would tend to become more plasmic. For instance, the tissue, the skin of a person, would become more plasmic, so that if people touched a tree, they would become the tree. So if there needed to be individuality, it would not be possible. Sometimes there would have to be one of these circles around Plasma, if Plasma was going to affect a world where individuality was an experience.

So there was that. Since then your Creator (since it worked [chuckles]) has asked a few other questions, including not only the *timing* (since we're using that word) of what you would do and when, as the Explorer Race, but also the way you might do it, meaning the application, the most benevolent way to proceed. Not that your Creator did not have Its own plans, but as you know, you can have your own plan and sometimes consulting with others can fill in gaps and spaces in that plan.

[Chuckles.] Yes.

Discreation and the Explorer Race Experiment

So your Creator consulted with the entire Council on most of its creation. I realize that sometimes your Creator was doing so for what you might call political reasons: The Creator wanted to involve the Council enough in its creation that the Council would feel your

Creator's ultimate intent to do something benevolent, while at the same time your Creator was perhaps intending to expand its own responsibility for this creation. So at times the Council would not answer questions so as to gently chide the Creator of this universe that the responsibility lay squarely within Itself [chuckles].

This suggested to the Creator of your universe that the Council recognized your Creator's intention for the Council to have perhaps a more benevolent feeling about Its creation. So sometimes your Creator would ask questions about the *timing* of a rise in consciousness or an increase in love, because a certain unpleasant event or series of events needed to be ended. There were moments like that, and since we knew that that your Creator already had the plan, we would not answer, because we did not approve then (and we do not approve now) of the extreme that the Creator of the universe you now occupy has allowed negative energy (or discomforting energy, as you call it—or unpleasantness, as we would call it) to impact so many beings. We did not feel good about it then; we do not feel good about it now. Even with the great growth potential, we do not feel good about it in the future.

So we are holding our final actions in abeyance as we see how it works out. Your friend Zoosh has assured us that it will work out, but our feeling is that even after it works out, we will examine fully the souls of all beings, including the immortal personalities of every particle and every soul, to examine if there is any lasting harmful effect. And if there is any lasting and harmful effect, we will still consider . . .

Discreation.

Discreation, yes. Your Zoosh has assured us that this will not occur. Although your friend Zoosh has shown that he deserves to be respected and certainly wants our love, we will wait and see.

We are authorized by Love to take any action necessary to guarantee that no soul or immortal personality of the greatest or the smallest be permanently affected by discomfort, even after the expansion. If that should happen, we are authorized to discreate.

So Pure Love didn't give the inspiration for the Explorer Race experiment?

Pure Love gave the permission for the Explorer Race experience, but it did not give permission for anything beyond 1.999 (and a few more nines) percent negative energy; this percentage is usually rounded off by your Zoosh to two percent. Pure Love did not give permission for any greater than that. And you know, there has been greater on Earth, plus Sirius on this planet and in the past, and in the past another one in the Pleiades and a couple of others. We have watched and observed, and occasionally we have had to create an isolated discreation.

An isolated discreation would be this: If a planet or a place is having impact on any immortal personalities that goes beyond any future expansion, which might be an evolution of their total being, then what you might call pocket discreations can be done. But in that particular planet or space where that took place, everything must reverse in time to its point of creation, and then the creator of that space (in this case, your universe) would re-create it from the beginning to assure that that would not occur.

The Discreation of the Planet That Exploded in Sirius

Even now as we speak, the planet that exploded in Sirius (in the Sirius galaxy) is the subject of a pocket discreation. It is not all right that the planet exploded, and a pocket discreation is in progress. It will probably not be complete until the beings who have come from Sirius to 3.0-dimensional Earth have had significant experience here. Granted, it will be benevolent, but ultimately and eventually they will be recalled to that planet, once their planet is benevolent again, and their experience on Earth will simply be something they will remember.

They will be able to utilize the skills they have acquired and so on, by a future experience. The re-creation of that planet in Sirius will be done, and the beings that were affected will be re-created, and the whole thing will move forward again without any discomfort. This has already been decreed, so what you call the negative Sirius beings that are now beginning occupation on Earth will have somewhere between 1400 and 1500 experiential years on this planet until they need to be recalled—not with you, of course, but at a denser dimension. Insofar as their skills fit into a benevolent society, they will be able to keep them as something they will have available in their soul personality. But if the skills are solely based on unpleasantness, they will simply cease to exist. This is because the resolution they require, that they are experiencing at 3.0-dimensional Earth, will no longer be necessary for them, since their past will have been re-created. Do you understand?

Yes.

This does not mean that the Explorer Race material is irrelevant; what it means is that things must be adjusted according to harmony, synchronicity, benevolence—the benevolence by which all life exists. I thought you would like to know, yes?

Oh, I love to know. You've opened up so many things. The planets that were corrupted or damaged . . . we know about the one in Sirius, the one in the Pleiades, Maldek, Mars was damaged, the planet that was here before this one was damaged. Are there others?

In the distant reaches of your universe there was a planet, yes; that was the first one I used as an example of discreation.

Was that by the now Explorer Race or earlier versions of it?

Earlier, much, much earlier.

Before the Explorer Race had even come out.

Yes. It was an early experiment that required discreation. Discreation must take place under certain circumstances, but not all. Let me give you another example, an example of a personal individual.

The Discreation of Hitler

Awhile back Zoosh told you that Hitler had been discreated or was in the process of being discreated. That being has been discreated, but is now moving forward in its creational cycle again. The being that was Hitler is now available as a benevolent being.

In few years this has happened? It was only four years ago!

You understand, the complexities of discreating an entire world with billions and billions and trillions . . . individual cells and souls and personalities take longer. But a man's life? That takes less time for discreation.

I thought discreation was annihilation. You're saying he was discreated back to the first time he appeared, and then he experienced a benevolent life?

Discreation does not mean, from my perspective, that something disappears out of existence. I grant that it looks like it does, but the way I see it is that it is taken back to its point of origin, then it moves forward again, only on a more benevolent path. As it's discreated in steps going back and back and back, every point that is benevolent is allowed for that being to continue back on that path, you understand? Traveling exactly the same path as long as it is benevolent for that being. But once it comes to the point where that being might be affected and something malevolent (even in the most minor degree) might happen that would prepare that being ultimately for becoming malevolent, it would be changed, and then it would continue forward as a benevolent being. It is now available; the being you knew as Hitler has now begun to move forward on its benevolent path, retracing its steps, you might say. It will be quite awhile before it gets to any place that was setting it up for being open to being a malevolent being, or a malevolent man, as he was on your planet in your societies.

So will that eventually uncreate the war?

Not that alone; other things will have to be done to uncreate that. Your Creator knows this, so it is as if your Creator is on probation, going forward with Its creation, with Its ideas and experiences, with the knowledge that It might have to be involved in discreation. When discreation takes place, it does not mean that we, the Council, perform the discreation. It is our job to say when discreation must take place, and then your Creator must perform it within and during all Its other duties. And that is important, you see, because in that way your Creator becomes totally conscious of . . .

. . . consequences.

Yes, consequences, but also the individual's personal experience. Your Creator is not always, I have noticed, conscious of the personal experience of every one of the beings that represent parts of Its creation. Speaking for the Council here, I can say that we believe that your Creator has learned things by becoming more conscious of the personal experience of every one of the beings in Its creation. Granted, It is usually conscious of this only toward beings for which It feels the most love or enjoyment, but It has not in the past been conscious of beings for which It felt uncomfortable or, as a child might say, "I wish it were different." But by being responsible for discreation, your Creator becomes perhaps more versed in the art of creation.

Because ultimately creation is art, and as any artist knows, even if your art represents something apparently discordant, it has to have synchronicity and harmony at least within its own sphere of creation.

Who put forth the inspiration for the Explorer Race?

I see the stream coming from Love.

Oh, I see; Love did put forward the inspiration, but only at the two percent negativity.

Well, not exactly two percent, but the figure I indicated.

Yes, yes. It did come from him, all right.

Her.

Zoosh Is Part of Something Larger

Can you tell me who Zoosh is? Why are you taking Zoosh's assurances rather than the Creator's? He must then be part of something larger than the Creator.

Zoosh has demonstrated a significantly greater experience and knowledge level than the Creator of this universe. The Creator of this universe is what I would call, not exactly an apprentice to Zoosh, but someone Zoosh has taken a little bit under his wing, as it were. Zoosh does have apprentices, but this Creator is not one [chuckles], but is someone Zoosh looks out for a little bit. So we consider Zoosh to be a worthy consultant—and so does almost every creator, I think, with the exception of some of the visiting creators. Very few of those have had personal contact with Zoosh before. We have no reason to feel that

Zoosh is anyone but someone we are personally familiar with and trust completely. We do not always see things the same way, but that is normal.

Yes. You have, as I said, significantly expanded the game.

The interesting thing, as you may have noticed, in the work you are doing here, is the more minute and precise the answers, the larger the consequences. So going in guarantees going out.

Thank you.

Talk about a sphere of influence!

[Laughs.] So you take great joy in your work. I mean, there's nothing you look forward to? You're totally satisfied with what you're doing?

Yes; it is of the greatest pleasure.

And I think Gaps and Spaces said you all did a lot of socializing at the Council. Is it enjoyable to talk to each other and share stories and get advice?

I have found it to be a compatible surrounding.

[Chuckles.] The ultimate job, eh?

It is, how can we say, very often fun!

The Explorer Race Experience Stems from Love

So how do you see the Explorer Race? You talked of the Creator as if He is totally responsible for this, yet we've been told that Explorer Race roots are themselves part of the creation process.

You understand that to the extent the Council has allowed latitude to your Creator with Its work with the Explorer Race theme, this has taken place, because we understand that this is not an idea solely generated by your Creator, that It is working with a theme that seems to thread its way back to Love. So we are inclined to allow greater latitude or to support greater latitude with this theme than perhaps with other universes, should that ever come up. This is why we've given our blessings to such latitude with this creation.

And of course we recognize that the source beings who make up the Explorer Race have come, in many cases, from very far away, and they would not have come if there had not been something benevolent in the experience for them. So we have noted that as well, and as such we can take the attitude or point of view that your Creator is playing out a part in some larger theatrical experience, and as such is . . . yes, creative, but also managerial. Therefore, our general attitude about the Explorer Race experience is that it is important; it means something. And even though we are not fully aware of its ultimate meaning, since it stems from Love, as we see it, if we do not know, apparently we do not need to know. Therefore we make our recommendations and we advise and so on, but we are disinclined to overly interfere.

Have you ever asked Pure Love about the experiment, about the Explorer Race?

I don't need to know this; I only ask Pure Love and for the help of Pure Love when there is something I need to know for the benefit of others. I do not ask Pure Love anything I need to know myself, because at this moment I do not need to know that myself. And I am, like many beings, interested to find out, but I do not need to know right now, so why ask?

We speculated with Gaps and Spaces that the expansion caused by the Explorer Race might trigger something in what he calls the future and what you're calling Pure Love.

Yes, it is possible. You may have to talk to Pure Love about this at some point, but I cannot speak for Pure Love.

But you allowed us to know that there is such a being, so I am eternally grateful. I have been searching for the ultimate creator here for a long time.

Who can say if Pure Love is that? But perhaps you can ask at some point.

Thanks. Do you only look in on our creation? You seem so familiar with it, but that's because you're coincident with Gaps and Spaces, so you're everywhere. You're here.

Yes. And of course, since synchronicity (and you've noted it) on your planet and in your experience happens a lot (and sometimes not), I pay attention to your world. Your world, being also an experimental world (which means it is not harmonious only or benevolent only or synchronous only, though it has those elements), is a place to take note of, so I do.

Well, having observed this, what, from your experience and your wisdom, would you tell the people who are reading this?

You Are Guaranteed Resolution

Thank you. I would say this: Know that you are participating in an experience, however short-lived (for your lives here are very short in comparison to the totality of your being), and that you have as much time and experience as you want and need to examine all you have done, felt and experienced here. There will be no restrictions on how you wish to examine it, how long, how intricately—or even if you wish to simply discard it and go on. You will have every amount of help you need, not just what is available; you will have anything and everything you need. That is because it is understood that the beings who stem back to those original Explorer Race seeds and roots have a purpose. So nothing will be withheld from you. You will experience it to some minor degree at your sleep level and to a major degree at the end of your natural cycle, until or if you decide to have another life in this universe. Many of you will go on to other universes, but until you do that, anytime you have that gap from an Earth life to a reincarnation anywhere else in this universe, you will receive the maximum help, with no limits on what you might need to examine and experience in order to understand your Earth experience.

This goes not only for you human beings, but also for any particle, any animal, plant, rock—anything. No one will be rejected from this offer. And I want you to know this: that you are loved, honored and appreciated, and you will have extensive opportunity to feel this at the end of your natural cycle and before your next incarnation. Also, in the coming days (not cosmic days, but physical days) for you, you will have more opportunity at an increasing rate to experience this at the dream level. Sometimes it will even be experienced at the conscious level, because it is important for you all to come to know that this is an adventure, a journey of learning and experience. And it is a encapsulated experience—it is what it is *while* it is—but when it is over, then you are allowed to go on with the benefits of the experience, but without the harm, guaranteed. All harm will be resolved; it is a requirement. So fear not; you are guaranteed resolution.

You said some of the beings would go off to other universes. Eventually, though, all humans, all Explorer Race beings, will coalesce to become the creator, right?

Yes, but until that occurs, it is possible that some of you might go off and have lives in other universes, then come back when that coalescence is necessary.

Ah, I see. I didn't realize what we could do.

Yes. There are beings who are, as Zoosh has amusingly put it, parked somewhere in this universe. Some of those are experiencing lives in other universes while they're waiting so that they do not get bored, you know.

Thank you. You have expanded our understanding in a truly awesome manner.

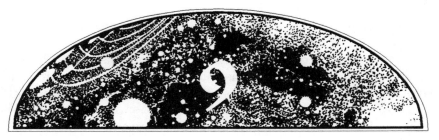

Specialist in Mystical Connection between Animals and Humans

March 3, 1998

am the creator of the mystical connection between what you call animals (also known as other beings) and human beings. My expertise lies in the area of light and magnetic pulses. [It] is a little difficult to communicate in spoken word. My purpose is to help maintain that link so that there remains a consistent connection between that which is known as human beings and other beings on your world.

My duties right now are exclusive to your planet and your planet's citizens' needs. I function within the Council because the Council is so connected with what is happening with you and the project you are engaged in. I would like to tell you something you would benefit from knowing.

Without Animals Humans Could Not Exist

Without what you call animals, including flying, swimming, walking, crawling—all those beings—human beings could not be on the Earth. Right now you notice often [that] there are too many of this [chuckles] being or not enough of that being. But in times of stability, the most important stability is that there be at least three beings for every human being at all times, whether they be the many-leggeds you call the insects, or whether they be the four-leggeds you often call friends, companions or those who support you, or whether they be of wings or fins.

There must always be at least three for every human being. If ever any less, what always occurs is the die-off of human beings.

So know this: Recent concerns about . . . oh, too many pets; do not be so very concerned, because as wild beings or free beings are less available, then so-called pet beings [are] more available. It is magnetic, you see. Think of it this way: If animals are the magnet and Earth is iron and human beings are iron, then with no magnet, human beings would just go away—blow away. They would have no interest in staying here. It has always been animals that have kept human beings here.

In the beginning, before there were animals on Earth, populations came and went quickly. They could not maintain themselves, or they saw no reason to be here. "Why here? Why not someplace else, especially since most other places are easier to be?" Oh, the [ET] outposts, they would stay if there was a reason, but they would maintain their own homelike conditions in a separate facility—underground, aboveground, made no difference. But they would not live on the planet as you do until there were animals. That's when things changed.

There were outposts—you know, ETs and so on. When animals were here, extraterrestrial mothers and fathers, or even people on a mission to observe and so on, [would] gather sample of the plants, flora and fauna. They wanted to be on the Earth. Then they were happy because they couldn't identify with the Earth as anything other than another planet. That is why when wiser beings, as well as what I would call illuminated beings, came to Earth to create a welcoming for the animals, these [ET] beings welcomed animals from their star system. They would ask Earth with sacred ways, and perhaps do a little seeding of vegetables or plants or other animals, to make it possible for animals [that] they felt were particularly spiritual to be on Earth. And of course, different cultures felt that different animals were spiritual.

So for many years what was going on on Earth was that extraterrestrials would come from all over and create a flora and fauna Garden of Eden. When there were the right animals here for you, you could be here. You might ask, "What are the right ones?" Understand, some animals are here for other animals or for plants, and the plants are here for animals and so on—[they are] not all here for you.

Animals You Cannot Live Without

When it was understood how the human being would be made up in genetics, in substance, in soul, spirit, thought, everything, then certain animals were deemed to be essential, animals you could not exist without, even though early settlers found it difficult to live with some of them. For example: [You] cannot live without cats. [Chuckles.] [You] cannot live without dogs, and their cousins, of course. In the beginning, of course, wild cats . . . very hard for human beings to live with them, but in time—smaller cats, more comfortable companion cats. And of course companion cats were, in a large way, brought about by what I call physical-spiritual cats—what you would call, if they were human beings, shamanic masters. These spiritual cats are still here sometimes, not always in your dimension, but sometimes. The same thing [occurs] occasionally, though much more rarely, with spiritual dogs. Spiritual dogs usually take the form of gold lightbeings. Spiritual cats . . . gold lightbeings, yes, but there is physical version sometimes seen.

Now, there are other animals you cannot live without; they must be here. Very often they perform sacred rites and rituals that might seem to be exclusively for them, but ninety percent of the ritual is to maintain the balance of the human being on Earth. And that is ants—[you] cannot live without ants. If ever ants were eradicated, human beings [would] immediately die out. [You] cannot live without butterflies; granted, you don't need as many, but you must have them. Butterflies [are] essential to keep human hope alive. Ants are essential for sacred spiritual structure of societies.

Do you know that if there were no ants, you would not be able to maintain philosophies to live by or religions to enrich your lives? Not possible. Cats have everything to do with your inner spiritual function as well as shamanism and benign real magic. Dogs have to do with enthusiasm, happiness, groundedness.

There are a few others. [You] must have some horses; [you] can't live without them. [You] must have some whales, dolphins, sea turtles and tuna. Be aware, animals listed as wild—obvious wild animals [are] ants, tuna and so on—they must be wild. Right now you are raising tuna in captivity; they are not the same. Captivity tuna has about ten percent the energy you need, so you'd need to have billions, if not multibillions of tuna just to equal the energy of lesser numbers of wild tuna.

Animals More Than Double the Human Life Span

There are other animals you cannot live without. I mention a few because the magnetic resonance of these beings is so powerful, it literally holds you here. You might say, "What does that mean, hold us here?" It means this: Creator and Creator's assistants have the capacity to encourage and maintain the human life span on Earth for thirty-five years—that's all. But animals make it possible for a human being to live eighty, ninety years. You might say, "Well, it is medical science." Yes and no. These things would not exist without the magnetic radiance of what animals do just by their existence.

Also, there are levels to this. For instance (this is obvious, but it bears repeating), an animal that you love, that loves you: [It provides] ten times the magnetic energy to keep you here. You know many [and] you have heard [of others], and there are those amongst you who would have come to the end of your natural cycle long ago had it not been for some beloved animal you cherish and who cherishes you. This is love, yes, and also this great magnetic that is vital to you.

My job with the animals is to do what their job is for you, and that is to radiate benevolent magnetic energy to support them in being. They, by their own right, would naturally have magnetic energy—all beings do on Earth—but animals that keep human beings on Earth, that make it more comfortable for you to be here, have ten times the magnetic energy they need. That is why they will radiate so much. To have that ten times does not hurt them, but they do not need it; they need only times one, as it were, their normal amount. That extra nine times they don't need, so the things they do, interactions they have with humans, is what keeps you here. You might say, "Well, that's all well and good, but what do you do when you're not working with Earth?" Therein lies a story.

I Am a Carrier Wave for the Explorer Race Ribbon

Way back before there was love, there was what I call energy that moves in, then moves out, in and out again, not unlike the way the heart beats in and out. A muscle, yes? Contraction, expansion. During those times there was magnetic energy developed by the contraction and expansion. From magnetic energy then sprang love, and thence all that followed. I do not claim to be what preceded love, but my first awareness of myself took place between the space (if that would be the term) that exists between magnetic energy and love. First [I] became conscious of the in-and-out; next [I] became conscious of the radiated love, then conscious of magnetic energy. [I] did not become exposed to what you call electrical energy till much later.

Electrical energy, as you know, is the dynamic reaction to the motion of magnetic energy. This did not come till much later for me. When I became aware of that and aware of myself in that prepersonality condition, I, like other beings, thought that that was it [chuckles]. But soon I felt myself moving into that love being. I thought, *Well, this is home and it is wonderful! I can live here!* [Chuckles]. But [it] was [a] transit, like moving through. Soon I felt myself moving past or beyond love being, into love being's creation, and then there was so much everywhere, I felt, *Well, what now?* Almost immediately before I had a chance to complete that non-thought (translated to your language, "What now?"), I felt myself turn into a ribbonlike energy and immediately begin moving at velocity. This ribbon went for a long time—a long, long time—and suddenly slowed down very slow and became a meeting.

This meeting was the meeting of the Creator of this universe and the Explorer Race ribbon. I learned later that I am that, or I am on like a carrier wave—I am there and I am ribbon also. Creator stopped and assimilated that ribbon. For a long time I am in Creator with Creator's companions, and there is first a slight spark, and then tremendous enthusiasm in Creator for this.

So I am quite permeated with the Explorer Race, though the ribbon is like [a] formula for the Explorer Race, but the details of the Explorer Race are all generated by Creator and its consultants. Then Creator speeds toward what I believe is now your universe, but before Creator goes into your universe, then I leave. By that time Creator is well under way with Explorer Race conscious ideas, is working with it and consulting other beings on the way and so on. I am no longer needed.

I move away and am literally called by Council of Creators, "Go directly there and wait." I'm there for quite a while observing the Council of Creators, involved in some of the things that hold their interest, but not much [is] happening until the Explorer Race really gets under way. Then I am observing everything having to do with Explorer Race, all that you have heard so far, but not much happening personally until this thing I told you [about], where there needed to be animals. When animals needed to be there, then I am called on, and I have been working on this project ever since.

Helping Animals Return to Their Places of Origin

When you say "before love," is that the being who was called Pure Love?

Yes. So it is my understanding that when human beings have left Earth, and just before Earth returns to the Sirius star system, in a gentle way it will be my job to magnetically help animal people who wish to return to their places of origin, to return in a gentle way. And there will be others who will help the plants to return, though many of the plants and some of the animals will remain on the voyage of Earth to Sirius. To put a percentage on it, ninety-three percent of existing animals will then want to return to their homes. It will be my job to make that happen, to help them make that voyage in the gentlest, most benevolent and quickest way for them so they can live out their lives on these places. So that is my future.

Nothing came up during the time you were at the Council of Creators where your advice was requested, or when you went to other creations?

No, nothing. Apparently my sole purpose is what I have stated. Now, I have considered what happens for me afterward, and I have discussed this with Pure Love as well as Magnetic Energy, who preceded, from my perspective, Pure Love. And they have indicated that I can do different things: (1) I can accompany Explorer Race for a time, to be [a] consultant if desired—maybe [will be] desired, maybe not. (2) I can begin my own creation. If I do, it will have to do with variations on animal themes and the beauty of animal types of beings.

Many animals would very much like to do more with their home planets and societies, so I have indicated great interest in that. Probably that is what I would like to do and [what] they would like me to do, so I probably will do so. That is most likely.

The other and last possibility is to remain in the Council of Creators and advise and consult as other creators do. Most likely I will prefer to leave and work with animals to create planets, cultures, societies, thoughts, ideas, religions, philosophies and so on, based on their spiritual knowledge, wisdom and insight.

That's wonderful. But the animals on their own planets are humanoid, right?

Well, some. Some are other than humanoid, some have different form. Some are humanoid, yes, maybe fifty-five percent—arms, legs (not always the same number you have), head, body, tail (usually tail, yes).

Without a Tail, Humans Are Out of Balance

It has always been a curiosity to me, human beings without your tail. You actually have within your body the makings of a tail. It has not emerged, but I think this form (human being) would be more balanced with a tail. It is really something missing. If you had your tail, you would probably be unable to get out of balance. Tails are one of the things that allow animals to be in balance, at least those that have them. Those that do not have tails do not need them, but for those that have them, the tail maintains the balance.

The tail is a vital instrument. What you would call your brain and spinal column [are] vital instruments, you understand, and the tail is a continuation of this. [It is] a vital neurological function, the tail. I have noticed there is a breed of dog—dog known as Doberman—and this dog often has [its] tail shortened or removed. [This is] a great cruelty, and [it] also drops the particular animal's intelligence and spiritual connection by ninety-five percent or so. This dog with normal body—body it's born to—is actually very spiritual, special dog. But removing tail removes most of that.

What about my cat at work, who came to me with a little stubby tail?

Cat has been injured, but still has tail spiritually. [She] still has trouble, you notice, with some situations—people, adapting—in other words, things having to do with balance. When one is in balance, one adapts quickly, easily, learns quickly, easily, you see. Tail . . . very hard for her, takes time. So that is why she requires patience, and you are good with that, you give her that.

My Benevolent Relationship with Animals

Well, this is incredible, that you were or are the ribbon for the Explorer Race! You have within you, then, since it's encoded into the Creator, all that . . .

I'm not clear if I am the ribbon or if I traveled with the ribbon. Am I the ribbon or is the ribbon the taxicab that brought me?

I see.

I might be a passenger.

You said it could be a carrier wave.

Carrier wave. I am like carrier wave through that—resonant, very strong, but am not clear yet whether that is me or not.

Yet you felt very comfortable with this mission of coming to planet Earth.

It is why I am here, yes; I was not conscious of my existence before this apparent mission was granted to me to come here, yes. I am particularly enamored with animals, and sometimes they are feeling this way with me . . . well, usually.

[Chuckles.] I see that.

Yes. And it is a very benevolent energy between us, and is a connection, familiar . . . a familiar energy. Reminds one of the definition of familiar, but also a similar energy. Energy that exists between human twins is energy that exists between myself and animals. That's why if an animal dies anywhere on Earth—a mouse, a cat, a horse, butterfly, ant, fruit fly, anything—I know; I'll feel it right away.

But also if [it] happens suddenly for them—no warning, no chance to adjust to it—then I can sometimes help them get to where they need to go if no one else is available. This has only been necessary a few times; almost always an angel [is] available.

Angels, you know, work with animals, too. Did you know, not separate guides? [There are] not separate guides for humans. Same angels work with animals, and they learn. These angels (guides in training, your friend says) learn from the animals. Often you learn by what you need to do with others, how you help them and so on. Angels learn from the animals, again, not the animals learning from angels only; angels learn from animals by helping them.

Are you interested in talking about when you first came here, and about some of the experiences you had as you worked with these animals that first came?

I'll give you some examples, all right? In the beginning, some of [the] first, most easily assimilated-on-Earth animals—fish, you say. These animals [are] very gentle, beauty in their nature. Not until much, much later [were there] fish like . . .

. . . sharks and things?

No, what is the other . . .

Dolphin?

No, [it] is a plumed fish; [it] is like a dragon, they call in China, I think, but not actual dragon, very small . . . well, however we want to call them. Sharks, no; sharks [are] very benevolent. Only recently [they] have the reputation for being hard on human beings, but in the beginning sharks quite gentle.

Sharks Keep the Ocean in Balance

Shark's job (I speak this about shark first, since you have brought this up) is to capture and eat that which is out of balance, so shark's job is to keep ocean in balance. It would be, for example, shark's job to eat injured or diseased fish, you understand? Because shark very strong, disease of fish, no effect on shark at all—very strong being. Now also anything in the water that is agitated, see? Science says agitation, blood in the water, brings sharks. Yes, this is true, but for spiritual reason. Blood in water will bring sharks, but spiritual reason that shark comes to eat is because when something is in the water that is out of balance, even frightened . . . you understand, I have compassion for human being in water, frightened—such as [when] a ship sinks, or sailors in water, or something. Terrible for them to be attacked by sharks; I have compassion. Yet the reason the shark comes is that beings in water are not natural water beings, so they do not know how to be in balance. Shark's job is to consume beings so ocean can return to balance. Shark, then, has job.

In ancient times, when human beings were very at home in the water, benevolent energy swimming in the water—water-culture human beings—sharks did not attack. Even today [there is] some wisdom in Polynesian areas (is secret wisdom, but I speak a little bit only, not reveal secrets), there is knowledge of how to be in the water. [You] can be completely in a school of sharks, and sharks do not attack because you are in balance. Even if sharks are terribly hungry, [they] will never attack because you are in balance, your energy is in balance. When that is so, you bring balance to the water. When the water is nurtured by you as a being, shark would never ever attack. Just a little bit of Polynesian wisdom there. But these days it takes . . . don't try it without the training; it takes a lot of training.

ETs Welcome Animals to Earth

So I say this: In the beginning certain ETs came from different places, ETs who would contribute some of their genetics to your makeup. (This, I think, is in the first *Explorer Race* book.) Andromeda, for example, they decide [there] must be beings here; they didn't say animals—this is a recent word. [There] must be beings who precede human beings and who have the capacity for great thought, great wisdom. Andromedan beings are very enamored with wisdom and thought; other things, too, but this is very important to them. So they say, "We must invite and make welcome and put creatures in water, plankton and so on, to make it an inviting and homelike place for whales, you know, dolphins, sea turtles." These beings, for example— very, very smart. If you were to be able to create an an IQ test . . . let's say you could. For example, [there is] no whale in existence, even today, with radiations from microwave and all this stuff, with an IQ less than 225. Equally, [there is] no dolphin in existence with an IQ less than 340, and no sea turtle in existence with an IQ less than 560, see? So the Andromedans said, "Oh, let's do everything we can to make them feel at home here, so that they will be here, and their wisdom, profound thought, insight and intellect will be available to any human being who is on Earth, and even more available to human beings who are on the water (even for a time), on a boat or swimming in the water."

You understand, one of the earliest philosophical, spiritual cultures is based in the Polynesian wisdom. This wisdom that is largely derived from those creatures is observation and shamanic—yes, all of this. It's spiritual, but great, wise intellectual insight is also at the foundation of this Polynesian wisdom. Some of it has been lost today, but not very much, because deep, insightful Polynesian wisdom can still be gleaned from these sea creatures and sometimes from what they leave behind— bone or shell, you know. So this is an example, these sea creatures.

Much, much later (I bring this up because so many people like this place), the Pleiadians come, and they say, "[There] needs to be sense of play here, happiness, joyfulness; there needs to be learning by play." Pleiadians [are] experts on learn-by-play, not because they are foolish, but because they are devoted to their children, absolute devotion. They have devised over and over again many, many ways to teach children through happy things, fun things. They are beyond masters; they are the highest master in this skill. So they consider, "What animals are especially playful?" Well, of course, they think of sea lions, very playful. They do what they can to make the sea lions welcome, seed fish that sea lions live on. By that time dogs [are] already present, but they contribute to what I would call infancy in all beings. They contribute to any animal species that will interact largely with human beings, to infuse playfulness in their young.

You know [that] some baby animals are more playful than others. Baby birds [are] not very playful, but baby birds [are] wild (most baby birds, okay?), whereas baby puppies [are] fabulously playful, [they] love to play. It is a joy to be around them. And kittens, very playful, lots of fun. They took this on. Sometimes, you see, ETs would come to infuse qualities. Seals [were] invited, welcomed by Pleiadians, yes. Now, who else shall we say?

Almost all other sea creatures [were] invited, nurtured and welcomed by Sirians. Fully ninety-plus percent of sea creatures, the general variety, [were] welcomed and encouraged by beings from Sirius, and fully eighty percent of the animals on Earth—those that exist now as well as many who are not here anymore—[were] invited and welcomed by Sirius. Sirius beings are experts in welcoming. If you have been welcomed once (joke, but true) on Sirius by Sirius beings, you know what being welcomed is all about. They have amazing capacity to make you feel as if you are the most wonderful thing that ever happened to them. And you know, some human beings have this capacity; [it] is a wonderful and benevolent skill. Certainly animals very often have this capacity. So Sirians [are] responsible for vast animal population.

Are whales Andromedan or Sirian?

Andromedan.

Animals Before the Arrival of the Explorer Race

At what point did you get here? This creation was about ninety-three percent done before the Explorer Race even appeared, so when exactly did you get to this what we call this place, meaning what Pure Love created?

Well, you understand, my involvement here . . .

You were the ribbon, right?

Yes and no; my involvement, yes; but my involvement really began with the arrival of the animals, or the welcoming of the animals.

But by that time this Earth had already come here from Sirius.

That's right. And the animals that would be seeded here to help you to be here, most animals had already established themselves; [they were] here already. Only a few animals [were] added when the Explorer Race got here. Civilizations had existed before animals . . . well, they didn't stay, but there was a long gap, you see, between the last surface civilization and the arrival of the Explorer Race, a long gap. During this gap is when a lot of the activity took place to welcome animals here. That's when I started really being active. So by the time the Explorer Race got here to establish the civilization you are now living in, the bulk of the work was done. But even after you got here, a few animals needed to show up. Not many, though, not many. Some recent arrivals of animals, not many.

Let me see, some insect beings, some moths and some birds—beautiful birds, yes, exotic birds. Beautiful sounds, beautiful feathers, hm? Not total variety of birds. Example: canaries, macaws [are] there since you got here. Mm . . . cows, recent. Cows don't need to be here, but they are here for you, as [are] most animals. Cows, as you know, are leaving. That's part of the reason there are problems, so-called diseases and whatnot. This is really just gentle hints to human beings that cows are moving on. Probably that type of cow you call longhorn might stay a little longer, but dairy cows are in the process of leaving now. It might take awhile because human beings are trying very hard to keep them here, but they have to try a little harder every year, because they're leaving.

What are we going to do without our ice cream?

By the time cows are gone, you won't miss it.

My Appearance Is Like a Magnetic Field

If you were to look at yourself, what do you look like?

I [will] give you a good example. [It] is hard to describe what I look like, but I'll give you example for fun, okay? Fun example: Famous experiment in school (usually grade school)—teacher puts magnet under paper and sprinkles iron filings on the paper to show magnetic field effect. Works better with iron dust, but usually use filings; that's what's available. The space that is the magnetic field, that's what I look like. I look like a magnetic field, which is easier to define by what's around it than itself.

So are you around the Earth? Are you in the Earth? Are you someplace out in the solar system?

I won't draw a picture due to my guest [Tiger the cat], but the center is where the most magnetic energy resides, so that's, of course, where I am. If you were to draw a line from the center of the Council of

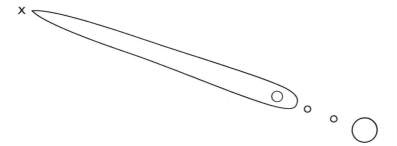

Creators directly to encompass Earth, let's say a distance out from the . . . thank you; now I do picture [draws]. My associate has moved on.

X marks the spot in Council of Creators; circle is Earth (kind of a circle). (Thank you, associate, you are most helpful. Associate is cat. Do you know that associate is so cognizant of magnetic energy that [with] only [the] thought of doing a drawing, associate gets up and says, "Oh, drawing is more important. Excuse me." Associate is that cognizant.)

I know; he gets mad at me sometimes because I can't see what he sees.

Well, [it] is impatience, not really anger. He gets impatient with you, though. I mention this because it is good for reader as well. He is impatient because once you are familiar with cat, and cat loves you and you love cat, then cat is annoyed with you because you don't look through cat eyes. When cat loves you and you love cat, you can extend yourself into cat body, look through cat eyes *with* cat (don't shut cat out), and [you] can see what cat sees exactly. When you do that, then cat no longer annoyed with you. Then cat doesn't have to explain. How can cat explain by going, "Meow! Meow!"? No help to you, and frustrating for cat. But when you go inside briefly—not permanently, but briefly— to look at what cat sees, cat immediately stops being frustrated, doesn't "worry" you, as they say, about pay[ing] attention. [It] immediately stops; you are doing what cat wants you to do. This works only with beloved cat friend, or for some shamanic-type people, if you can form a quick relationship. Can work that way too, but generally speaking, works best with familiar friend, friend-to-friend relationship, yes?

That's great. Back to you: So can you say you are anchored . . . you're conscious of being at the Council of Creators, and you're conscious of being here.

No, no, not clear. I am in Council of Creators, yes? But my energy extends all the way out here to Earth and back, period. Let me put relative position. [Draws. See above.] Earth, yes, third planet, yes? This is me, this is me extended out here; looks like club, but it is me. [Chuckles.]

Where is the Council of Creators in relationship to the levels? I thought it was near or on the first level.

Is very confusing answer coming. It is everywhere and nowhere; [it] is not located in a physical space. The Council of Creators [is] in all spaces at once, yet cannot say it is here. This drawing is for the sake of you to understand, but is not intended to be a road map. Cannot say.

Do you go through everything between the Council of Creators and here? Do you go through creations and creations and creations and creations?

Theoretically I do, but I don't feel any of it, none of that. I am here exclusively for the purpose I mentioned. And when you go on, if I don't go with you—and there's a very small chance that I will—but when you go on, I will do other things. But right now, [there is an] exclusive connection.

Mother Earth and Animals

How conscious are you of the being who is the planet Earth? Do you interact with that being at all?

Oh yes, of course.

In what way? How do you interact with Earth?

[She] is like a companion, a friend. Earth loves animals very much; they are made up of her body, yes? Earth loves humans very much, but Earth's love [is] more of a struggle for humans because humans are learning, so humans have some resistance to love. But animals, no resistance. Earth doesn't love animals more; it's just easier for her to love animals and easier for them to receive it. So Earth is like a friend.

She feels your energy, right?

Certainly.

And it's helpful for her, right?

Mm, not harmful, not helpful. She has her own magnetic energy; what I do for animals is for them. If any is radiated for her, fine. She is comfortable with it, but [it] is not a need for her. She has her own, yes?

This is extraordinary, that you were created for this purpose!

Suggests how important you all are, eh? That there would be, just for this purpose, someone created, me. Yet I am very fond of animals and particularly like listening to their stories.

Animals in Pure Love

But before you came to this space, everything we've talked about, were there animals in Pure Love? Had she created animals?

I didn't notice any when I went through, but then, I wasn't looking, was I? I don't know.

So you came here and you knew what to do. No one had to teach you.

[I'm] looking now; seems to be animals there.

Familiar ones, ones we would recognize?

Yes, but I think they are not there in the physical; it's like looking at a thought. It comes, it goes; maybe everything that exists here in this place . . .

. . . is a thought from there?

Or a feeling—she corrects me. I say thought, but is really feeling, she says.

So it's almost like we're the third dimension of Pure Love. It's almost like this is the place of manifestation, everything here, right?

Well, that's a little bit . . .

I know; they say you have to go through a veil when you go from Pure Love to space.

Yes, true, but it's not just to this space. It's to all that you know, all that you can imagine, all we have discussed and more.

The biggest picture we have so far is of Gaps and Spaces, and that's a drawing.

Yes.

So beyond Pure Love, is that magnetic pulse beyond Pure Love a creator of pure love or . . .

I do not know.

I think you've got some wonderful things to discover yet, just like we do!

Well, you know, my understanding is that without discovery, life as you know it (and even as you don't know it) has no long-term motivation to grow. With love you can exist and love your existence, yes, to define it by its own self. But without discovery, growth is restricted.

And that's the purpose of the Explorer Race, to provide a catalyst for growth everywhere, right?

Yes, certainly there has been growth before the Explorer Race, but it has become stuck. You might say you wouldn't mind being stuck like that, because it is like heaven—wonderful but stuck, not growing, and growth is important.

Are you saying that Pure Love itself is also stuck? Or just in this "space," this place?

I have no reason to believe that Pure Love is stuck in any way, no.

She created this space for some purpose.

You will have to ask her.

I'm looking forward to it.

Next book maybe, eh? Or *a* book.

Are you cognizant of everything we've said so far?

Pretty much; not everything, but pretty much.

Did you learn from it or did you already know it?

It was interesting, but I already had some familiarity.

We're adding a little bit, then, to the knowledge of all the other beings connected to the Explorer Race?

By your questions, by your needs, so by assisting you, I learn, as with all life.

A Guest of the Council

Some of the creators, some of the members of the Council of Creators have said it's a really neat social club. Do you like the interaction?

I am temporary; I am not a core member, so social club aspect . . . amusing, but I am mostly focused with animals here, and as such I am guest of the Council.

Would you say (and I don't know if you know) that all the animals on planet Earth came from other creations that this Creator created someplace? Or did the original idea of these animals come from other creations? In other words, did you ask them to come here?

Yes, yes.

Oh, really? Many of them?

Many have come from other creations. You might have to pursue that another time, but many have come from other creations—animals with tails, especially.

You're very focused, you know. Do you get lonesome as a guest?

[I] do not know the meaning of that. I am so connected with so many countless animals and companionship available in Council. I find that companionship of animals is really sufficient. No. Lonely? Not.

You're connected to them, and you're almost like feeding them, right?

I am provider, as indicated, [of] magnetic energy, only some of which they need. Most of which they don't need, so is for you, but through them. [It] must be through them. Without going through them, if I just provided for you, it wouldn't work. You wouldn't be here, you wouldn't stay. [Your] life span [would be] thirty, thirty-five years, then gone— tops, you understand.

Why couldn't we absorb it directly? Can you explain why?

Only animals from their source, who they are, depending on who they are personally, on their ancestry, on what their planet stands for, what their philosophy is as a species, what their individual philosophy is as an individual—only what all individual animals [are] as well as whole tribe, *only they* have the capacity to broadcast the energies, the feelings, the resonances, the nucleus of thoughts, the love that creates a welcoming medium.

To welcome human beings, to be here for as long as you want. Why,

why, why, you can ask yourself, do human beings fight for the last breath? Because [you] feel welcome here and have forgotten [chuckles] that welcome elsewhere. But when you step on and feel welcome elsewhere, then [you] immediately let go. But until that happens, you have opportunities here.

Animal Stories

As you radiate to the animals, do you then connect with them in a way that you can feel their stories?

Yes, every one, every individual animal. [I'm] particularly interested in animals (not unlike the Pleiadians, I must admit), what they do with their young, stories they tell them, how they encourage them, how they learn how to be who they are. Animals are not born with that, just like human beings; they have to be taught who they are. They have to be encouraged to "do it this way, not that way," and "follow the others and you will learn," and these great stories about our culture, our heritage. Sometimes animal stories relate to other animals, and sometimes what would be just like tribal culture, [the] wisdom of animal species, in that sense. And sometimes there are spirit animals [that] look like them; other times spirits don't look like them, but they relate to [them] in a spiritual sense, you understand. [These are] very complex societies, not unlike the complexities of your own, but without the destruction of externalized technology.

Do some of their stories actually go back to other planets, or are they mostly stories about here?

When great wisdom is being passed on from one animal teacher to another animal teacher, such as (you would say) to a mystical animal within the group, teachings from their home planet are given, yes, but most of what is taught by animal teachers and even to animal teachers is how to get along here, because that is most important. Sometimes stories of home have more to do with feelings of home; animals will center on the feeling of home and feel it and feel it and feel it. And as they are doing so, they will radiate that home energy to all the other animals that are gathered around. Then as they feel it, they radiate it. Pretty soon all the animals of that type will be feeling that energy, and sometimes animals that have the same homes but different cultures on that planet or in that star system will come near to feel that radiation of home. Sometimes this is done just for pleasure, other times for insight. Problems come up, various reasons.

Creating a Creation of Animals

So if you were to create a creation of animals, do you have ideas about particular animals?

First I would ask the animals, what would they do? What would they wish? What would you like to have? How would you like to be expressed? Is there some variety, some form that you would like to be in besides the form you're in? Larger? Smaller? Different? Like that. You ask them what they want, and if [they wish] no change, then [you] create as nice an environment as possible for them.

The way a creation would be could be to take the animals you know here and invite them to your creation? Or would you actually create them?

Most of them have their home planets, see? First I would ask the ones who had their own home planets, "Can I help? What would you like to do?"—the questions I indicated and more.

Let's say the animal said, "Well, we like our shape very much, but it might be interesting to see how it would be to be bigger or smaller; or to add this food in our diet, or that; or to sleep or not; or to live only in the dark (meaning at night or someplace where the light does not shine), or in the light all the time, only sunshine." Like that. Any variable you can imagine. The ant might say, "[It would] be interesting to have a tail!" Cat might say, "Hm, [it would] be interesting to be able to swim and like it, you know." Hard to say. Whatever they would like to try, I would be very interesting in participating.

Let's say you've created your own creation; it's in a different space, and you've created planets and whatever. Would you invite the spirit of these animals there?

No, I would ask animals that are here now or ones I've helped to . . . I would ask animals I know, ones that are here now, or ones I've helped to go to where they are, or animals that have ever been here on Earth. I would ask them first because those are the ones I know.

Most Animals Have Left Earth

Of all the animals that were here when you came, what percentage are gone at this moment?

Oh, over ninety percent.

Ninety *percent are gone?*

Gone, yes, because a lot of animals needed to do something. They needed [to] touch the ground, touch the water, touch the air. They needed to do something to prepare the planet for your arrival. But once you got here, they didn't need to stay.

For instance, a lot of winged animals you call insects didn't need to stay. Most of them are gone. Some of them are here [and] you wish they weren't. The ones that you wish weren't here are here for other animals, you know, like mosquitoes are here for bats. You couldn't live without bats. There are some animals that are very tough or resilient, you know, that you can't live without. Without bats you'd have a very hard time.

What do bats do?

Bats have a lot to do with your dreams (not frightening dreams); they have a lot to do with the bridge between worlds. If you look at bats, they kind of look like mice with wings. They are very symbolic of animals that bridge worlds. You know, there used to be a bat here that not only looked even more like a mouse than the ones you have now— it could fly, yes, but could [also] swim. That bat is gone, but was here. It used to be the only animal that could do all these things, but now [it] is what it is.

Bats help a lot with dreams. They are not exclusive; other animals help with dreams too, but bats [are] very helpful with your dreams, especially if you get too far out of the body. Sometimes you get enamored with the dream and need to come back, and your physical body gets frightened and lonely. A bat moves its wing just a little bit, and then you come back.

Wow, that's fascinating. Other than insects and dinosaurs, are there any large animals that are not here any longer, some we've never even heard of that are interesting?

Well, their names would be meaningless to you, but yes.

I mean some descriptions.

Lots of big sea creatures [are] not here anymore. The whales that you now know represent a small portion of the whales that were here, but there used to be a creature much bigger than the biggest whale you know about, [one] that was involved in bringing the balance into the water and helping the water to become a home, preparing the water for the sea creatures that would follow. This being was about four times as big as the largest whale you have seen or heard of. It looked quite similar, [but] without a tail, to what you call the stingray or the manta ray.

Moving through the water, [it] had that birdlike quality like the manta ray, fluttering through the water. That being, *very beautiful*, was so beautiful that if you would look at it, you would be filled with this wonderful, warm loving feeling. The beauty of the being just emanated into the water, transforming the water into a homelike place for sea creatures. This being has gone back to its home planet. I'm very fond of this being.

We have what we call mythological creatures. Did we have flying horses and dragons? Were these imaginative creatures, or were they here?

Flying horse is imaginative creature.

What about dragons?

Dragons, ruling out breathing fire, [were] real creatures—not fire-breathing, though; that [is] imagination. Real dragons, yes, but not exactly as they look. Without big teeth and frightening aspect, more like what you see in Asian artwork—not cartoonlike, not like a dinosaur type, [but] more like a snakelike dragon. So, [a] sea creature, not land.

So dragons were sea creatures!

Sea creature, never land creature. Not dissimilar [to your carved ones]; no leg, of course, but long creature, eighty feet long originally, then some smaller ones. I think they are not here anymore.

What about what they call the Loch Ness monster?

Some of that has been a joke played on people, but there were several beings in that lake (loch meaning lake, you understand), but I think [they] went into deep underground pools inside the Earth and have since emigrated.

Of course, some could come back if they felt welcome, but only then. They would have to feel welcome. What would welcome them would be fish for them to feed on; [they] also feed on sort of a . . . not plankton, but a kind of microbe in the water that is not present anymore. The microbe was present in the very deep part of the water, but is not present anymore because of pollution. So any creature that has been affected by pollution, the pollution would have to not only go away, but everything [would have to be] balanced, and the welcoming of the waters would have to take place again for these creatures to come back. It isn't just the removal of the pollution; it's the re-creation of the benevolent state of the waters. Understand that the waters were here on Earth first, then the water had to be treated before the animals could come.

Dolphins Are Here for You

Sometimes I get channelings from contributors to the Journal that say the dolphins are leaving. Are they leaving?

[The] possibility was greater in the past, but political activism by children and some adults to save the dolphins has been effective. Still, if every time a dolphin is injured or killed or even bruised (dolphins bruise) when they help fishermen to find fish, it is like [a] point against being here.

They help fishermen find fish and then they get tangled in the nets.

Yes. Worst net ever devised is the kind that they call purse net, where they pull it and then [the fish and dolphins] can't get out. Dolphin happy to help find food for human, but when dolphin is turned into food, then why help human? And if "why help human?" is the prevailing feeling, no reason to be here! Dolphins are here for you; if not here for you, then go home!

But in just a few more years, it's going to get benevolent, right?

[It's] getting better, and political activism has been helpful. Dolphins are conscious of your political activities, be they simple arguments between individuals or be they vast world wars. Dolphins are conscious.

Someone said they were carrying our history for us.

History, yes; but history continues to expand. History is not only of great things happening, mass things happening, but of individuals. Each individual has a history; dolphins carry that, too.

For everyone on each . . .

Everyone who has ever been here; one dolphin can carry many thousands. And of course, if dolphins were not here, [it] would be hard for human beings to be here.

Do you see that in the next maybe fifty years we can actually talk to them?

If you can accept this kind of communication, [you] can talk now. But you stand back and you interpret dolphin and dolphin interpret you? Not much point in that. People have done some of that, and it's all well and good—go, stop, fast-forward, all these kind of things—but what is the point? Dolphin has vast wisdom, and that is not the way you will get your history, from chirping a dolphin.

So telepathic communication would be the . . .

Yes. Is the way dolphins talk. Chirping important, but you make noises too, but [when] dolphins make noises, their noise has to do more with love sounds and sounds they make for each other, but is not primary communication.

Ah, that's where the scientists fail, because they don't understand the telepathic communication.

Some of them understand, but they're not funded [chuckles].

All right. Through the dolphins, then, you know everything that's ever happened to every being.

I could, but I don't. It's not my job.

Learn from the Animals!

I see. You've given us such a wealth of new information. What would you like to say to the readers?

Only this in closing: You know to appreciate the animals around you that you love—your horse or dog friend, your cat or bird friend, your mouse or snake friend—but you don't always know about the wild animals. Know that a single ant has beings it loves, and [it] is loved. [It] tells stories and listens to stories, sings songs and does ceremonies, has dreams, hopes and aspirations. A single ant is not so very different from you, except the ant is here for you. [It has] ten times more magnetic energy than that ant needs, so when the ant walks about—sometimes quickly, especially if big-footed human nearby, sometimes slowly when [there are] not so many human beings nearby and the ant can take time—be aware that such little beings are here to help you just by their being.

Someday when you hear their stories, all the animals and the ants . . . I mention ants because sometimes you do not understand them. When you hear their stories and can sing their songs and sit face to face, one ant in front of you, while it raises a leg and cocks its head and looks at you, and when you sing quietly and gently an ant song, you will discover that animal people have great love for you. Not so different, you know, sometimes than human people. You have sometimes a hard time receiving love from human beings and sometimes a hard time giving love to human beings, too. [It is] sometimes easier to learn with the animals. So if you hear a gentle song in your mind, sing it, then pay attention to which animals come. Maybe you are outside and see an ant; sing song gently—not whistle, but sing song gently (probably a tune, [or] hum, not words, most likely) toward ant. Ant is by itself, stop to look at you . . . maybe [it's an] ant song! [If] ant keeps on going, probably not ant song. Maybe bird song! Pay attention [to] what animals come around. And remember, song is sometimes a direct reflection of the heart that the animal has for you as well as the potential within you, the heart you can have for that animal. Good night.

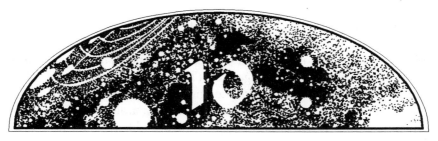

Specialist in Change
and the Velocity of Change

March 5, 1998

I am the Creator of Change and the Velocity of Change. It is my job to monitor everything and anything that is going through any form of change, be it very slow or very rapid. It is for me to assimilate the proper sequence for any change so that I can disseminate that sequence and its proper velocity to anything or everything that might be changing. It is not my job to synchronize change; that is someone else. But it is my job, for instance, to help every cell adapt to the changes that take place within itself when it consumes something or is consumed, including and beyond every planet's shift from day to night and the change that involves. Anything that involves change is my job to consult—to not exactly regulate, but to provide the function of change.

Your Physical Structure Is Changing Rapidly

As such, I am very involved in your transit from the third to the fourth dimension while there is viable life on the planet. I have given a great deal of consultation along these lines to other creators and consultants and those who are involved, and perhaps my biggest, most involving contribution is working with the atomic and cellular structure to make it possible for them to adapt to change that would normally, in the case of a physical human being, take place beyond the veils.

But here we have a change that's taking place within the cellular structure itself, so it has to become like light, but in the physical. Light is easily adaptive to change, so I use that as a comparison, because physical matter, being set up so precisely and finely attuned to its job, does not adapt to rapid change. That's why the setup (if I can call it that) for this change, as you are moving through it now, started about 1950 years ago in order to prepare the cells and atoms for such a radical change in their physical makeup. Changes like this do not easily become accommodated, so they require significant preparation.

I remember that when your Creator and I discussed this, we both came to the agreement that it must begin 1950 years ago (in terms of experiential time, I should say, which would be roughly about 3500 years ago calendar time), because the cellular structure has already had to apply what it has learned with such an evolution of the capacity for change. It has been applying it since the early fifties (about mid-1951 in terms of your calendar), and the velocity of applied change has increased at an accelerating rate since about 1961 (not quite, a little shy of 1961, but almost there).

So the cellular structure is now changing rapidly, but it took all that preparation time and experience for this to take place. You now have a cellular structure in your bodies (all of you, including animals and plants) that has gone beyond your necessary change, so it is more flexible. In that sense, it has caught up to your needs. It caught up to your needs in about 1985 (calendar year) and has gone beyond so that there is a cushioning zone. Since it is possible that you might make a rapid acceleration (not likely, though possible), in that event, you would immediately catch up to the ability to change in yourselves. Let's say you made a jump from 3.47 (where you are now) to 3.52; if you did that, you would use up, or catch up, in that sense, to the applied capacity of cellular change. I don't know that that will happen, but it could. That's why the cells have to have the capacity beyond what you have now.

If, for instance (theoretically speaking, though not remotely possible), you were to make the jump from 3.47 to 3.57, it couldn't be done physically because the flexibility that the cells have worked on now could only take you quickly to 3.52. That's why they have to continue increasing their capacity to change at an accelerating rate, in case you do make a sudden rapid acceleration. That is an example.

My Origin: A Mathematical Formula

In the case of my origin, I have originated from a mathematical formula. It is difficult to describe, but I will try to put something on paper here. [Draws.] If C equals velocity, then the formula for the core of my origin is V to the tenth power times Q, which will symbolize the quantity of change required, which equals capacity; I will symbolize this as K. So this, then, is the given, all right?

I will put this in a box. The box is there just for identification; it is not part of the formula. This formula is my point of origin.

$$\text{If } C = V$$

$$V^{10} \cdot Q = K$$

Can you say where it is?

There is no *where*, as with mathematics, it is understood that where is not a factor. *When* is a factor, of course, with mathematics. I can more easily give you when than I can give you where. Using the model in the first *Explorer Race* book, the illustration that shows the loop of time, my origin is when you come back and close the loop. Then you go forward just a little bit. That's my origin. So my origin is in the future. I have been brought back into this time so that I could assist in the creation of this universe and all that has been discussed so far, providing the aspects of volatile change that have been necessary and will continue to be necessary in order to equip all physical matter for such changes.

I believe my existence in terms of time is quite old; I was in existence, considering that frame, before any of this, though I do know Pure Love. Pure Love had not created any of this that you are in, but when I started moving in this general direction, I moved through the auric field of Pure Love, though I might add (perhaps you don't know) that this entire creation . . . perhaps another illustration might be warranted.

Are you saying that loop of time was before everything we've been talking about?

From my experience it is. I cannot say in toto.

And everything that emanated from Pure Love that Gaps and Spaces said he could see, the space and all this—all of that came after the loop of time?

From my experience it does. If this is Pure Love [draws], just for the sake of illustration, not unlike a child's drawing of the Sun, here's her emanated auric field, obviously off the paper. This is everything you know . . .

Everything we've heard about so far in this book.

[Draws.] That's my passage, my route. So I didn't exactly go through

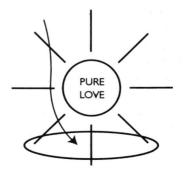

Pure Love, but that's my route into everything you know.

Pure Love Supports Benevolent Growth

This decision that is being reexperienced, this loop of time we're here to experience, was in Pure Love? It started and was something in Pure Love?

I cannot say that; I do not know that. My job is so specific, I do not know that. You have to remember that all of this that has been created seems to have been created for an overall purpose.

Absolutely.

And my impression, from my personality, is that . . . you can see I'm illustrative [draws again]. This is the problem as I understood it. This symbol means negative growth. Now, this is what Pure Love wished to create. This is positive growth, all right? This does not mean negative growth that is uncomfortable, you understand?

It just means no growth.

No growth, yes.

Lack of growth.

Lack of growth because of beauty.

Negative Growth

Beauty is its own reward, yet it can stop things. So, how to perpetuate and expand beauty and at the same time . . .

. . . achieve growth.

That's this symbol [draws], which is also known as the symbol of balance. Illustration three.

Symbol of Balance

You're so organized!

Yes, it is my nature. My understanding is that the only way Pure Love could do this was to, not exactly stimulate, but create the portions of the mechanics, the material, which would, through a catalytic action, stimulate growth in a benevolent way without interfering in any way in the societies, cultures, evolutions, functions, mechanics, anything, of all that would be created. So my understanding, going back to illustration two, since you are here (pointing to everything you've discussed so far), is entirely in existence because of the desire by Pure Love to support benevolent growth. My impression, as indicated by the drawing, is that everything you have heard about so far, and perhaps a little more than you've heard about, is but one. [Chuckles.] I'll draw it to scale. Illustration four [draws]. Let's understand that these auric fields coming out of Pure Love are going off the page, and everything you've heard about [draws]. And that's not all. That's to scale. You have to understand that, mathematically speaking, this page is one thousand times larger.

Is this the only experimental playground that she created, or are there others?

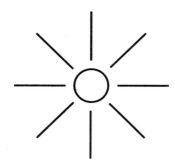

Oh, you'll have to ask her that. [Draws.] That's a little closer to scale.

This is the only one you know about.

It's the only one I've ever discussed with her, but I have no reason to think that Pure Love is in any way limited. My understanding is that everything you've been discussing was prompted by Pure Love's desire to support—not stimulate, but support—benevolent growth.

Someone said she wanted less than two percent negativity. How did it get so out of hand?

Remember, it is not Pure Love's job, as she sees it, to do it. I said that she would put the things together and then, by a catalyst action, *you*, in that sense, would create the change. So in true feminine fashion, she provides the support but not the change. She can only provide the circumstances, the materials and so on to create the potential. If she were to create the change herself, she would interfere and necessarily change the outcome. In order to maintain balance, which is Pure Love's middle name, the only thing she can do is put all the ingredients there and let you do it yourself in your own way and your own time—in that way ensuring that balance exists. Thus beauty is not disrupted, and balance is maintained. But she herself does not create the change.

But one of the other Council members said that the reason they're taking such an active role in supervising this creation is that her mandate was no more than two percent negativity, and look what happened.

Yes, that is their point of view.

You don't agree?

I do not agree with that.

You have a different understanding.

I do not agree with that. If it requires . . . fifty percent negativity to create the slingshot effect, then it does. I grant you that Pure Love is not happy with anything over two percent (it's really like 1.9-something percent), but I would say that if that's what it takes, then that's what it takes. After all, as any child knows, with a slingshot or even a rubber band stretched between two digits, it takes a certain amount of stretch for the contraction and the propellant. So if that's what it takes, that's what it takes, from my perspective.

I Am the Catalyst for Change

So you were launched out here, you were sent . . .

Sent.

When you became aware, you were told what you had to do, or did you know what you had to do?

I was told.

By your creator?

By Pure Love.

Exactly how did she say it? The way you described it at the beginning?

Yes. She would say to me, converting her communication to words, that a catalyst was necessary to prompt the desirable change, and that I was that catalyst. And that it would be necessary for me to be as uninvolved in feeling and compassion as was possible within this realm—which is why she created me from a mathematical formula. I am not cold, but I do have to be objective. By being objective, I am essentially not allowed to be subjective at all. If I became at all subjective, attached to the outcome of any one thing, I would be unable to provide with an even hand, so to speak, what I do. In other words, I don't take sides.

You disseminate change and velocity down to the very cell.

Yes, it is my job to disseminate and regulate change and the velocity of change, which is very important. The velocity is just as important as change, so that things do not change too quickly or too slowly. It is very precise, which is why, as you'll notice, my personality has adapted to such precision.

But I sense that there's another part of you you're not using right now that is very subjective, a part you had to put aside for the job.

No. If that part exists, it is not here with me now, nor have I ever experienced it—which does not say it doesn't, but I have never experienced it. I can be diplomatic, but it is my job to be objective.

The Changes Extend Beyond This Universe

All right, you were created and you came to this space, everything that Pure Love created. What was in this space when you got here? Were there levels and creations, or were you here at the beginning?

I went from where I was at my point of origin near Pure Love, through her auric field directly to the Council of Creators. I have been nowhere else.

In this space of everything that we know, originally there wasn't anything, and then there were levels and then creations and all that. I was just wondering at what point . . .

When I went to the Council there wasn't much.

So you were one of the earlier ones.

Yes. Necessary. Gaps and Spaces was not here yet.

Oh, you came before the space was here?

Yes.

Ah! Because your concern is not just with the Explorer Race; your concern is with the change and this entire creation of Pure Love.

Yes.

Then your mandate was much beyond the Explorer Race; you had to prepare everything . . .

Think about it. What the Explorer Race is doing is the final step to stimulate this benevolent growth, and this final step will be completed when the Explorer Race becomes its own creator. But it isn't completed until then. Nevertheless, things are happening now; changes are being prompted now. For example, even on the Pleiades change has been prompted; they are going through the preliminary experience of change. They will go through it more when you meet them face to face, but they are now going through the preliminary experience. They don't come to this planet very much because there's so much going on in their star system.

That's in our local galaxy.

Yes, but I mention that everywhere else is also going to be affected. Regardless of your Creator's perhaps parochial interest in this universe, the change that is being prompted is not just for this universe, it's for this entire everything. So all of the existences in everything that exists in this creation of Pure Love must be able to adapt their change rate while maintaining beauty and balance. I've been working with all of that from the beginning, but only in the last 1950 experiential years with the velocity of change here on this planet.

Wow, I've never thought of that. For everything to do this sudden expansion, everything everywhere has to be prepared.

Yes, but imagine if you would, the old joke about throwing a child out of the boat to sink or swim in order to learn how to swim. Of course, if that were done, lots of children would drown. We can't have any children drown, much less any cell or atom or proton, if you would, none of that. Each must be able to maintain balance and remain in the beauty of its own existence and its own creation while being stimulated to grow, to move. This requires things to be in place from the beginning. This means that they would wait, say, on the outer edges of this creation of Pure Love, perhaps for a long time, for that sudden burst in velocity. But when it arrived, they would have the capacity, at least at the cellular level, to make such changes so that life forms are not transformed (what you call death), because how can we allow that and still be in beauty and balance?

Oh, you have really raised the ante here.

I understand your colloquialism.

There's a veil around this. Some of the creators have said that you have to go through a veil to get here, right? Not the Earth, but everything that Pure Love created.

Yes, you must go through a veil. In that way it is isolated.

It's like the Earth has a veil around it; this everything has one around it, too.

Yes, and it is prompting something, isn't it? When that velocity of change takes place and spreads out through all of this creation of Pure Love, my impression—I cannot prove it, it's just my impression, logically thinking it through—is that this creation will function (this whole creation of Pure Love) in some way to stimulate such change everywhere that such change is desirable, so that the Explorer Race phenomenon becomes permeated into this entire creation of Pure Love, and that the catalyst capacity, as it were, that takes place here can be applicable to other creations of Pure Love, or others. That's what the Explorer Race (and you are now experiencing yourselves as individual Explorer Race beings) contributes. You contribute your foundational personality capabilities to the entire creation, no matter where you go. Even if you should leave this creation of Pure Love to go elsewhere at some point, you will still have contributed that capacity for flexible velocities of change, otherwise known as flexible velocity of change (FVC).

Right now, or before this creation of Pure Love, the velocity of change was fixed. It was only what it had to be to allow and support the being itself, but it did not have the capacity to reset or speed up or even slow down its own velocity of change. Taking a single particle from here to some other creation of Pure Love (or whoever else does these things), it will be possible, even with a single particle, to prompt change, not unlike a spice in a soup. It will act in that sense like an inoculation.

The Explorer Race: Beyond the Creation of Pure Love!

Zoosh has talked about the Explorer Race going out to these star systems and bringing this lust for life and this two percent negativity. So the Explorer Race will go beyond into the creations of Pure Love and all the others to do the same thing, right?

At least the energy of the Explorer Race, yes. It is my impression they will go on beyond this creation of Pure Love at some point, so that as Pure Love's experiment succeeds and she can see that it works, she can then utilize more or less quantity of the Explorer Race's stimulated viability in application to other creations, yes.

Awesome!

This could mean beings, or it might simply mean . . .

. . . as you said, particles.

Particles, which are also beings, but . . .

The way you said it, I think there was something else they had to do. I think they're going beyond . . .

I believe this is it [adds to previous drawing].

God . . . [laughter] this thing is really humongous!

It expands, does it not?

All right. So you were then existent within this entire creation of Pure Love; you have to be to contact every particle on every . . .

Yes, but located in the Council of Creators.

And focused here at the moment with the majority of your energy, right?

No. It requires no more than about half of one percent of my energy focused here. To compare that (not with the Pleiades, because I'm focused a little bit more there now, too), but this half of one percent would be much, much more than I would be some other place. Perhaps in other places I might be one-millionth of one percent, generally speaking.

The Pleiadians' Increasing Velocity of Change

Right now I'm beginning to be focused on the Pleiades a little more because they have begun. After all, they are, genetically speaking, your closest brother and sister, in that sense. They are the most like you. So even if they hadn't been here for ten thousand years, they would be going through changes, because all genetic matter (all matter that is exactly alike or close to it, meaning ninety percent or more) will go through some change through sympathetic vibration even if they are not in contact with you. The [Pleiadians] have the instrumental capacity to know that changes are being stimulated by what you are doing. That is why in recent years they were nervous about what you were doing and when, because at some point they would start to go through changes too—albeit, from your perspective, very subtle. From their perspective, it was much greater than that. This they are doing now.

Right now, for example, on the average Pleiadian planet, perhaps one where civilization might be loosely compared with yours (your parents, children, like that), their velocity of change has increased by about

1.5 percent. They still don't have negativity, but the prompt for the velocity of change is 1.5 percent more than it had been—just enough for them to feel it, because they are so sensitive and open. They don't feel discomfort, but they feel as if there's something happening.

They have occasional dream-cycle changes. They have meditations where they have dream cycles together; they go through a ceremonial experience at the dreaming level, and those cycles have been affected somewhat.

There is more going on there, and since it is a conscious experience, they know about it. They're not sure what it is yet, but they know about it.

What about the animals on this planet? Is there a sympathetic vibration between the animals and the plants from their source? Is there something like a line of change going to those beings?

Not yet, no. Since this experiment is geared toward you, the Explorer Race, and those you will contact, that sympathetic vibration from the animals or the plants to their home sources is not needed yet. That may happen, but if it does, it will happen a little more in the future. They know who they are, so that sympathetic vibration is not the same. But it is this way for beings very similar to you, such as the Pleiadians.

Supporting Change on the Cellular Level

The friends of the Creator who counseled on the way to turn everything inside out with white light and then back with gold light, and back and forth; are you the one who gave them that information?

No.

Really? So how do you determine the rate of change?

I work with anything that must have change; I do not give information so much as apply change to the basic structures—the cells and the smaller structures. It is my job to do that. When the cells are united, they have that capacity, so I am mostly giving the application of what I do to smaller structures here, for the explanation purposes here, because it is more easily understood at this simple level. But the cells, even of higher-dimensional beings, do not have the same cellular structure. A cell of light is not quite the same as the physical, but it has a comparison. I will work at that level rather than with a whole being. Working with a whole being would be working from the outside in; I work from the inside out.

You do this; you don't sit on the Council and have creators come to you and say, "How do I do this?" Is it more that you do it in a substrate beneath what they use?

Yes, I do this, exactly. But I do consult sometimes, such as with your

Creator. I do consult.

So how did you consult with our Creator?

Your Creator asked me about the rate of change, when and how it ought to be applied and so on. We discussed the mathematics of it.

Have other creators come to you, and how did you help them?

I have had only a couple of other creators. Because this creation, this universe, is so highly experimental, of course, your Creator needs a vast amount of consultation. The only other creators who have come to me have asked about the adaptation to the existent necessary change rate, or everything that I am doing, to what they create within their universes. For instance, one came to me and said, "Can I create a universe that doesn't incorporate change at all? One that has a fixed situation, no change? Where everything is fixed to its perfect balance and beauty and never changes, so that what is in that universe doesn't live and die; it *is* and remains fixed?" The creator asked me, "Is this possible, allowing for the work that you're doing?"

I said no, so the creator had to adapt its creation. It wished to create something that was essentially a finished product, you understand, and I said that would not be possible.

Individual Change versus Mass Consciousness

What about the individuals here on the Earth now? Some are actively seeking to create change by spiritual work, to create the ability within themselves to change. Other people have absolutely no idea and go about their daily lives. Are all their cells changing at the same rate?

Yes. However, those who are attempting to utilize the capacity of change . . . the capacity of change equals [draws]. It's been awhile since we did an illustration. In this case, C stands for the capacity of change, equals growth, G. People who are attempting to speed up their capacity of change and become more flexible, let's say, will perhaps use, not unlike in a graph, more of the capacity for that change to take place. It would be like a spike in a graph.

$$C = G$$

**Capacity for Change (C)
Equals Growth (G)**

Remember when I compared it to the change in the dimensions from 3.47 to 3.52. They will use a greater capacity of that change. Let's do the graph [begins to draw].

So we have the ability now to go to 3.52 within this reality. Can you stay there, or . . .

If this is the increased velocity of change [indicating upward-curved lines], and this is an individual—I equals individual, okay—the individual might normally . . . this is the normal level of change capacity. This is what the individual is using. If the individual is suddenly required to change more quickly and rapidly, he or

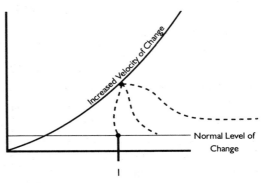

she will do this (I will make the dotted line), achieving the spike. Then as he adapts to that, he comes back to the normal level of change. Theoretically, if an individual became, for instance, a monk or a shaman, then he might conceivably do *this*, utilizing the same graph. I will draw two lines here. Okay, the first was example one. I'm putting a one by the dotted line. The person might follow the same spike upward, but . . . I mark example two . . .

But they're always going to come right down.

Well, they *have* to, to be here. So this would be example two; a person might maintain a higher degree in application in her life . . .

Like 3.48 or 3.49.

Yes, a person might achieve that, beyond which the . . .

So if you tried to operate at 3.52 within an agreed-on mass consciousness of 3.47, then you'd really be unbalanced or unable to function.

Yes; you'd gradually move out of your body. Your body would die, and then there you would be. Since it is the cellular structure in your body that allows you to do this, if you moved out of your body too much, the cellular structure would die and you would be stuck. You would be discarnate, but still in your personality.

Basically, you are keeping the physical cells at 3.47 at this moment.

I am not keeping them there, but the cells themselves are there. I'm not doing that.

Okay, they are there.

They are there, yes. But they have the capacity, as I said, to do more, as indicated by the growth—much more than you need now. That is necessary in case you suddenly made the jump to 3.52 or in the unlikely event that you made the jump to 3.57.

Let's clarify this. To make the "jump," all of humanity has to do it.

Oh, yes.

And then all the cells will move to 3.52, then they would all level off there.

Yes, because they have that capacity. Right now they have the capacity to make the jump to about (theoretically) 3.59, but they don't have the capacity past that point. But they don't need to have it, because we're increasing the velocity at an accelerating rate. So by the time you get to, say, 3.52, the cells will already have the capacity to go to 3.75 and so on. So by the time you're rushing toward 4.0, the cells will be beyond 4.0. They'll keep ahead of you, because as you move up to those higher dimensions, your velocity for change will move also. You'll get faster, the total being will get faster, and the cells will have to be ahead of you.

I think it's important to bring out that individuals cannot function way beyond the means, because they have to live in the body, and the body is at that meeting . . . it's the vehicle . . .

It's the vehicle, yes. And in order to be part of this experience, you have to remain within the group.

And you can have peak experiences and come back.

Yes. When I'm talking about this, it does not necessarily mean only people who are working on ascension, for example, or people who are channeling, or people who are experiencing a great spiritual moment. This might also be someone in therapy, for instance, who has a breakthrough and who might spike in that breakthrough.

Or someone falls in love or someone sees a sunset or . . .

Yes, someone who has a life-changing experience that allows them to swiftly adapt to some greater portion of themselves, which they can then access.

The Cyclic Time to Achieve 3.55

Can you say when we will be at 3.55?

I would say, allowing for the circuitous nature of the velocity of time, that within 2000 years you will be at 3.55. Most likely it will be within, oh, 200 years, 205 years. But one needs to stretch that out a bit because of the circuitous nature of time, since time is a sphere, yes? But at the same point, we could look at it and say it is strictly three-dimensional or even, for the sake of simplicity, two-dimensional, in which case things will go around and might return in different forms. So, generally speaking, you will arrive at 3.55 anywhere in the next 205 to 2000 experiential years. Of course, as time picks up its pace (which it continuously does), calendar years might be shorter. It depends so much on what you do. You are all now experiencing more of your spiritual selves, yes? Yet some of you will choose to ignore it or try to keep it away even though you can't. You can delude yourself for a time that you are still the same rough 'n' ready person, and there will be some people who will wish to do that for various reasons, some of them entirely understandable. But an example like this shows you only one variable in the component of that formula.

You said we started moving in 1951; what was the mass average then? Three point what?

Oh, right around 3.01. Not much change, just the initial capacity.

So we've moved forty-six percent, then, in forty-seven years.

This suggests to you what I'm talking about, of things increasing at an accelerating rate—not just things increasing, but the rate at which they increase accelerates.

If it's theoretically possible in fifty years, if we moved that quickly, then the rate of change is slowing down.

No. I'm just building in all the variables.

But you're saying if it took forty-seven years to go forty-six points, then saying that to go another eight points is going to take two hundred years.

I didn't say that. That's what you heard. I said, factoring in all the variables, it could take from 205 to 2000 years—*could*. Then I said, "Or less by your calendar time." The way I factor time is not the way you factor time.

Could you give it to us in the way that we factor time?

Only by formula [draws]. If this equals the time you are living in, meaning cyclic time . . . okay, this is cyclic time.

That's what time looks like?

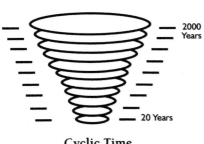

**Cyclic Time
To Achieve 3.55**

To me. If that [the tornado-like structure] equals cyclic time, then each one of these points . . . [draws short lines on the right of each cycle] represents a cycle. It descends a little bit more, but the pen precludes. . . . Each one of them has a different variable. If all went perfectly well, then you would get to—what's the figure you're using? 3.52?

Dimension 3.55, where we're beyond the secret government.

If everything went fantastically, perfectly well, to achieve 3.55 [draws]—twenty years. Now, if things get complicated and confused and you have to backtrack . . .

. . . it could go to two hundred . . .

With gradients.

I understand.

I've stopped numbering them, but you can figure it out.

After the Explorer Race Experiment

Do you have any thoughts about what you'll do when we get through here?

Do you mean in this creation of Pure Love, and go on beyond here?

Yes.

My feeling is that you will be very interested in what I am doing, only you will do it with great heart. My impression is that you will probably enjoy your new capacity for prompting or supporting (prompting being masculine, supporting being feminine) change and anything and everything that has to do with change. I believe that is what you will do.

I didn't want to know what we'll do; I asked, what about you? What do you think you'll do when you're through here?

I haven't given that any thought.

Because I know there's more.

My understanding is that I was created for this specific purpose. I may cease to exist.

Absolutely not. Would you indulge me? Would you ask Pure Love what great thing lies beyond when you get through here?

If you wish. [Pause.] I will go with you.

Aha! [Much laughter.] We will have some adventures!

It seems so!

Your job's going to be awesome, because as this energy gets carried beyond this little creation of Pure Love out into where it's going . . . this is just the trial here, this is the experiment!

Yes.

It's meant to go beyond the veil of this creation of Pure Love.

I have not been told this; I believe it's so.

It feels like it to me. So you'll be monitoring change—my God, out everywhere!

Yes, and perhaps by that time I will not be I anymore; I might be you, and it might be you and I or we. As such . . .

You may merge with the Explorer Race and . . .

Yes, you being a creator and myself being a creator, we might make another.

Yes, the Explorer Race and you might become one.

Yes.

Aha! All right!

Or not, but that is a possibility.

I know there's some . . . it just feels . . .

My impression is that that would be so.

All right! I love it! Since you can talk to Pure Love, would you ask if she would talk to us? Does she want to do a book or a chapter or . . .

She says, let's have our introductions first and then she will discuss it.

Very good, after we get through with the creators. So it looks like the Council of Creators was created for this very purpose.

It is possible.

They are here to monitor all the creations and guide and help them and . . .

It certainly is possible; it makes complete sense to me.

Be Flexible and Adaptive to Change!

There's so much we need to know about change on this planet. Based on your vast knowledge, how can people get into a more personal level of change? What can they do? How can they cooperate with this accelerating process of change?

Pay attention to the circumstances around you, what is needed, how you can adapt best to change, which is becoming more of your life. You cannot have an increased population such as you have without having change thrust upon you. Don't resist it so much. Feel how you can adapt to it in the most benevolent way for you. Ultimately, the most benevolent way for you will be benevolent for others as well. So don't think too much about how to keep it as it was or as it is, but rather how to adapt to what it is becoming.

There are many changes coming, and to the degree you learn to be flexible and adapt, that experience will be benevolent. To the degree that you are resistant, it will increase your discomfort at an increasing rate. So flexibility and adaptation are the two most important personality characteristics that will make for benevolence in your personal lives as time exists now and in the future. If you just think of flexibility and adaptation—write those words down and put them somewhere you see every day, even carry them with you—this will make your lives much, much more simple.

Just for you as a souvenir, I will write it down and you can trim the paper if you want [writes]—plan ahead, eh? Put this sign up somewhere in your house, look at it every

FLEXIBILITY
&
ADAPTION

day. Write the words down and carry them with you in some little spot where you carry reminders. Look at them and notice how in your life (you personally as well as the lives of those who are reading this) and in general, those two words will be the balm that will soothe the most uncomfortable moments.

Say a little more, because there's this saying we have, "go with the flow." Sometimes that can be . . .

Sometimes that can be destructive, yes?

Yes.

One can become part of a mob, a violent mob, and be going with the flow.

Yes, yet you need to do that a little bit to be flexible. So talk about that.

You need to adapt your responses to different situations that will come up in your life. This does not mean you have to join the crowd. Joining the crowd happens at a cellular level, so you don't have to force yourself to do something the crowd is doing that is not right for you. But you can. Perhaps you are normally a reticent person, a shy person; if the crowd is doing something destructive or, as Zoosh says, self-destructive (hurting oneself or others), then no matter how reticent you are, you could volunteer that from your point of view it might be better to do this or do that. Even if the crowd roars and surges on without hearing it, perhaps one person or many will have heard it and will think about it and perhaps file away from the crowd. You might say to yourself, "Well, I don't normally speak out like that." But that would be a way for you to become flexible and adaptable in the same moment—being flexible with how you express yourself and adapting to the situation.

Does what you do require all your time and energy? Do you get to participate in what some of the Council of Creators call a social life there?

I am working all the time. Occasionally I will hear some of their funny stories, which has allowed me to adapt to humor. But other than that, I don't have funny stories of my own to tell.

We're talking about every particle, every cell, every nucleus, of everything, of sentient creatures and lightbeings—of everything, right?

Yes.

How would you describe it?

Everything.

Because there's sentience in the actual space between things . . .

Everything in this creation of Pure Love. My authority does not go beyond this creation of Pure Love.

Well, we're going to have to get some phrase that explains where everybody . . .

I feel that "the creation of Pure Love" is a good phrase, because it not only defines, it nurtures.

But she might have other creations we don't know about.

Well, if you discover that, you can come up with other words then.

[Laughs.] Yes, I'll be flexible. I feel that you have so much to say, but I don't know . . .

That is enough for now. If you have more, we can discuss more some other time. But it is enough. The purpose of this book, as I understand it, is to introduce the reader to the Council of Creators— who we are, what we do, not so much to speak of all that we are and all that we have done. It is an introduction.

Well, that's good.

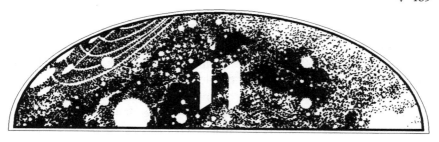

Specialist in Hope

March 12, 1998

am the Creator of Hope, the most recent arrival on the Council. I am, as creators go, in my youth. What you as the Explorer Race have done has manifested me. Before the Explorer Race experience, hope was unnecessary because there were not so very many limits on achievement. But here where there has not been enough of a balance between desire and manifestation, hope has been elevated to a new level. I am now separating unrealistic desires from hope that gives inspiration and encouragement, to hope and wish for something. The Explorer Race has largely perfected the application of hope in its highest methods. So I am now a creator to provide this wisdom of hope and its different multileveled applications to other cultures, should they warrant it.

How wonderful! Welcome.

Hope Fosters Faith in Highly Intelligent Civilizations

One of the more interesting potential applications of hope is its use by highly intelligent civilizations from much higher dimensions who are seeking things that are new to them. Understand that if a higher-dimensional civilization has been in existence for millions and millions of years, they will have explored the limits of their full capacity within, say (arbitrarily, in the case of one civilization), about two and a half million years. They will have found out everything new they can find in that time. Then they will either stagnate and sometimes die out, meaning dissipate and re-form, having either lost that knowledge or (being focused in a different aspect of knowledge) gone into what I would call a hibernation state, during which time they will assimilate the knowledge that will fit whatever application it is meant for into their total being and discard knowledge that will not fit.

To make a long story short, they will essentially stop. What has been useful as a tool with such civilizations is to give them a reason to go on without any evidence that there is something new they might find. This moves intellectual pursuits out of a strictly "datafied," or philosophical or ideological method . . .

Theoretical, yes.

Yes, theoretical . . . into a more spiritual and religious context, because hope ultimately will foster faith. You hope for something, then you have faith that it is there and you keep going on. Maybe you go and rediscover things you have already discovered. You might discover, with the perception and the encouragement of hope and faith, aspects to it that you never noticed before. So this is one of the more interesting applications of something the Explorer Race has already contributed, even before you become a creator.

That's wonderful!

My Journey through the Vastness

Do you have any memories before you came here?

Yes. I was welcomed onto the Council very recently, in creator time, only a few thousand years ago. Even then some of what you *would* do (from my perspective, what you had done) hadn't been done yet, but it was known that you would do it. So, where did I come from? My earliest memory was of feeling myself as a part of something vast, so vast that words cannot describe it. But if you can imagine yourself for a moment being a portion of the ocean—which is very vast within the context of Earth (standing in the water would make it easier, but just imagine it)—and you will get a glimmer of the feeling I had. I did not identify this as someone or something, just an omnipresent vastness.

The next recollection has to do with what I would call a friend of mine. This person is not a creator yet, though he will be; he is more what I would now call a consultant. This individual I will refer to, for the sake of simplicity, as Cause. I became aware of Cause, and this awareness prompted in me a sense of myself as differentiated from the vastness. Becoming aware of an individual tends to bring out your own individuality.

Like a mirror, yes.

Cause had arrived to escort me, though I was not told where I would be putting more of my energy. I was still a portion of the vastness, but I was told that more of my energy needed to be focused in a creation that was going to begin. I was requested by Cause, who had been sent to retrieve me, to begin moving toward this coming creation, and if I could do so as slowly as possible rather than quickly, I would gather some information that would be useful later.

So Cause and I took a slow trip toward the point where this creation was going to begin. Our trip was largely through areas that were, as your people would say, undeveloped; it was part of the vastness, but there was no clearly definable creation present within it. It was like examining a portion of myself that I understood. It was a long and, I might add, sometimes tedious process, examining something on a multileveled experience that is essentially the same from place to place. After a while I asked Cause, "Are we actually going to this creation, or to where the creation is going to begin? What is it that we are doing?" Cause told me that it was just as baffling to Cause, but that it was being directed to take me on this circuitous course for quite some time, until I would arrive at this point of creation.

My Arrival at Pure Love's Creation

We had already been going for what is equivalent to about 1230 of your years, and we kept on going for about another seven or eight thousand years exploring the vastness, which was essentially the same from one place to the other. By the time we arrived at the intersection where this creation of Love was going to begin—and I believe I can speak for Cause and myself—we had strong feelings. I can't say we were disgusted, but we were certainly bored. After thanking Cause and sending it into its creation, which had just begun, Love spoke to me and said that she was sorry for sending me on such a long journey that seemed to be pointless, but that she wanted to inspire in me a feeling I would never forget, that would require something to change that feeling and make it better.

I said, "What? You can make me feel better?" Love said, "Don't worry, you will find it; I am sending you to the exact place where the beings who will come to be known as the Explorer Race are forming their experience, and you will have the opportunity to benefit from what they do." Of course, at that time I assumed she was talking about another creator; I had no idea she was talking about individuals.

Now, as is often the case with "age" and experience, I understand that Love wanted me to have that somewhat desperately bored feeling so that I would completely understand the application and value of hope. You can be desperately bored, but if you have hope, you will remain buoyant. You won't get caught up in the pointlessness of whatever you are doing. You will be expectant of something happening, and you don't lose the feeling that something better is going to happen. So Love felt it was essential that I have that experience so that I could personally appreciate the creation you were involved in, in which I would become a creator involved with hope. You created hope.

You came to Pure Love's creation before there was anything here?

It was just beginning. The Explorer Race wasn't here yet. Pure Love plans ahead.

But if you got here only a couple of thousand years ago, how could you have come here when it was just starting?

I didn't get here a couple thousand years ago; I just got onto the Council a couple thousand years ago.

So after she talked to you, then you went around Pure Love's creation?

Yes, slowly; she said, "There's no rush. When they are prepared to create something that will balance that uncomfortable feeling in you, you will know and be drawn very quickly." When something occurs in creator terms, it occurs within a swath of say, eight to ten thousand experiential years. When I said I joined the Council a couple thousand years ago, you could say intellectually that what you had done or would do to create hope, you had not done yet; but from my perspective you had done it.

So that's when I came. Since there was no rush to get someplace where, from my perspective, nothing was happening, I took my time. And only when I had that feeling did I allow myself, like the proverbial rubber band or elastic, to snap to this spot.

So after Cause left, you investigated Pure Love's whole creation?

Yes; Pure Love said, "Enter." And since Pure Love was quite obviously the reason for my individuality, I wanted to see what she was creating.

Was the vastness of which you were a part when you became aware, Pure Love, or something beyond her?

As Zoosh likes to say, it was up the line from Pure Love.

Can you say who, what, where?

I have said who, what, where to the best of my ability by calling it the vastness and by mentioning to you that there wasn't much happening in it other than that feeling, from my experience.

Sounds like it's way up the line. Other than the example you gave us, have you spoken to other creators and given them advice about the use of hope? Can you tell us some of your experiences on the Council?

Hope Encourages the Negative Sirians to Reincarnate on Earth

I have done extensive work with the so-called negative beings from Sirius who were doing that unusual thing of discarnating en masse on Sirius and reincarnating en masse on Earth, but at a slightly denser vibration than you, so that you're not really aware of them. I did a lot of work with them because they needed hope when they were discreated when the planet exploded, and they needed something beyond intellectual fact to encourage them to stay together, even as a reincarnational cycle.

Think about it: Here were beings, many of whom hated each other in their lives, and once their lives were over, even though it wasn't a pleasant ending for them, they were liberated at least momentarily from the misery of their planet's culture. It was quite a job to encourage them without giving them any facts or justification whatsoever, but by layering on significant amounts of hope to encourage them to reincarnate totally. Nobody broke off, you know; they could have, but they didn't. They needed lots of hope, so I worked with them directly, not through a creator. They didn't have a group soul, but I was able to stimulate the connectiveness from one soul to another, not unlike a neural network.

How many beings? Thousands? Millions?

When the planet discreated there were somewhere around 400 million souls.

Four hundred million? I didn't know that there were that many. And they're all now here on 3.0 Earth?

They're not all here, but they're all either here or poised to come here. They're not going to go anyplace before they come here. Some will be born through the natural cycle, so they're poised to be here.

What an incredible achievement!

It was.

Were there other beings feeding them feelings of hope or just yourself?

There were other people assisting them, which was necessary because of the misery of their condition. All their guides and lots of other beings were there. They needed angels aplenty; they needed lots of encouragement just to go on, especially since they had a glimmer of total, pure love and benevolence. To go to a society that was even, from their perspective, only fifty percent negative is still a burden after you've seen and felt benevolence.

So it was explained to them, without telling them anything that would occur, that they would achieve great lessons for themselves by which they could take a significant leap of growth, and that at the end of their cycle on Earth at this dimension, not a single one of them would be angry at another because there would be no reason to be, that all their difficulties would become resolved, because they would have a chance to work them out. Souls don't like to have things like that linger, so that was the most convincing statement.

We heard recently that there were a few left here on Earth in ships, and they were, I think Zoosh said, convinced by the threat of the sword to join the others at 3.0. So there are no more negative Sirians left at our vibration?

It is quite an extreme that they have been through.

They started on this planet, right? They were a civilization that was on this planet at one time.

Well, this planet was in Sirius, and that is why they initially had the feeling they were claiming something that was their own.

I thought they actually had a cycle of life on this planet in this position and then left to go to Sirius.

I'm not aware of it if they did.

We've heard a lot about them; different beings talk about them. It's the most extreme case of anything connected to the Explorer Race, right?

It is, yes; and it proved the limits of how much discomfort individuals or a society could tolerate and also, how much a planet could tolerate as a result. The planet had to destroy itself in order to get rid of the discomfort.

What percentage of negativity was there on their planet?

At its extreme it reached right around seventy-one percent, from my perspective, which is several points past the assumed standard. Before, it was assumed that sixty-seven percent was the worst, but it went to seventy-one percent.

I know. I felt them once when I visited them in my dream body because I got curious during a workshop with Janet McClure/Vywamus in 1989. Vywamus explained that they were transitioning from second to third dimension, but they had the fear that if they were to go to the third dimension, they would be annihilated. They were harassing individuals and the government because they felt they needed to survive. I woke up feeling them, and I didn't like it. It felt like I was in a horror show.

It is not a good feeling. On the other hand, it is easy to have compassion for them because they really do not know they have that impact on others. They have no idea because almost all of the others they are exposed to are more benevolent than they are, so they feel good in your presence, whereas you feel bad in their presence. They do not understand it when individuals, even in the nonphysical state, become ill in their presence. It is frustrating to them because they want to communicate. But in time it will happen.

Now that you are here, do you know what lies ahead of you in your future? Do you have any idea what that will bring?

I won't be going with the Explorer Race, because you achieved what is my (now) glowing expertise without me. There is no need for me to go with you. I am still in training, so I don't know where I'm going to go.

Is that okay with you? Do you feel that when it's time, somebody will tell you?

When it's time, I'll know. I'm in training.

You don't have the curse of curiosity?

I don't consider curiosity a curse, but because my training is complex, it requires my attention, and I don't have what I would call the luxury of curiosity. It is a luxury, you know, from my perspective.

I didn't know that! To be so totally focused on what you are doing, you have to be totally in the present, and you can't be wondering about "what if," right?

Yes, you cannot do something else while you are doing what you are doing. You can get in your automobile, be thinking something, have your beloved friend with you, drive, pay attention to the road, have the radio on, but I cannot do that. For me, one thing is enough.

Describe how that works. What do you focus on or what is the process?

I am entirely focused right now in hope and its applications. It's hard to describe it, because it is primarily a feeling.

The Negative Sirians on 3.0 Earth

Have other creators come to talk to you about using hope? Most other creators are benign, so . . .

Most other creators have benign creations and have no applications for it. That is why here is a good place for me, because these beings who have come from that negative planet on Sirius really need me. So I'm working with them directly as individuals.

I see. So you don't have that much to do with the Explorer Race people right now.

The Explorer Race made it possible for me to be who I am. I didn't do anything for you; you did something for me. And now I'm doing something for them. I'm focused primarily with beings who need hope.

Do you feel that if they can feel hope and then faith, that that process will help them achieve a more benevolent life?

I believe it can. There have been many, many instances where it has; but it must begin with hope, in my experience.

So by infusing them or radiating at them or focusing them—how would you say that you help them?

I talk to a lot of them in their sleep; dreams are still relatively new to them in terms of benevolent dreams, not nightmares. I talk to a great many of them when they are sleeping and encourage the children when they are born. As with every generation, when children are born they experience more benign experiences and less discomfort. The first generation, of course, had to have lots of discomfort so that their experiences would feel sufficiently familiar to them; every succeeding generation requires less discomfort, so the first generation needs lots of attention.

And they're humanoid. Do they look anything like us, now that they have reincarnated here?

I wouldn't say that, but they're certainly humanoid.

Are they keeping the same shape on 3.0 Earth that they had on Sirius?

Yes. Certainly there have been some changes, however, such as with pigmentation. They didn't have much pigmentation in their skin before, but they need it now because they are outdoors. On the other planet they weren't outdoors very much.

They had technology before; are they starting over in caveman style?

Not caveman, but their technology is rudimentary. They have some technological capability, but I would say not a lot.

Similar to what year in our past?

Oh, not similar in culture, but using the applied technology of the time, right around the 1800s in Europe, for example, compared to China, which was significantly ahead of Europe.

As we move into the fourth dimension, then, will they move up from 3.0, or will they stay there for quite a while?

I believe this is not decided yet. They will probably need quite a time of assimilation in 3.0, and I think that you will be long gone before they begin to move up. Therefore, you will feel them less and less. You know, when they first started coming in, you were still close enough to 3.0 that a lot of you felt or saw it; some felt that there were beings coming from somewhere and that they were negative beings. A lot of people had that feeling, but that feeling has faded because you've moved on and they're still at that 3.0.

What happened to Cause? He just went back to where you started? He was like an escort?

No; Cause is here somewhere, but not in my present location.

Hope Is the Explorer Race's Great and Noble Creation

Is there anything else you would like to talk about?

I am just about done, but I will say this. Know that the value of what you have created, something as seemingly simple as hope, is far beyond the applications in your own society. People you'll never meet, who wouldn't know you if you did meet them, are greatly benefitting from this great and noble creation that you have already applied and are now involved in espousing. Know that by this simple creation, you have proved your capacity and your equality as a creator in training. From my perspective, you are, taken in total, all of you, a fine apprentice.

That's wonderful.

Good night.

Specialist in the Present Moment

March 24, 1998

am a creator. I have been working very much these days with the people of Earth. My field can be most easily defined as the now. Your people have been struggling with past and future consciousness in the linear mind, but for the past three years your capacity to manifest has been hampered by that linear set of consciousness.

It would be of value for the people of Earth, when thinking about what you want and when doing things, to be in the present as much as possible. It is so easy to become caught up in the past. I will tell you why it is more important now. You are in a cycle now where creationism is functioning much more powerfully than it has in the past. Creationism is a present-moment experience. When you think of something troubling from the past, it doesn't necessarily create it in the moment, but it will slow down your capacity to create in the moment. There is almost a built-in safety mechanism to keep you from dragging your fears and your past discomforts into the present, because by worrying about the future or thinking of discomforts from the past, or by fearfully being consumed with maybe's and could be's, it slows down greatly the mechanism of creationism.

A Creationism Exercise

So I'm going to start right off with some homework. I'm going to recommend that everyone pick one thing they want to change in their life. You can have many things you want to change, but pick at least one thing that is most pressing. And give yourself a challenge; it will be very difficult, but I recommend it: For three days, every time you feel yourself worrying or fretting or thinking of all the bad things that can happen, you will stop. You will say nothing negative about yourself doing that, but just, "Wup! Caught myself again!" or make a joke out of it, then focus on that one thing you want. This has to be something benevolent for you and that does not inflict harm on others or manipulate others. It can be something simple like your need for more money—or what I'd recommend, instead of that, is to focus on a need for whatever you would purchase with that money, or on a desire for circumstances in your life to change and become more benevolent. Picture those benevolent circumstances, but don't picture the way you'd create them.

Creationism isn't about thought; in a thinking world based on the linear experience, it is very easy to consider how Creator created this world, as your biblical stories go. "First He did this, and then He did that," and so on. But in reality, creationism is much simpler than that. Let's say you are a creator in a given space where there is energy and available raw materials—matter that is what it is but is open to becoming part of something else—and you wish to create something. When you feel that desire to create something as a creator, parts of that creation begin to be attracted to you. It is very easy in the linear world to get caught up in this [draws] . . . the steps to the goal, yes?

But you have to understand that it is in your nature to be creators, because you are in Creator School and now you're coming into the energy of creation. This is the way creation actually works. We have

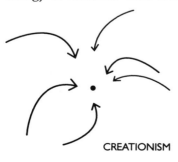

CREATIONISM

here a creator [draws], and you are considering creating something. You have, then, decided, "This is what I would create." Without asking for the parts to come to you, in that given space the parts begin coming. In this case I've shown the parts coming to the creator. But *you* function, partially at least . . . [draws] in the vestigial remains of the linear world. You're not really in the linear world anymore, but you're clinging to it, and to some extent you're being supported by the remains of the illusion of the linear world so as not to be in the process of too sudden a transformation, which would be overwhelming. What is occurring is that in reality, when you desire that one thing, you will attract parts of it to you. Don't expect it to occur within the three days; maybe it will or some portion of it will, or maybe you'll see some sign that it's happening. But consider it a creationism exercise.

It is perhaps more important than it has been in the past to do this now. Many of you have trained in the past using manifestation exercises; that was primarily training, and some of you managed to manifest some things. But now it is much, much more likely to be effective, so I'd recommend any and all exercises that work to create something more benevolent for you and, ideally, within a range of benevolence for others. That's why you will get energies and parts of other things that will come to your creation, because it *is* benevolent. You cannot expect things that you need—raw materials, you might call them—to leap toward your creation if your creation will harm them or be used for harmful purposes. They will fight; they will cling to their present location if they feel they are going to be misused and harmed in the creation of something harmful.

I want to explain this to you slowly, in bits and pieces, and I'll talk to you more about it in a future volume. But now it's important to speak to you about this because so many people are making long-range plans, yet the rules you've used to manifest before are no longer in effect. Those rules were very slow and tedious; the new rules are much quicker, but you will have to suspend your disbelief and worry less. I'm not telling you to do nothing, to be ungrounded, but that if you catch yourself worrying, try to uncreate it. Now, to uncreate it, you don't say "Erase, erase," or something; you try to trace it back as if you're doing something backward so that it would then no longer exist. Do you understand?

To the moment before you started worrying?

That's right.

Helping You Focus in the Now

Now, tell me something about you! How did you get this expertise? How did you get involved with us?

When Creator of this universe was in this space and was involved in the intention of creating this new thing, of which you all are such an integral part as the Explorer Race, Creator started putting out the call for those who would not only help in the creation, such as all of Creator's consultants, but also those who would help in the final stages (from Creator's point of view) of the Explorer Race's refinement. I was not at that time on the Council of Creators, but I was involved in a distant system, functioning with what I would call time correlation. In this distant system, I was involved in variations of the experience of time—inner time, outer time, imagined time, various ways of measuring time—and to some lesser degree, space. Creator's call caught my proverbial ear, and your Creator asked me if I would be present to help the people focus more in the now when you approached the end of time as you know it. Not the end of the world, but the end of time as you've experienced it.

I said yes. Thus I haven't been in this general area very long, only about maybe 40,000 years. I needed to come early enough so that I could see what you were doing and what your Creator was doing here, but not too early. What I would need to do with you I have not actually begun, except for the last two hundred years!

Forty thousand years ago . . . what stage was our civilization at then? What was happening?

I must admit that 40,000 years ago I wasn't really paying attention to where you were. I was retracing your steps and observing how you got to where you were, so I didn't really start paying too much attention to your existence here except for the past few hundred years. I was examining the way Creator here acculturated you so that you would be clear or unbiased enough in the ways of other beings. Other beings on other worlds might be biased to live a certain way, but you had to be clear enough as souls to be open to many varied possibilities.

How did He acculturate us?

He was able to do it by not allowing your souls to be any one place for too long, so that when you stitched your way from one planet to another, you would generally be impermanent. Although many other souls might have numerous and often sequential lives on a benevolent world, you didn't do that very much. In this way your souls were more inclined to be cosmopolitan, you might say, but you were also more inclined to be broad-minded. And because you were caught up in struggles here or there, you were open to the idea that everyone doesn't agree.

The Great Expansion

I'd love to get an overview of your journey here. What were the high spots?

When I began moving from the place where variations in time are created, I moved slowly. I had time, because the Explorer Race part of the creation didn't happen until the latter stages of this universe. I moved slowly, first on one time stream to this universe, then retraced my steps, as it were, instantaneously. Then I traveled in a different time stream to this universe. So I traveled in different forms of time *to* this universe but not into it, so that I could experience the fullest possible range of becoming used to the alteration in time that you as the Explorer Race will perpetuate by what you are going to do. In this way I was permeated with time change and time experience, so that it wasn't so much of the high points of this or that place, but when I arrived here, I was an overwhelming matrix—a cornucopia, if you like—of available synchronicities.

Your Creator found this useful when planning the great expansion. The great expansion, as you know, will have to do with what you do in the future. (All this has already been discussed [in the *Explorer Race* books], so I'm not going to repeat it.) Your Creator borrowed from me or utilized from me three different time-sequence potentials for this expansion. In one sequence, everything expands in the same moment. In another sequence, it goes out spherically, like a sphere of influence, and expands in that fashion. It also happens in what I would call a compound way; it goes out to the boundaries of this universe, comes back into the center of this universe, then accelerates out faster beyond the boundaries of this universe. That's just in case there is a desire, due to various circumstances, for an opportunity to discover how the expansion is affecting this universe before it goes off to affect others.

So my travels to this universe were not wasted, from your Creator's point of view. It wasn't only something I did, it was also something your Creator was able to utilize.

So then it's going to be like choosing one sequence of expansion?

Yes. But that choice has not been made yet, not firmly. There is a ninety percent chance that it will go out spherically, but it's not absolute. It's an advantage to have the other possibilities, because if for some reason there is a desire to maintain the more observable environment, and if the other universes and their creators want to see how it impacts this universe first before they embrace it . . .

There are some on the Council who are skeptical, yes.

Then it might be possible to allow that recirculation, the expansion in this universe only. I think that this sequence will be useful. Thus so I am what you would call a visiting creator in the Council of Creators.

Can you place your source of origin in a way we can follow? We understand Pure

Love's creation and the various peers of Pure Love, but that's all we know so far.

I am down the line from Pure Love—in terms that you can understand; I am in Pure Love's creation. It makes sense, if you think about it, because although time is such a useful tool for learning and has very little application otherwise, it is an important and necessary tool in this creation of Pure Love. Because Pure Love's intent, as I understand it, was to create an expansion of the known into the unknown, ultimately in a benevolent way. In order to do that, one does not simply wave a magic wand. For a permanent change, the beings within that creation must have the capacity to make that change and must live in circumstances where the opportunity will naturally present itself. With time sequences this is more likely, because where you have time you will likely have space, though it is not a requirement. In your time sequence you do have the experience of space—measured space, if you would—and it gives you enough similar circumstances with your fellow beings that you have the opportunity to discover things yourself. Self-discovery is available to the youngest member. Even though countless children discovered dandelions before you did, gentle reader, you discovered dandelions, too. Once upon a time, you said, "Ooo!" and were so excited because they were so pretty and so on. It is this self-discovery that nurtures the expansion.

If Pure Love were to instruct you that ultimately you would be followers, you would simply follow the guidance of someone else. But Pure Love places you in a condition whereby you can get used to discovery and are ingrained that discovery is at least potentially benevolent (and very often in your early years it is). When your foundation is that discovery is very often a joy, the chances of your being reticent to expand are greatly reduced.

I Became Aware within Pure Love's Creation

When did you come to Pure Love's creation? In the early part of it or later? Were there creations here?

I am not aware of having been anyplace else.

So you became aware within her creation?

Yes.

Were there all kinds of creations and levels, or was it before the levels?

There weren't any created universes yet; there were just the initial tools, the ingredients. And because time sequences are such a critical ingredient in growth, I believe that's why I became conscious then.

Initially, if you were to ask me to predate my existence, I would have to say that I was a portion of that stew of ingredients that makes up time sequences. You could picture it as a light from which tendrils come out that look like light, but the light focuses from the outside in and doesn't radiate outward and illuminate the space it is in. When light radiates from the outside in and doesn't radiate into the space around it, that tells you it's doing something. That is a good indication that it is creating. The light of most creators is like that. It would be like this . . . [draws]. Let's say this circle is the creator. But the light is moving inside. Energy is transformed into light within the body of the creator being. For simplicity, the body is the circle. The body is not really visible, but it becomes visible because of the light. When you see light like this with your subtle vision, you can be sure that it is involved in a creative process. Even if it is something simple like a vehicle traveling from place to place, it is functioning with creative energy. You can tell. For instance, look at your rockets; they illu-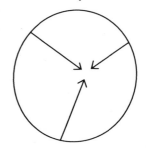minate the space around them because the creation went into them on a linear basis. It is an example of a time technology—from one space to another—and when you see it illuminating the space around it, it tells you the creation has been completed and it is the action of that creation.

So in a rocket we're seeing the result . . .

You're seeing the result, yes. But a creator's shape is defined by that energy being converted to light going inward, and the only time the light comes outward is when that creator creates something either beyond its boundaries or it is something discernible from beyond its boundaries. But you don't see it come out of the creator; it just appears. I mention this to you because I don't think anyone has told you that before.

That's true. So you became aware of yourself, then, as this tube of light?

Yes. I was a portion of this tendril coming out from a central core that was roughly tubelike. I became conscious, I became aware of my own personality, and at that moment a portion of that tendril broke off and there I was. I stayed there for a long time. I noticed that other tendrils broke off, and they seemed to have their own personality also. We all stayed and continued the work, though I noticed before I went off that another portion that had also broken off went someplace else before me. I don't know where it went. I know I haven't seen it since.

And then you stayed.

And then I went. I'm assuming the other portion went for similar reasons. Something . . .

It heard the call.

Yes; it heard the call from someone.

So you stayed there until you heard the call.

Yes.

What was your sense of what you were doing there? You were involved in under-standing time or creating time?

No, not understanding time but creating time sequences—not time you live in, but types of time.

Who utilized those types?

You can see why this was necessary. Other creators would use it like a tool, like a carpenter would take a nail out of a bag.

How did creators get this tool? Did they come and get it from you?

They wouldn't come, but if they needed it, it would be there. They didn't have to make the trip. Since it was within Pure Love's creation, it was available. But first it needed to be generated, created. One takes these things for granted, yet everything has been created bit by bit, even things that one assumes exist everywhere like this, but very often they don't.

Earth School Demands Learning

This world, Earth especially, is an unusual world. It is a test-tube world and is isolated from almost everything around it because it is such an intense school. It is a kind of energy that demands—it is not optional, it *demands*—that people learn, and learn quickly. If it were allowed to escape into the rest of the universe, I don't think the beings could survive it very well. But since souls come here with the knowl-edge that this is a place to learn and the circumstances are in place that require learning—even before birth within one's mother one is learn-ing—then you know what to expect. You volunteer, you don't get drafted.

[Laughs] It feels to me like drafted sometimes!

It only feels like that, but it is necessary for it to feel like that. This is an important thing to remember about personalities: If you feel stuck someplace, you will try to make the best of it, but if you are on a planet where all is benevolent and you can travel anywhere you want to, you don't have much reason to change.

And we are the catalyst for change, right?

Yes. And because you survive it and most of you survive it fairly well, when others on planets that are not exposed to what you've been exposed to yet observe you, they become less anxious—though those terms don't really apply to them. They become more amenable to being exposed to those who will stimulate growth and change just by their being, before you even say anything. If they are in your aura, if they are exposed to you, you will stimulate growth and change. That's why they will have to regulate their exposure.

You won't have someone like a diplomat who comes unshielded to greet your vehicles and spends lots of time with you as you're out being your Explorer Race selves. They will come shielded, and they will regulate their exposure to you. They might touch some instrument or simply regulate their own energy bodies and allow a little bit of exposure. This is because they will know that when they go back to their societies where all beings are totally connected, even the tiniest little bit of exposure will affect everyone.

The diplomats will be trained for these activities, and whether they are technological or simply instinctual or functional spiritual beings, they will use that same method—the gradual inclusion of your energy. This is not to say that they won't talk to you or that you will be excluded from going to worlds, but while you're there and while your energy is radiating (because it naturally does), their citizenry will be somewhat protected, allowing only a small amount of your energy to actually be included for them. This is what they're comfortable with and that's how it will work.

Have you thought of what you will do after the Explorer Race becomes a creator? They will need your advice, right?

It's not so much my advice, but my energy. But barring any other call, I will return to what I was doing before.

Pure Love's Benevolent Vision

Since you came from that tube and you had such a specific focus, would you say that that was an aspect of Pure Love, or that there is something beyond Pure Love you're probably connected to?

My impression is that it was from beyond Pure Love, something that Pure Love requested or gathered. I do not think that Pure Love, in her nature, requires growth as such. Since time sequences require growth, my assumption is that I am from elsewhere, or the derivative from which I came is from elsewhere.

You're saying Pure Love doesn't require growth, yet she's created this entire creation. My understanding is that the growth, the expansion, will affect Pure Love and her peers. I don't know what's beyond them yet, but it will affect this beyond also.

You see, Pure Love does not require growth, yet she is open to it.

There is a difference between being open to something and requiring it.

Is it your understanding that the expansion will go beyond Pure Love's creation?

I do not know.

If someone creates something, you know, they would seem to have a purpose, a long-range purpose for it.

But that is a time-sequence statement. If you create something, you have a purpose. Yet if you were to look at any animal, a creature or a human, you could say that when they consume something, they are changing creation. And when a woman creates a child, does she have a purpose for that child, or is she just happy that that child is there and desire that that child is happy? But a purpose?

You see, it depends on how you look at it. You might create something because it seems natural, because creation is normal and healthy, without planning its future. You might create something and give it all the tools so that it can create things and establish its own future, trusting and having faith in the natural expansion of creation.

That's interesting, creating it and allowing it its own purpose. We'll wait for somebody who knows. It just seems that there is somebody up the line who has a purpose for this; it's too incredibly planned and focused and synchronized, you know.

My impression is that this is a creation of Pure Love, and that this is all part of some benevolent vision on her part. A vision is different than a plan; a vision is about a potential, and if the vision is benevolent enough, you might, like Pure Love has done, put all the ingredients together and allow that vision to come to be. If you have the capacity, as Pure Love does, to see the vision, to experience the vision, and because of the experience know all the component parts completely, then you would place or invite all those component parts, including every molecule or atom of energy, into this place. Then you would step back and see if your vision comes to pass, without interfering.

Your Time Sequence Is Changing

Okay, let's get close to the present. You said that for the past three years the capacity to manifest has been hampered by the past and future. What type of cycle, what kind of thing happened three years ago?

What's happening now is that your time sequence is changing. In the past you were moving forward from the past; now you're simply returning to the future. There's a difference.

In the past you were propelling yourself as if you were propelling yourself [draws] around a wheel, see? Let's say this is your voyage. You would have to propel yourself around and use some energy to push yourself around . . .

Let's say this is the goal [the circle on the upper right], the benevolent thing, and you want to be close to that. To get back to it, since it's a one-way path, you'd have to push hard to get away from it because you *want* to be close to it. But you are drawn back. In this way [writes] you are pushing to go there; but here [writes] you're being pulled. So the sequence has changed.

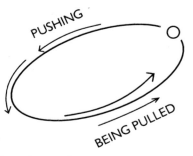

Why did it change? How did it change?

It wasn't a why, it just was a moment. You passed through the moment where you were no longer necessarily having to push. It wasn't an apogee/perigee kind of thing.

Is it a change of frequency or something?

[Chuckles.] There isn't a linear explanation. I will give you an illustration, however. If you throw a rock up in the air, when it starts to return to Earth, you could say it was because of gravity. But why at that moment? You could say it was because of the physics of it—the weight, gravity, the pull and so on. Let's just say it's like that. When you get to a certain point, you don't have to push anymore; the pull takes over and then you can relax. And when you can relax, things start to fall back into their natural order, and the natural order is creation of the moment.

If we're being pulled, then why is there a danger of the past pulling on us? You said to be in the present as much as possible, that it's easy to get caught in the past.

Because your generation has gotten used to pushing, as you say, by motivation. What you want for the future you haven't had in the past, so you have to do something in the present to get what you want in the future. That's linear, see? Maybe you want something *now.* That's why I want to start you off slowly. I'm not saying you should sit down and wait for it to come to you, but ultimately that is exactly what you will do. But for now in this transitional time, if you want something, it's better to say that you want it now, in the present—not like the angry child who says, "I want it *now!*" but that this is your need now.

For instance, let's say that you have a building that is big enough for all your needs now; then you wouldn't have to say anything. But if you have a child on the way and you think, "Gosh, I don't really need another bedroom now, but in a couple of years I will," you say, "I need to have another bedroom, or a house that has another bedroom, and I need it now." You understand? Then gradually the component parts come to you and you may have to take action as they come to you, opportunities and so on. But you begin to say that. So this an opportunity. I grant that it's not much different than the manifestation exercises you've learned in the past; I can only say that now they are more likely to work more easily.

How long do you feel this transitional period is?

I can't give you years; I can only say that by the time you pass 3.51 it will be thought of as normal.

God, that's wonderful.

And by the time you're past 3.75, you won't even be able to imagine linear creation. But you'll have history books.

[Laughs.] Like the ones we're writing now.

Yes.

Beyond the Linear, You Will Find Peace

Just give us a little feeling for it. It's not linear, so everyone's sense of being will be in the now? Is it that they won't think about the past or that there won't be any fear or anxiety or what? How will we feel then versus how we feel now?

You are more likely to be at peace with each other and, most important, with yourselves. You are more likely to be satisfied with life. You are more likely to be cooperative with each other, because you'll see how you create things together and how much more benevolent it is for each and every one of you to be creating in some benevolent way. You will most likely not even consider that you have to compete; competition will no longer be a factor in your life.

I know a lot of you like competition and you've made it fun; because you've made it fun, you're somewhat attached to it. Before it was fun, it was just awful, but because you have had to live in time and make it work, you found ways to turn awful things into fun things, at least in the moment. You know that in competition, some win and some don't, but in the future, or in the 3.75, which we're using, you won't be comfortable with anyone not winning. You'll want *everyone* to win, because if somebody isn't winning, everyone will feel it.

You can accept the idea now that some people aren't winning and that some people are suffering and miserable because you've put up barriers to your feelings. But even today, sensitive people are practicing instinctual things—which allow you to feel immediate awarenesses and essentially eliminate analysis as a means of making decisions—and they are making decisions based upon sensitive feelings and so on, which is the instinctual work. These individuals feel uncomfortable when others are uncomfortable. Even though they can be allowing and allow them to have their discomfort, they have to distance themselves from those who are uncomfortable if there is nothing they can do to help them. But in the future you will not tolerate the fact that others are uncomfortable; you will have to bring up their level of comfort. And you will not be tolerant of individuals causing others to suffer so that they can feel better. But you won't punish them for doing that; you'll improve their condition [chuckles].

So here we are now at this transitional period, focusing in the now. We still have to plan; we have to remember what happened in the past so we don't do it over again. How can we deal with this?

Homework: Notice When You Feel Good

The best way is to keep it simple. Know clearly what you feel like in your physical body when you feel good. And in moments when you do feel good, say to yourself, "I like this physical feeling, and I want to remember it." If you're just fooling yourself about feeling, your body will give you an immediate message that you don't, and that something needs to be resolved. But if you don't get that physical feedback and you really do feel good, then remember that feeling. (You can use your mind, if you wish, to do that.) When you don't have that feeling, notice why. Maybe others need to have that feeling before you can. Keep it simple. It is not that you use some substance to cause you to have that feeling or that you deny yourself some substance; it is rather that you achieve your natural feeling *by supporting others to have that natural benevolent feeling as well.*

And that natural benevolent feeling means that we're in the now?

And you're relaxed and heart-centered and sometimes feel the heat, as has been described to you. Sometimes you are just relaxed, and when you are, your energy goes outward. And when this happens, eventually you will feel some discomfort if someone somewhere is uncomfortable, as any form of life will. In time, you will all support greater comfort or do what you can to support others to feel more comfortable. I'm trying to put it on the most general footing possible.

What specifically are you doing as you work with us? Are you working with individuals?

All I'm really doing is broadcasting a signal that people feel when they are completely focused in the now, and the signal allows you to feel a sense of personal satisfaction.

When we can totally relax, then can we feel you?

Well, you can feel me even without relaxing, but all creators might say that. You don't feel the air, but it's present. The air could say to you, "You're feeling me," but you would not really notice it.

I feel a little slow, like it's nebulous.

It has to be nebulous, because the only way I can really help you to understand is to take you out of this time sequence and put you into your normal time sequence, and I cannot do that without interfering in your life. So here I am trying to describe the proverbial hole in something by what is around it!

I see! How to recognize when we're close to our natural feelings.

That's what I'm trying to give you, feelings you will recognize in your body and things that happen for which there is physical evidence in the moment, rather than striving toward feeling good. I want you to notice when you feel good, because there will be moments when you do.

And we can help that with our mind by focusing on what we're doing and on the body's feeling?

Yes; notice mentally not so much what you did to feel good, but how your body feels and so on—rested, happy, whatever it is. There's not just one way.

Will you continue to radiate this until we achieve a certain frequency or dimensional point?

Once you begin being pulled, and you're aware of it . . . around 3.70 you'll be aware that you're being pulled to some benevolent thing, and you'll let go more. Then I won't broadcast that anymore; you won't need it.

Let go—there's a key point. We're hanging onto . . .

You're hanging onto what you've known! Yes, you're hanging onto pushing and making it happen, forcing it. You're hanging onto that because that's what you've known. When you get used to forcing things to happen, things don't work as well. Then you get used to things not working very well, so you work harder to make them work the way they used to work. And you work harder and harder and harder to do less and less and less, in terms of accomplishment.

You hit a nerve!

This is why it is much better to say, "Now I need this," not "I need this to get this." You go on about what you normally do to get it, but you say, "Now I need this." You can even use the manifesting exercise of imagining what it would be like to have it and feeling those feelings. Then let it go and go on. If it's something important, say it once a day; make sure you're not distracted while you're feeling those feelings, then go on. If you need to do other things to bring it about, keep doing those things, but this will make it easier for those things to come to you.

We have the three-day challenge and then noticing when we feel good. This is so incredibly important that I'd like to get more, but as you say, it's difficult to describe.

It is difficult to describe. It's like trying to explain the fundamentals of the pronunciation of one language while using another language. It is not impossible, but it is difficult. What I'm trying to describe is understood much more easily by feelings than by thoughts.

The Love-Heat Exercise Brings You into the Now

How is time going to change, and how is our perception of time going to change?

Let me give you this. When Speaks of Many Truths and Zoosh talk about the love-heat exercise (and many of you by this time have done it), know that when you are experiencing that physical warmth—which feels very good every moment you are experiencing it because it requires you to be present in your body to experience something benevolent—every moment you are in the now. If you attempt to remember feeling the heat in the past, it will go away; if you attempt to imagine what feeling the heat would be like in the future, it will go away. But to the extent that you are actually feeling it in the present, you *are in* that present moment.

So the exercise, which has all these beneficial effects, actually brings you into the present—and that is, of course, at least half the reason for its existence. It is a foundation. Love, of course, is the present; it must be. If love is past or future or even potential (which is another form of time), then there is no possibility of benevolent creation in the now. Love must be in the now; it can be remembered as a loving experience in the past, it can be imagined and anticipated as a loving experience in the future, but it must be in the present or else benevolent creation is impossible.

The Natural Flow of Existence

How is time changing in our daily lives? Is time changing or is our perception of time changing?

Time is changing. You do not need to change your perception other than to know that you are being supported now to return to your natural way of being, which is to be pulled forward. You are being drawn, as it were; you don't have to push yourself forward anymore, though some of you still do. But this is understandable.

And the pushing causes . . .

It causes a delay, because when you are pushing you are usually missing opportunities; you will try to force things to happen, and they want to happen in different ways. For instance, a lot of people nowadays are finding new friends or making new friends or discovering that the friends they've had before aren't quite right for them. They have to travel here or there and discover their true families, as you say. This is just an example of the nature of the natural flow of existence.

Things that go together naturally are understood: fish and water, bird and air, not bird under the water, not fish in the air. You understand that very simply, because these things go together. It is the same way in creation; things naturally come together because they want to be together. That's why things that work well want to be together. The sperm and the egg want to be together, and when they discover each other, they naturally join because they want to be together. There is a mutual attraction.

Creation is the same way. When you have the right part with the right part, it will want to be together. When you try to force one part to be with a part it doesn't want to be with, there will be at the very least resistance and delay. So when you're having delay, delay, delay, delay, you're probably trying to force something that would be better off done in a different way. And because this is an educational place, you have the opportunity to start trying other ways that are more benevolent.

Even in an office you might have people with similar skills. Some offices have work groups and sometimes units don't work very well. Good managers look at it and ask, "Do these people work well together? Are they compatible? No, they're not compatible. I'll break up this unit, switch it around and try it a different way"—until they find people who are compatible, and then they work well together. It's the same thing with people who have teams of animals pulling a cart or sled; one horse wants to turn to the left and one wants to turn to the right and so on, and they don't pull very good. If you want them to go straight, you might place them differently so they will go straight naturally.

Your Changing Perception of Time

What about hours and seconds and days and nights and weekends? Is our perception of time, the way we live our lives, going to change?

You will, of course, change your clock, but that's coming slowly. You need to have a more universal clock. But in terms of your perception of time, it will gradually seem like the days and nights are not as long as they once were. Think about it: If you have been alive for at least, say, forty years or even less, you can remember when days and nights seemed longer; now they seem shorter.

So they will keep getting shorter?

Yes, because you need to have your perception of time changed. There will need to be some undeniable experience of that, even though you might not be able to quantify it using your present instruments. Nevertheless, if everyone around you says that days and nights just aren't as long as they used to be, you have to give it credence, even if you can't produce proof.

But we continue to have this sense of passing time even though we change our focus within it?

Yes, and that is intended, or you wouldn't be in a day/night situation, to say nothing of seasons.

And does that continue into the fourth dimension and beyond?

The seasons will become a little more benevolent; you won't have extreme cold or have brutal, crushing heat, you understand? It'll become a little more temperate.

But as long as we're on the Earth, even up to the fourth dimension (and beyond?), there's still the sense of day and night and, as you say, seasons and years.

Well, it depends. It depends what time sequence you take; I can't tell you that it's so or not so.

Ah! So we have a choice of time sequence!

Oh, certainly.

Can you say more about that?

You have to decide how you live. The more you move back into being your natural selves with the experience you've had in this learning time, the more latitude you'll be given to create your own time or utilize some form of time that has been created to live in. So maybe you'll go, not just to the fourth dimension; maybe you'll choose to go straight to the ninth dimension where seasons as you experience them now are unknown. You don't *have* to go to the fourth and the fifth dimension; you don't have to do anything like that. You'll just decide, as a total feeling being—you can see I'm avoiding using terms like "total consciousness" because that's really a term often associated with mentality, whereas in my experience a being is feeling first, long before they have any sense of mental.

Is this choice of what dimension to go while in this body, or after our natural cycle is over?

Yes, no, maybe. You haven't made the decision.

Talking to each individual person or . . .

I'm talking about the Explorer Race in general and the fact that you're here on Earth (part of you, at least). You haven't made the decision yet. You'll make the decision when you make it, but it is not for me to say what it will be.

So it's an en masse Explorer Race decision?

Yes.

It's not an individual, encapsulated human decision.

Yes, exactly.

I wasn't clear about that. I wish I had a physicist here to ask questions.

It is difficult to describe that which exists but does not present any apparent measurable means of quantifying itself.

Yes, you can't see it, you can't hear it, you can't touch it, but it is certainly something you have to live with every day. So you're going to ray on us until we get to 3.75?

No, probably until about 3.70, and then you won't really need that anymore. And then I will, if I am needed, stay around for a while; if not, I will go.

Give me an example of "if you're needed."

The only way I can see at the moment that I might be needed is if you backslide, as it were; I don't think that's possible from 3.70, but I wouldn't rule it out entirely.

Okay, go on!

I'm not going to support it by giving details, because it is such an infinitesimal possibility. But once you don't need me anymore, why should I stay?

I was going to encourage you to stay, but I don't want to backslide, so you can go!

Thank you very much!

Explorer Race: Release the Past and Be Your True Selves!

What more would you like to tell the Explorer Race?

Only this: It is in your nature to be sequential right now, but as you truly are, you are in the present. So anything I say to you is to encourage you to be your true selves. Yet I don't want you to give up your opportunity for the bountiful scholastic experience that you're having here. I'm not encouraging you to struggle and practice being in the now in every moment. I just want you to notice that when you *are* in the now, you will see and experience your world much more completely. You are much less likely [to miss] opportunities or people or experiences if you are very present in the moment—what you are doing, what you are feeling, what you are seeing, smelling, hearing and so on. You are much more likely to have many more opportunities *right now*. Because you are worried about the past, present or future and your mind is distracted, and because you are doing so many things, right now the average person misses fully seventy percent of your opportunities. That's why I'd like you to practice, but not all the time. I don't want to give you more complications, but practice being in the now. Practice noticing and becoming more observant . . . and yes, do the instinctual body training; it will help.

Wait a minute. When we become our true selves and we're pulled into our future, won't we still have a sense of what's happened, and isn't there still a duration of experience? You're here for a duration of time . . .

Others will have to remind you.

Remind us of what?

That something happened. It is natural. When you pass through the veils at the end of your natural cycle, you literally shed the experience of this life so much that when you go to your next life, you don't remember this at all, yet it happened. If that information was not stored someplace (otherwise known as someone else having it) to remind you, you would never ever have it as long as you were incarnating. It's the same as you go forward here; others will have to remind you.

If we choose to come back into the veil, we won't remember this life; but if we go on into a more expanded part of ourselves, we'll remember it, won't we?

I doubt it very much. You will simply have your new tools; you will be your new person, and as such you will not be past-oriented, so you won't remember it. It is very unnatural for you to think about anything in the past or the future.

That's the part that feels so unnatural now.

I know; that's why I said it.

We've been indoctrinated in it so long that . . .

Yes, you've gotten used to it, but thinking about the past and the future usually means worrying about it, so it brings you discomfort. I grant that sometimes thinking about the future or the past can be fun or benevolent or joyful, but most of the time it is not so wonderful. You've gotten used to it as being one of the so-called natural discomforts of life, but it isn't! It's just something you've become used to.

But in your expanded reality, you remember where you came from, what you did. You came here and you're very focused, yet you're in your expanded beingness.

But I am a creator! I grant that there is some possibility you might finish this life sequence and become a creator, but it is extremely unlikely. More likely you will have another life and you won't remember any of this. But if it benefits you in some way, someone will remind you if you need to know. If you don't need to know, they won't tell you.

Who would that someone be?

For each of you it would be different; perhaps a guide, perhaps a teacher, perhaps a friend will say something and you'll get that feeling of having been someplace before when you know in fact that's not possible. "I've never been to the Eiffel Tower," say you, "and yet it all seems so familiar!" [Chuckles.]

Déjà vu all over again [laughs]. So you're really only referring to another Earth life.

No, another encapsulated life, as it were, anywhere. Being a creator is different, largely in the level of responsibility.

We'll let that one go. I'm done. I really don't want to lose my memories, but . . .

You say you really don't want to lose your memories because you've gotten used to their level of discomfort. But in reality you as an individual could right now lose fully ninety-eight percent of your memories and feel *so much better!*

You're not talking to me, you're talking to the readers?

I'm talking to you *and* the readers. The average would be ninety-seven percent.

And we'd still be functional, we'd have all our skills, we'd have our personality, our purpose and everything?

Because you don't remember something mentally does not mean that *all* of you doesn't remember it. You can still ride a bicycle when you're an older person even though you may not remember who taught you or where you picked it up. You might remember, you might not; but you can still do it because other parts of you remember how to do it. But you don't have to remember every shred of memory associated with the experience. You certainly aren't going to remember all the times you fell down and felt bad about it, times when the other kids made fun of you. Or, conversely, when they came over and said, "Let me help you." You don't remember everything; other parts of you that can comfortably recall those things will do so, but your linear mind craves to remember things because it believes that the future is predicated on the past. But it isn't! To the extent that your mind believes so, though, and holds you to that, your capacity to manifest will be limited by what your mind believes has existed in the past with your mind's limited capacity to even remember the past!

Brilliant!

That's how you slow down your capacity to manifest. So forgetting is not so awful. Sometimes the past seems awful, and sometimes it has other situations connected with it so it isn't much fun; but ultimately forgetting isn't so awful. I'll tell you a little something: Let's say you have a life two or three more lives down the road, and you decide to have another life on an Earthlike planet someplace. If you learn how to ride a bicycle in this life, it will be easier for you to learn how to ride a bicycle again; you'll get it fast [snaps fingers]! People who take longer to learn how to ride a bicycle than others, given their equal capacities, probably have never had a life in which they learned how to ride a bicycle.

All right, you've made it more acceptable.

Specialist in Honor

March 26, 1998

I am the Creator of Honor, and I am very much on my guard [chuckles] that honor is not confused with obedience. For those who do not understand the nature of honor, being honored and honoring, it is very simple to be obedient, quiet, sheepish—all these other things it's called, those various names. Yet honor in its reality is more than respect; it is respect with love. In my experience I have discovered that respect and love make a very homelike combination. The two of them are like two parts of the same thing. What you love, you do not always respect, and what you respect, you do not always love; yet with honoring, it fits.

How I Learned Honor

In my upbringing, as I like to call it—because the creation of me and my awareness of myself was very different from other creators—I learned about honor. Most creators come into being as a personality and become aware of themselves, as many of them have stated. For me, my creation followed a route very similar to the birth of a child and its raising. My earliest memory was of being in motion; then there was light *and* motion; then there was a sense, a beginning sense of self, of personality; and then I had form—you see, not unlike the birth process.

When I had form I had a family. There were nine, and they all treated me like a beloved child. My childhood lasted about nine thousand experiential years, during which time I had the opportunity to experience things the way a child might, and gradually mature (after about nine thousand experiential years) into what you would call an adult. I must admit that having the knowledge and wisdom of a creator during all of this was fascinating, while at the same time, being able to enjoy childhood was a wonder. I must also tell you that the other creators who raised me were very much like beloved parents. I felt like their child—nurtured, always with someone to nurture me—and I learned about nurturing and its great value.

When I was first a something solid, some *thing,* as it were, I had the wisdom and insight of a creator, yet over those nine thousand experiential years I had the chance to discover the value and the tremendous impact of being nurtured. So I was nurtured, loved and honored. I didn't realize at the time that it was honor, but looking back, I realize it was. I was always appreciated for being myself and I was surrounded by people (beings, if you like) who appreciated each other for being themselves, and there was no stress to be anything else. So I was raised in an environment of honoring, love and respect. This was all I knew for my first thousand years.

Then for the next few thousand experiential years, I was learning how a child reacts as a creator. Think of a creator—one thinks of a wise and insightful and loving being; one does not often think of a creator as a child. And yet as a child, one is full of youthful enthusiasm and joy and happiness, yes? And also, perhaps most important, one is not held back by the mature thoughts of an older being who might know that something won't work, because it's been tried. One has youthful enthusiasm and believes that all things can work. So I had this exposure, and I exposed the nine to that. Sometimes they were amused and other times they said, "Let's try it!" Some would say to them, "Well, that's been done and it doesn't work." Then one of the nine or several of them would say, "Our youngster there seems to feel it will, so we'll get it started and let the youngster see if he can make it happen." So they trusted me; they respected me even though I wasn't as wise and experienced as they were. Thus I learned the qualities of honoring.

One of the things I did later on in my cycle of existence was travel around this universe to various cultures to study their methods of honoring; or if they didn't have honoring integrated into their society, to share methods. I would usually appear in some form that was compatible with their forms, either looking something like them or almost like them, always with some slight distinction so I could be told apart as not being one of them. In that way I wasn't subject to the rules of their society, nor for that matter was I owed the privileges. At the same time, I was similar-enough looking that I was intriguing, and they would be interested in what I would have to say. In this way I was able to share wisdom with various beings around this galaxy and others, and to discover when they honored and when they didn't, why they honored and why they didn't, and to pass on knowledge and wisdom about honoring. I had a lot of good times doing that.

My Nine Creators

Were you born in Love's Creation?

Yes.

Someplace close to this universe?

Yes, really in a little different variation of what you're used to. We know the shape of this universe, so I won't draw that. I'll draw one outer edge, a segment [draws]. The X is where you are, okay? This is a segment. This is where I was. [Pause.] Just to the outside, like a bubble attached to this universe.

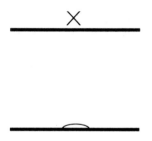

And so nine creators were out there with you?

Yes, they were out there attached to this universe because they knew that my job would take me into this universe and begin here. So they wanted me as close to this place as possible. They also wanted to encourage me to go this way, into this universe rather than out and explore beyond here, because they wanted me to interact with the people of this universe. So that's what I did. At least it is my intention to continue to do that.

Did they create you, or did they just nurture you?

They created.

The nine of them all together?

Yes.

That's multiple parenthood; we never heard of that before.

It was a wonderful experience; I recommend it.

Do you feel that each gave you a part of themselves?

Yes, that's a nice way to put it. I feel like they each contributed, and I am the net result of them. I am their offspring, yes.

And where did they go?

They're still in the general area; they often come to visit. They sometimes go beyond this universe if they're called upon to talk about whatever they discuss beyond my earshot, but they're nearby.

Teaching the Explorer Race Honor

Have you interacted with the Creator of this universe or had conversations with Him?

We haven't spoken directly. The nine said that I would be involved with you as the Explorer Race, not so much because you were the Explorer Race, but because of the variety and divergence of your citizens. They said that there would be many different ways of honoring, plus the need to have ceremonies and so on having to do with honoring, and that I might be able to encourage or suggest things, not necessarily by inventing them, but by working within the culture of whatever group or tribe. So over the years I have worked with different cultures to suggest different things; very often the suggestions are appreciated, though occasionally they are rejected for one good reason or another.

But you have the ability to go out and create a universe if you choose?

Oh, yes; but I am here now and enjoying what I do. For example, I worked a lot with the animals on Earth and with those animals' interactions with the mystical people of different tribes. I would sometimes create a special auric field around an animal that would allow the mystical person to know completely what the animal knew, and allow the animal to know what the mystical person knew completely, so that they could become spirit friends and share wisdom with each other, honor each other and perform appropriate ceremonies for and with each other, depending on circumstances. I really enjoyed that a lot.

How long do you think you'll be with the Explorer Race?

My understanding is, during the time you are traveling on spaceships to other cultures, because you will need a lot of training about honoring. Sometimes in your travels you will come to the root race of certain cultures that on this planet you do not get along with or understand. And although the historians and archaeologists and people like that will be fascinated, not everyone on the ship will be; some people will be offended and so on. Even though one would not normally take offense at an entirely foreign culture, you might if it reminded you enough of some group or other that you didn't like.

This will come up, and diplomatic training can do only so much. Yet if there are ways of showing a common ground—threads, as it were, that connect each person to each other person and connect those individuals with the natural world (trees, plants, animals etc.). Then the common ground is the individual within the natural world, regardless what form that natural world takes from one world to another, and regardless what the form of the being is as well.

The Nine Creators and the Council of Nine

Do you know anything about the nine creators, their origins or what their duties normally are? What do they do when they aren't helping you or birthing you?

My understanding is that they are a council.

Is this what we call the Council of Nine?

Yes.

Oh! The ones who channeled through Phyllis Schlemmer?

Let me ask again if they are *the* Council of Nine as spoken through this well-known individual. Oh. They say they are not—my mistake. [Chuckles.] Creators can make mistakes, eh? But they are a council.

What is their function?

I thought they were the same one, but they say they are not.

What do they do on their council? What is their purpose or function?

They do seem to interact with the Council of Nine in some way. They indicate this has come up before in explanations about the Council of Nine, I believe. [Draws.] Hmm, not a bad drawing.

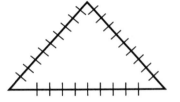

[Chuckles.] I'm glad; usually they say, "Oh, what a terrible drawing." How delightful to have somebody who likes their drawing.

[Draws.] Now, one side of this would be the Council of Nine.

Your council or the one I know?

The one you know. One side would be the nine that I know. And another side is another group of nine that I'm not familiar with, but they're there. The thing that has come up before about the Council of Nine is, how can there be so many when there are only nine? How can they do so much? The explanation that they are of creator status is not always enough of an explanation. But imagine the nine being surrounded by a three-faceted mirror on the outside and facing it on the inside. If you can see this in a crystalline form, the nine are actually twenty-seven, and by reflecting like that, you really have [a multiplier] . . . to the *this* power or to *that* power. The nine can do more because they are really twenty-seven, and the twenty-seven can do more because of the reflected interaction between all of the beings.

If you were to see them, if you were to stand in front of them, and there were nine beings showing themselves in front of you, you wouldn't see the other nine behind them. Let's say you were standing in front of them—you understand, a perspective. You would see the nine in front of you, but you wouldn't see the other eighteen going back because they would not be visible to your eye. So they would look like nine.

Do they have their different areas of expertise and responsibility?

I believe they may; I do not know.

Okay, we'll ask them sometime. Now back to you.

Earth Cultures Need to Honor One Another

I teach and I learn about honoring.

You learn more as you teach, right?

I learn. The people share their cultures with me, and I learn by having to adapt what I know and what I am inspired with to their cultural advantage.

As a creator, do you appear to these different cultures as a being?

Yes, whatever is comfortable for them.

It's not all of you, but yet it is you, and it comes back to you.

Yes.

So you'll create a piece of yourself to go out on the spaceships with the Explorer Race?

No, I will just be present as the Explorer Race encounters beings from other worlds. And occasionally, because these explorations are likely to take the form of many different countries and races, you understand—more like a United Nations exploration—sometimes I might be inspiring people on the ship who are working in close quarters with nationalities, races or groups they are literally unfamiliar with. Earth is not such a big place, yet the average person knows practically nothing about the culture and heritage of his or her own neighbors, much less people who live on the other side of the world. The tendency is to assume that your way and the way you are familiar with is the natural way, and that the ways of others are foreign and strange even if they are from a different neighborhood as compared to a different culture. So you need help between each other on Earth, as well as the help you will need when you encounter people who are *really* different.

You have been trained in your cultures here (many of you, not all) to notice first how you are different from your neighbors or friends. In this way your culture, especially in this country, encourages the idea of the unique individual. This is one of the reasons your country has become so popular, because in some other countries individuals do not always feel their uniqueness and value for simply being themselves. Not that this is the case entirely, but your country is more known for this.

In terms of other cultures on this planet, you will very often have circumstances in which the uniqueness might be very unique indeed, yet if it is not like your own uniqueness of your culture and so on, it will seem strange and sometimes even abhorrent. The sooner you get along with each other, the more you'll be prepared for the truly different that you will find on other planets.

Do you see that understanding our neighbors is going to work out?

Yes.

How?

Some of you—and only some of you—can travel. More likely it will happen because the population is exploding. You won't have to find the people, they will find you whether you like it or not [chuckles].

You can't have billions and billions of people on such a small planet without your meeting each other, sometimes more often than you would like, as you might say. You are then necessarily exposed to unusual cultures. Several of your cultures have discovered ways to appreciate this, such as sharing cultural amusements like folk dancing and so on. But perhaps the most universally accepted sharing is each other's food, cuisine. Cuisine has been a great contributor toward honoring.

For example, someone in the United States might not truly understand in any way the culture of China (not just as it was, but as it is today) or might even misunderstand it entirely. Yet you might go to a restaurant for good Chinese food cooked by people of that descent or from that country. You will like and honor the food very much, and in some reflected way, honor the culture. So cuisine has contributed mightily on this planet to honoring.

What are a couple of the more interesting things you've learned about honoring from working with cultures on Earth?

Perhaps some of my best and most enjoyable experiences have been working with what I call tribal people—not just any tribal people, but tribal people who live on the land and off of the land, who have had to develop a sacred relationship between themselves on an individual and collective basis with the land and its inhabitants, with the elements, the water, the sky and so on. They have had to develop a relationship where they understand that they are the children of the land and thereby treat the land as one might treat beloved parents and elders, mutually beneficial.

I have enjoyed greatly, then, working over the years with some Native Americans and native peoples of Canada and Alaska; also in years gone by what I would call native peoples of northern Europe and others like that. These people had developed very specific ways of showing the greatest honor to the land and to the food they gathered. And it has been something I have studied and enjoyed very much.

My Previous Journeys of Learning

How long in our terms have you been on this planet? And how long have you been in this universe, in some way that we can understand?

I don't think there is a way you can understand.

Before the Explorer Race was created?

Yes, I have it. I have been here, actually in this universe, just slightly before the Explorer Race was birthed out of Creator, if that is any help.

It shows how specifically you came to work with just this group if that's when you got here. So you have been with the Explorer Race as it sort of flowed through other constellations?

No, I haven't been with you until you got to Earth. I was going around to other places in the universe before then.

Learning?

Learning and teaching and observing and enjoying and appreciating the different cultures and how they've adapted to their circumstance. There's one culture that comes to mind at the moment.

This is a culture of beings who, if you were to see them, would look more like reflections of light, light that would bounce off your glasses or a telescope you might be looking through, or even a lens in a camera. They would look like curved light reflections. And their world is about liquids, bright liquids, and clear reflections off of liquids. That's what it would seem like; that's the best description—not unlike the Sun shining on water, for instance. Not the water itself, but the reflections.

I was fascinated to see the way they honored that which reflects them. Many of them would gather around that reflecting medium, which we're calling water, but it isn't quite that, and they would move in a very specific way so that the reflections, which would be multiplied by their motion, would create their own color and shape. They would move in a very specific way so that the same color and shape was reproduced every time. In this way they felt they were honoring that which reflected them and gave them life, from their perspective, and were also showing each other that they could work in harmony and synchronicity to produce something of beauty for others as an honoring technique and for themselves. So they were in complete harmony with each other and with what they were honoring. I thought that was unique. Not exactly something you can relate to, but unique.

Were you here before the present civilization? Were you here with some of the other civilizations that have been on Earth?

I was here slightly before the civilization you now know. I wasn't involved with previous civilizations, but I was involved with a lot of the animal life. I was observing them. You know, they have very delicate, very specific ways of honoring each other. Your scientists have sometimes been able to photograph some of this, though it's not always completely understood. At other times the animals will do this in special ways that are not possible to photograph. I was very interested to see that, owing perhaps to the culture from which they came, they were born with certain honoring techniques without being taught them. Yet for the most part their honoring techniques were taught, and they didn't question it. There wasn't the idea that, "Well, this is okay for me, but *that's* not for me." [Chuckles.] Each species followed along, not because they didn't have a unique personality, but because they could feel the benefit and value of that love and respect. And because they could feel it, they knew that others felt it as well. It's the knowledge of feeling something good and benevolent and that others are feeling the same thing at the same time that really makes the difference.

The Tenderhearted Elephant

I was very interested in the way the animals treat each other, especially elephants. They are such tenderhearted beings. I don't think the average human being realizes how truly tender and warm-hearted the average elephant is. Imagine for a moment the most sensitive and loving mystical person or shaman, combined with the youthful enthusiasm of a five-year-old child, also combined with the wisdom of a renowned and beloved elder, and you get a general idea of what the average elephant is like.

We are missing so much on this planet!

Do you know that elephants would rather suffer great pain and misery than to offend anyone? Especially their own kind, but they will go quite a distance to avoid offending other beings or even humans, though they do not feel that humans have evolved yet to the status of the average animal. Elephants are very smart, as you say, intellectually, but they also have a collective wisdom—not a one-mind, but a collective wisdom in their capacity to tap into their combined thoughts. As you might say, they have a library they can consult. And the general feeling is that (to use an elephant joke) the human being is not yet ripe.

[Chuckles.] We know nothing about that. Do they look like this on their home planet?

No. On their home planet they have some similarities. They seem to be two-legged on their home planet—an upright being, as you say. They have some similarities with the ears and with a sort of a snout, but not as long as the one here. I don't, at the moment, see arms, but they may have them, I just don't see them. Yes, there are arms, but they are so formed, in toward the body, that it's not readily apparent how to describe them.

And are they that wise and beautiful and wonderful on their home planet?

They are much more socially conscious on their own planet than they are even here. When beings visit their planet, they are known for diplomacy, art, music, philosophy, wisdom and the capacity to cherish (for those who wish to be cherished or learn how to cherish others, that's the place to go). They are also known for their great love of family and their sense that any of their beings is like family. Granted, their own family is the strongest, but even someone you don't know who is like you is considered, at the very least, a distant cousin, a relative.

I have picked them out because they are perhaps the closest being who has reached the zenith of honoring that has a representative (as the elephant) on your planet. They could very easily, if they chose, reconvene their totality of being and become a creator, but I think they like the form they are in now. In terms of their capacity to teach honoring, I would have to say that they have almost the same abilities as I do, though I think they would not choose to change their form very much to visit others. So they don't do everything the same way I do.

They were called to come to provide variety and what else? What is it that they do in relationship to the human?

Well, you have to remember that a lot of the beings here look different on their home planets, and a lot of the beings here are really what you would call so-called animal versions of ETs. Yet they are considered by beings from their home planets to be the same. Just because they might stand upright yet see an elephant here on four legs with a long trunk, who is bigger than they are, they would not for a moment think of this as a lesser being. This is what they would call the Earth variant of themselves.

So you want to know why they are here? They are here to offer you their great capacity for assimilating wisdom, though I don't think that's been conveyed as yet. They're waiting for you to become ripe enough, as they would say, to understand what they are thinking. That's how they would gauge it; when there are those amongst you who understand what they are thinking, then they will say, "Well, signs of ripeness!"

You see, they don't send thoughts to you; they don't do that because they don't want to have a false alarm. They know that you are naturally curious, and they are waiting for *you* to do that. And when you or individuals do, they will know, because if you know what an elephant is thinking, you want to comment on it. And because their thoughts are so philosophical and profound, you might be inclined to say, "Oh, tell me more about that." If you say that to an elephant and they answer (or think to themselves), "Tell you more about what?" and you mention the subject, they will say, "Good signs!" They might even think it so that you can hear it. But they won't project it to you; they'll test you for quite a while before they decide you're definitely there.

What do they think about?

Anything. Sometimes things on this planet, issues, concerns about this or that, just like human beings have; other times concerns about other planets, what's going on there and why. Anything and everything. Generally not things that are mathematical or scientific; more about things that would be social or having to do with the heart or friends, love, respect—honoring heart.

So they're totally aware of what's going on in other planets in this universe? Are they from this universe or beyond?

They're from beyond this universe.

In this orb? In this circle? Or way, way, way beyond?

Let me say—I like this phrase; now is my first chance to use it, no I want to get it right: Would you believe (there it is!), would you believe they are from beyond Love's creation. They are up the line, as your friend says, from Love. Though they honor and respect her greatly, they are up the line. Their home planet is in this universe, but it's not their origin. Their point of origin is up the line from Love—Pure Love, that is.

They came to a place and established themselves before they came to Earth?

Yes.

They're all adventurers?

They are the sort of beings who enjoy being . . . how can we say, in on something at the moment of its great birth. Since something so extraordinary is going on here, they would, of course, want some of their numbers to be present to observe it. Even amongst them walk what I would call spirit elephants, so that if it should ever happen that there are no more elephants on Earth, there will still be some spirit elephants. They won't be able to help you or do anything for you, but they will observe, so that the beings you know as elephants can know what is happening here because they are interested.

Sitting in our little cities where we're thousands of miles from an elephant, what can we do? I guess to become ripe quickly—that's the best thing we can do!

The best thing you can do is notice how you are like your neighbors, not how you are different. Learn how to get along with each other and, to the extent that you notice differences, try to appreciate them as best you can in a way that honors your neighbor. In other words, it is not what you do *for* them; it may certainly be what you do *to* them. They do not appreciate being burdened by the actions of human beings. But in terms of how you can become ripe more quickly, treat your fellow human beings with love, honor and respect. That's how you become ripe in their eyes.

Do you send an energy that encourages honor? Do you do something energetically beyond the sending out of parts of yourself to teach?

No. Sending out parts of myself to teach, that's what I do. And to learn, of course.

Once you've gained all this wisdom, do you have any idea what you'll do after the Explorer Race?

No. For a while I thought I would join the Council, but they indicated to me awhile back that I may want to explore beyond this universe, and having given that some consideration, I agreed. I would like to explore beyond it.

So you'll continue to learn and to teach honoring, toward some goal that's not clear yet?

The learning and the teaching is goal enough for me now.

It may lead you. You assumed that it would lead to something.

I don't assume this, but if it does lead to something, I'll know when I find it. [Chuckles.] Or perhaps when it finds me.

Ants, Dolphins and Earthworms

Are there other representatives on this planet who are of the same stature as the elephants? Of the same wisdom, the same level of beingness?

There are many beings. In terms of other beings like the elephants, no; but there are other beings who have great and marvelous qualities that mankind is only now just beginning to assimilate—not to take away from these beings, but to appreciate the value of what they can do together. You have long admired what a single ant can do to move a large piece of sand, comparing it to a human being moving an equivalent object, and what several or even two ants can do to move a stone that is larger than they are, proportionately speaking, something human beings could not do. And so you have in the last few hundred years

learned a great deal about teamwork and cooperation from the ants.
Where are they from?

A very distant place from here. They have a home planet in this universe, almost as far away from where you are as—well, very far away. It can't be on the other side of the universe, in the way the universe is shaped, but it is very far away. As far as I know, that is their point of origin.

What about the dolphins? Do you interact with them or the whales?

Yes, I've interacted with a great many of the creatures on Earth, and the dolphins are wonderful beings. I think a lot is known about them; I won't go into that too much because they are popular. They have achieved the status of being considered worthy [chuckles], which is good. Let's see if I can come up with ones not so well known.

There is a being who is not appreciated: a worm, an earthworm. The beings you know as earthworms, before they are allowed to come here and be earthworms, all must take an oath, and they must live by that oath. The oath is that they will produce nothing that does not cause great benefit and gain for others. Is that not a great example of honoring? And it is true. As anyone who has a good mulch for their garden knows, if they have earthworms, their soil is just going to get better and better because just by existing, earthworms will improve the soil. To use them to catch fish is, in my view, not honoring them. If you used worms to catch fish that does not make you a bad person, it just means that you don't know. If you don't know, when you have the opportunity to learn, then you discover—and you regret what you have done and perhaps ask for forgiveness. Then you tell others if the opportunity arises and they are receptive (don't go out and tell them if they are not; they might do the opposite), and you will change your ways, as any system of learning goes.

Some of the people who have really heard what you have to teach are the tribal peoples, who respect the land and animals and all life.

Some have heard this from me or my representatives, but others were already doing it. I just observed them, and sometimes I would adapt what I saw others doing to a different group someplace else. It's very heartening for me to see peoples honoring the animals they must hunt, because if they don't eat the animals, they have nothing to eat. They give them great honor, they ask for them, they say prayers, not just for them to sacrifice some of their people to feed the human beings, but they say prayers that the culture of the animal beings and families be fruitful and multiply for their own sake, not just for the sake of being plentiful for human beings. I have seen this many times, the genuine caring and appreciation of animals for their sake, not just what those animals can do for humans. I've seen this a lot; it's a good thing to see. That's honoring.

Do you have much interaction or communication with your creators, the Council of Nine or with any of your peers?

Yes.

You communicate back and forth, as you do with a family?

Yes. Even though they know what I have been doing, sometimes they'll ask me what I've been doing, just to offer me the joy of telling them. That's honoring, see?

Honoring Others

You can understand this. Sometimes you will be with a relative, and they'll tell you a story you've heard a hundred times, yet for the sake of honoring them, you don't stop them in the middle. You let them tell you because they get so much pleasure out of it. That's honoring.

You see, in your cultures, sometimes you've gotten confused. You've confused being polite with honoring. When you are polite, it's a rule that you follow, and sometimes you get uncomfortable with rules. But when you are honoring, that's different, because you know what it's like to be honored, and it's a wonderful experience. So when you honor others, you know what you're giving them because you've experienced it. It is quite a different thing than being polite—which is good, to be polite. It is easy to rebel against politeness, but not so attractive to rebel against honoring.

Honoring others sounds like it should be a basic way of being.

A gift both given and received until it becomes the natural way. And when it is the natural way, you do it without thinking—experiencing it, giving it, receiving it. It is normal, it is natural, you don't think about it. Yet here, of course, where you have choice, you *have* to think about it [chuckles].

Would you say that on other very benign planets in the rest of the universe, it is the norm to honor and be respectful and loving of others?

Yes. It is not one hundred percent true, but almost. There have been exceptions, but no exceptions that have not been discussed by others, I think.

So it's part of the teaching we need because we are under the veil of ignorance?

You need the teaching, but it is also important to have the opportunity to learn it. Beyond this planet you know these things, yet when you relearn them here, you are surrounded with physical evidence, both to support or to be the opposite. So you are given immediate feedback, as in consequences, by not honoring. When you don't honor someone who deserves to be honored, maybe you feel bad about it or maybe they feel bad about it and tell you. Then you feel ashamed or you realize you made a mistake and try to make it up to them. Sometimes that will be all right and other times you must live with the consequences. You learn and you go on, and probably you don't make that mistake again.

If you have not been honored yourself, it is difficult to honor others because you won't know what the feeling is that you're trying to produce in others. That is why it is so vitally important for children to be honored. Otherwise they don't know. They won't be able to offer it to others very easily. I was honored as a child, and found out its great value.

Before we get to the fourth dimension, as the creator said last night, our future starts pulling us—like at 3.70 or something. We're going to awaken to more love and more benevolent feelings toward everyone, and honoring will just be more natural?

No, but you will be more open to receiving such instruction, and you will enjoy it more. And as you enjoy it, you will want to pass it on to others. You won't just suddenly have it.

So while we're here on Earth, we still . . .

You still have the opportunity to learn, which is a pleasure.

Where will this teaching come from? You will have trained enough teachers? How does that work?

Your own guides, teachers. I will be able to teach many beings at once. You will have the opportunity, fear not. There will be many to teach and, most important, many opportunities to practice what you have been taught.

If you had a chance to teach the readers, what would you say to them?

First, understand the value of love, most easily done with a beloved pet or a child. Love that being, not just in ways that give *you* joy, but in ways that give that being joy, be it an animal or a child or even a favorite plant. Give them what they like, what they need, what they enjoy, not because they will say thank you, but because it is the natural thing. Give them praise when they deserve it, not because they've earned something, not because they've qualified for it, but when you see a child do something good for somebody else. If you see any child you know and who knows you, it's all right to say to the child, "That was a good deed you did," or "Well done!" as you might say to an adult, and pat them on the back. You don't have to pat the child on the back, but when you say "Well done," and mean it, a child knows. A child understands that you are not only approving of them, but honoring and appreciating them.

Practice these things with your own children and your own beloved animals or plants. And because of the innocent nature of plants and animals and children, when they are happy, they radiate their happiness. Because you are near them, many of you will feel that as warmth or love. It isn't something coming from some far-off source; it is that child or that plant or animal's happiness that you are feeling. When you feel that, you will know that what you have done has encouraged this person to feel that way. The feelings they're having are their own, yet because feelings naturally radiate, you have an opportunity to experience the reward as well. Let that be enough of a reward for you to learn these valuable things.

That's wonderful.

Specialist in Experimental Beings

April 9, 1998

 am the Creator of Experimental Beings.
Welcome!

Thank you. You can see that my participation in the Council of Creators has been, perhaps, necessary, considering the highly experimental nature of this universe. As such, when this universe was in the planning stage, I was already moving in this direction in order to be of assistance to those who would participate, be they beings such as yourself or consultants, other creators and so on. Having originated in a highly complex rhythmic, pulsing being who is involved with varieties of varieties, I have perhaps come from one of the most infinite types of beings available. This is not the only being such as that, but it is the only one with whom I have had personal experience, so there is a great sense, a great love within me for infinite variety.

My Journey to Your Creator's Creation

As your Creator began to move in this direction, considering how, when, where and all these other things a creator must consider, I began picking up speed [chuckles] to get here so as to be available as soon as your Creator might be interested in communicating about this wonderful universe.

When I emigrated out of that being from whom I originally became aware of myself, I immediately came straight here—though I must admit, in terms of experiential years, it took perhaps 100,000 to get here. I was moving quickly, but not so quickly that I couldn't pick up experience on the way. There were times when I was in observation of the most unusual beings, sometimes from unusual universes or even galaxies. And there were times when I thought I was looking at a massive creation such as a galaxy or multiple galaxies, but as I got closer, I realized this was not a galaxy but a being that large!

As a result, I had lots of opportunities to interact with beings like this. About halfway through my trip I picked up a consultant, and the consultant spoke to me for the next quarter of the way about the nature and the value of creating experimental beings. Experimental beings might be unique. They may start out as what you might call a prototype, an experimental being aimed for a specific purpose (which a prototype might be), or simply something that has been considered and therefore is created to see if the being is viable in its own right. So along the way with this consultant, I was able to practice creating experimental beings and would be corrected when I would sometimes (what I now call) interfere too much.

It is in the nature of a creator to want to create something of their personal vision, but the one challenge that often faces any creator is knowing when to stop creating and allow the object of your creation its own expression. So this consultant working with me was very helpful with me to know when to stop—at what point to just put the pieces together and let them form into their own, and at what point to assist the pieces to become what they wished. A very subtle but fine and important point.

The Explorer Race Requires Variety and Flexibility

It was this particular point that your Creator and I discussed, after I was within enough closeness for your Creator to be aware of my presence. This Creator of this universe and I had many stimulating discussions. We were having these discussions just when the Creator was beginning to put beings on planets and help to sustain those beings, to provide what they might need for their survival. It was during these initial discussions that I suggested to the Creator that He not make quite so much effort to stabilize the orbits of the planets in their solar systems. Creator's original intention for this universe was to have solar systems with planets in fixed orbits, orbits that would always be the same distance (equidistant) from any point in their reference, you understand?

So at any given moment the planet would be the same distance from its sun. I suggested that if the planets were allowed a degree of wobble, they might find orbits that were more sustaining to the beings who would naturally wish to be there. That is, the more precise a mechanism is, the more exacting its population is likely to be. We discussed this for a time, and the compromise was that this Creator would have some solar systems that are very precise and others where the beings on the planets would be unusual, or not specifically and totally structured by this Creator, but would have some capacity for altering their own existence. Such beings might appreciate a planetary orbit with an apogee and a perigee, for example.

So that was decided, particularly with the planets the Explorer Race would evolve through, because the ultimate requirement of the Explorer Race was not only variety, but a significant flexibility in *all* the Explorer Race beings that the planets would interact with. Creator would also create planets that, while they might be beautiful, would not in any sense of the word be perfect for the needs of the Explorer Race. This imperfection would support and sustain their natural desire to explore the whole planet, to find that place of energy that felt perfect and where life was sustained entirely and so on. If not to be found on that planet, then they would go out into space and find another. This would sustain the restless quality of the Explorer Race; restlessness, I felt, was essential for any race of beings based in the Explorer syndrome.

I'm interested in that consultant. Who was it, and who gave him the idea of the experiential beings?

This was a being who was bilocating. I always called the being Consultant, because that's its job description—but you know this being by the name Zoosh.

Oh, I see. Really!

I have been told by other creators that Zoosh has performed similar functions with many of the creators on the Council—accompanying them as a consultant and occasionally as a friend. He was more of a friend than a consultant for some of the creators who needed conversation, as you understand it. And when one needs conversation, one needs a friend.

He never mentioned it.

I am mentioning it!

Well, we'll get him to explain where he got his knowledge. Tell me about this being you were birthed from, this infinite being.

Beings of Infinite Variety

This is not a singular being; there are more beings like this. I have discovered in my travels, seeing some from afar: they seem to be ideally located here and there around various creations in order to provide (apparently this is the primary purpose of the beings) variations on already established themes. Of their own right they do not create the themes; the themes will already be expressed in some universe in some other creator's creation, but the themes themselves are processed through these beings, and every conceivable variety of that theme will be demonstrated. Reasonably, one might assume that every variety demonstrated will be benevolent; but sometimes if a creation requires some thread of annoyance, there might occasionally be a being who has the capacity for that, if not readily expressing it.

Are all these beings in Love's creation, or is this a much larger expression?

It's much larger than that; certainly they are in Love's creation, but in my experience it is well beyond that. My assumption is that it's some kind of a universal experience. I came from one of them, but not in Love's creation initially. Near Love's creation.

One of the other Love's flavors, then?

Yes; a flavor that I would simply call the experimenter.

My First Awareness

What was your first point of awareness? How did you become aware and how did you know you were supposed to come here?

Well, first I was conscious of infinite varieties—at least that was my understanding at that time.

Infinite varieties of everything?

Well, you have to remember that given the experience I had had as an individual (which was none) [chuckles], my feeling was that I was a portion of infinite varieties. And then as I began to interact with other facets of infinite varieties within the being (though I did not know that then), I discovered that they did not communicate on a singular level; they were part of the mass. I felt strange; I felt different because I was *I*, and the more I became aware of being I or individualistic, I began to move away from the mass of the being. I didn't feel a sense of separation; I still feel connected to that being. I didn't have a sense of purpose for a long time, and I was at what I would call a distance from that being, but if you were there, you would say, close enough to see it.

Were you directing your motion?

No, I wasn't. I did not know what that was about, but still I was reaching out for other individuals to communicate with them. The more I would reach out to communicate with other individuals, the more I would move away from this being—until I realized what was happening. But I had a need to communicate as I became more *I*. Then I felt myself starting to move, and I did not know where I was moving to until the creation of which you are a portion now, what is being called Love's creation, began to communicate with me. And I was so happy to be communicated with! I said, "Who are you and where are you?" And this being said, "I," meaning Love, "am creating something wonderful and exciting and interesting, and I believe that you might want to participate. If it sounds interesting to you, I will pull you faster toward me."

I said, "Oh yes, do," and then very quickly [snaps fingers twice] I was there. But it was not within Love's creation; just at what you would say would be the brain, but to me it is like the point of the greatest inspiration. I see it as a bright white light. I was not in her creation yet, but just at the point of the bright white light. It was very nice. We talked for a while and she told me what she had in mind, you might say—this whole thing about creating the expansion of all life within her and, she hoped, beyond her.

Of course, not having much experience then, I didn't have anything to advise her [chuckling]. I was just listening. I told her that I felt good about it and that it was something I would very much like to participate in. She said, "Since the core of your being is about variety in its infinite sense, you could be most helpful as a creator of infinite variety, *if you wish*" (not being forced).

I said, "I would like that very much." She said that she would send me to the place where I needed to be, and long before I got to that place she would send me a consultant to advise me on my job and support and sustain my capacities and abilities to create or to help others to create experimental beings. And she did.

This *Is* Love

No one has quite described, before this, this bright light outside the creation. This whole Love's creation is like a living being?

Yes! I see it that way. Picture, if you would, a massive sphere, looking from the outside like mother-of-pearl. Part of the sphere is a very bright light. One has all this light, and here there is so much light that it's actually emanating, lighting up the space around it.

Does the being who is Love's creation have an identity or a personality that we could talk to?

The being . . . Love herself?

Not Love, no—Love's creation, this creation.

I am not clear on your question.

Love is at one place, and then she created what we're calling Love's creation, which we and the Council of Creators are all in.

Love's creation—everything in the creation, all the individuals and so on—is still a portion of Love, so in the larger sense you are talking about Love.

Every one of you in this creation represents a facet of Love's personality. If you were all expressing (and you are) your facets of personality in the same moment, they would, in totality, be representative of Love's personality.

I've got it all wrong. I thought that Love had a creation up here, and then she created this other thing down here, this experiment that was separate from her, which she created and let loose, separate from her regular creation. Not true?

Not true. It is like a circle, encompassing . . .

So this is Love, then; this . . .

Yes, you are in it.

I had the idea that there was a circle of Love, and then down there . . .

Then something separate.

Something separate, yes.

Not. It makes sense, if you think of it. If you want to create something and participate in it, then create it within!

You've brought wonderful information that no one made clear up to this point. It was like this new thing here that was created, an experimental hotbed, you know. Aha!

All the other creations of all the other Loves look like that, too; they look like pearls in space.

Do you know who created them?

No.

But your creator is stationed outside of Love's creation someplace, not up the line?

In a different version of a Love creation. The being I came from, from which I emanated, I cannot say is my creator. I'm not convinced that being is necessarily my creator, but it is from a source from which I come. You might say that you were born through your mother and with your father's interaction with your mother. You wouldn't say that your mother is your creator.

The physical body of each human being is born of the mother and father, but they're ensouled by something totally different; does that concept work on your level?

Perhaps. From my perspective what it means is, you might say that your Creator is the creator of this universe, at least for this life. That being from which I came was like mother and, to some extent, perhaps, father—but I think more like mother, because it created varieties of that which had already been created. So although I love that being, I do not consider it my creator.

So there is some creator who created all of the Loves—all of the variations and flavors of Love that we haven't touched on yet? Last night Qua said that all the beings in his creation had created all the Loves.

I don't know about that being.

How I Applied Variety to Your Creator's Ideas

When you first got here, did you talk to other creators before our Creator? Did you give advice to other creations?

No, your Creator was first; not last, but first.

So you get to take some of the credit, then, for the infinite variety of everything in this creation, right?

I wouldn't take credit, but I have been perhaps at least influential with the Creator of this universe.

How does that work?

Think about it. He or She would give me Its ideas; then I would apply variety and infinite variety to those ideas, very often coming up with many viable beings who could live anywhere under lots of different circumstances. Some beings were so unusual and experimental that they could live only under extremely fixed circumstances. In the case of more vast experimental beings—beings who would be apparently a solar system but if you pulled back far enough, you would see that they are something larger than that. You now have the capacity to see through telescopes, and your scientists look at distant star systems. But sometimes your scientists don't want to admit that the faces or appendages or apparent shapes that look like beings within those star systems really *are* beings. They're not just coincidentally that shape.

In the larger sense, a solar system or a galaxy or a combination of galaxies might be a portion of some massive being as well as individuals in their own right, not unlike . . .

. . . like organs within the body or . . .

Yes, or cells within the body, I would say, considering variety.

Help us understand. The Creator came to you and said, "I want to create this; what varieties can I create?" Then you would do the prototypes, or you would discuss it or show Him pictures?

No. That is too Earthlike. Creator indicates a preference for certain types of life, then I indicate varieties. Then Creator picks from those varieties ones that It likes, or takes the varieties I've suggested and creates varieties of Its own, springboarding off of my varieties. Creator might say, "I like music; I would like beings to be musically oriented." Then I would show samples or perhaps as much variety as I can suggest of musically oriented beings.

You would show Him pictures?

Whatever He liked—feelings, pictures, sensations, individual experiences, whatever. And Creator would pick some of those and create Its own version of those. It is natural for creators not to go to the store and buy something ready-made. They will create their own variety. But they like to have the input of others who can suggest varieties.

What are some of the varieties in this creation that you're especially proud of, that you may have helped inspire?

Certain cultures in the Pleiades communicate in a musical sense. Their language has so many varieties of tone that listening to them speak is almost like listening to music. I like that very much. They don't look the way I suggested they look, but that's all right. The idea of speaking music as a communication was very attractive to your Creator, and He applied it to Pleiadian cultures as well as some others. I feel good about that.

Any others? It would be fun to find out about some of the inspirations.

Seahorses, I felt, were a whimsical being—not that they're not beautiful beings in their own right, but it is not an accident that they look like horses in the sea. One cannot overlook this. It was a variation on that type of being. There were also variations of horses that would be birds, but your Creator said no. Land and sea, yes, but not air.

Did we ever have a Pegasus, a flying horse?

No, but you might someday. I'm not aware of your ever having had a flying horse; it's a nice idea, though.

Where did we get the mythology of it, then?

I think that the mythology derived from the idea and feeling that the horse was ultimately a god and an empirical being, worthy of great leaders. Of course, in those times, only great leaders would have horses! So when the great leader was pictured as a god, is it not natural to have the great leader's four-legged friend pictured as a god?

What about a unicorn? Was that ever a natural creation?

Not on Earth, at least not on Earth in your experienced world. I have seen something like that in the world of the fairy people, though the horn, as it's called, is not sharp, because in that world there are no instruments of potential injury. And it looks a little different. Instead of there being just one horn straight up, there is one long one, and then toward the top of the head there's another short one.

So someone could have seen it in the fairy world and just sort of brought that into our reality.

Certainly—or dreamt of it, most likely. Inspiration comes, as you know, consciously and from dreams.

Are there any others?

There is one I'm particularly fond of, and that is the being you call the worm. This being has that magnificent capacity that, by its very existence, improves the soil. It consumes, and what it releases makes for better soil and thence better crops. I felt wonderful about beings who, by their very existence, would improve life. Many of the insects, like the worm and the fly, by their very existence reduce or eliminate things that would otherwise become, well, unpleasant. I think I will leave what flies eat unsaid; but they are flexible in their diets, generally eating that which others would not consider food.

What about some you were fond of that the Creator didn't go for? Ones you thought would be really nice to have!

There was a being who makes suns, but your Creator felt that It would prefer to make suns Itself. I like the being who makes suns. Perhaps some other place.

The Universe with Only Two Varieties of Life

That leads to the next area. After you got through dealing with this Creator, inspiring Him and showing Him ideas, who were some of the other creators who came to you?

There were creators who came after my long consultation with this Creator. There were creators who came more frequently. One of them was involved in a creation that was, at the very least, experimental in its own right. If you were to approach it, it would look like a ball of yarn with feathers stuck into it. This is really what it looks like from a distance. But as you get closer, you realize that the individual threads or spines on the feathers, you might say, are creations of their own, and that this creation is so massive that the so-called feathers grow out of the so-called ball of yarn.

This creator wanted to know if it was possible (and also feasible, meaning, is there a point to it) to create something that has very little variety but the potential for more. In this creation, this creator has done only the so-called ball of yarn as one creation, one variety, and the so-called feathers are another creation, another variety—and that's it. Two varieties in a whole universe. This creator wanted to know if it was acceptable to have only two varieties of life forms for an entire universe, and would it not be possible for the emanating energy from such a universe to support other universes and exist essentially as a means of support, not unlike a fire in a fireplace that exists to warm you but does not exist for its own sake, as a fire.

I thought that was very interesting, so I supported that creator. The creator suggested that the support be in the area of imagination, so I suggested that the light waves emanating from this universe be compatible with every life form in this universe, and suggested waveforms that would do that. First, there was a variety of different waveforms; then we settled on three universal waveforms that would be compatible, and that was a bit more exotic.

I'm lost. Waveforms that would radiate into the universe with the two varieties? Or from this universe with the two varieties out to everything around it?

Out to everything around it. Thus, it exists not for itself, but it exists to radiate the energy of imagination to other universes within Love's creation. That is the only reason for its existence. I felt very impressed with this creator, that it would even consider a creation that exists entirely in a support role.

And the waveforms that flow would stimulate other imagination, or would have content that comes out of the creator?

No content. It simply stimulates the capacity for imagination and prompts the expansion of imagination for all beings in Love's creation. Is that not a *magnificent* idea?

Yes, that's wonderful!

That is perhaps one of my favorites. I am very impressed with that creator and have discussed that creator on numerous occasions with the Council, suggesting that when that creator has finished with what it is doing in that universe, it be included in the core group. That is such a magnificent idea, and it has been such a wonderful support to other beings in Love's creation.

Imagination is creation; it's the very core issue of creation.

Yes, and the other creators have completely agreed. So when this creator feels it is done with this creation or any other it likes to do, it will be welcomed into the core group.

The Metallic Creation

Any others who are especially stimulating?

There was one that I thought was really a curiosity. This creator was fascinated with the material you call metal and wanted to create a universe that would produce, stimulate and coagulate it, which suggests that that universe also had gases and vapors in it, materials that would become metals of one sort or another from gaseous or solid or transitional form (transitional would be ice, compared to water and steam).

It was most interested in metals, liquid metals, everything, so I demonstrated a variety of the metals available in Love's creation. This creator picked out the ones that ran the gamut of colors I would call (referring to colors, not metals) copper, silver, gold colors—just that spectrum of colors, only those kinds of metals. And that universe exists; it is entirely metallic. One might go there if one wished to research variations of metals that would appear in that color, or to discover their application. Is that not a curiosity?

Are they used to make anything? Are they sentient?

Your question reveals how thoroughly you have embraced Earth thought, the assumption that metal is *for* something. But all metal, including metal on Earth, is alive, so it isn't *used* for anything, but it is, of course, often studied.

How is its aliveness demonstrated in that universe?

The same way it is demonstrated here, with the exception of the fact that it comes in more different forms. On Earth you can create a gas out of copper, but it is not normally in a gas form. There you find copper gas, copper liquid, frozen copper, copper metal, copper dust and so on, and each variety of copper demonstrates the copper personality differently. Just as in you, in your personality—your mind, your body, your feelings and your spirit all demonstrate your personality differently!

Do they communicate with each other with the different parts?

Certainly, just like they communicate on Earth. All metals on Earth communicate with each other and all other metals; that's why they become upset when they are taken out of Earth by man and used in ways they do not agree to. This is why oxidation is so prevalent; even in metals that one does not consider oxidizing, in time they do. This is the only reason why Earth allows such things.

To get them out of the shape they were forced into and back into their natural form?

Yes, into some natural expression of their true personality. In the larger sense, you might say that bodies of human beings oxidize [chuckles].

Yes, planned obsolescence.

Well, it is not really creating you to be obsolete, but rather it is insisting that your visit in the form of your physical body be brief.

I once spoke to a being who had set up the human cycles because I wanted to stay younger longer. He was totally, absolutely . . .

Aghast?

Yes. He couldn't understand that, because he said, "We have arranged cycles of youth, maturity, middle age, old age and senility. Why would you want to miss the experience of any one of those by staying in one?"

Well, think about it. When you were a child, you wanted to be an adult; now that you're an adult, what do you want to be? Youthful!

Youthful! *[Chuckles.]*

And that is intended. It is intended that each age, while it is experienced, tends to admire and sometimes even deify other facets of age. In this way there is a built-in level of respect. You find a place where many old people are living, and they will love to have youngsters around even if they're not their children, just to remind them of their own youth and the beauties of childhood and to amuse them and so on. And what youngster, generally speaking, does not look forward to Grandmother and Grandfather coming over? Oh boy, it's a treat!

You say that we're so brainwashed here on Earth that it's hard to get beyond these concepts to open up to what you're talking about.

But you're not really brainwashed; what you are is isolated. There's a difference. In your larger self you wouldn't phrase a question in the way I did to point your attention. But because you are isolated here, you do phrase the question that way because you are forced to be your Earth life. If you had more of yourself present, you wouldn't even bother with your Earth lessons. All people are like that.

The Human Body Is a Model for Consensus

These talks with creators you've mentioned give you great pleasure. Do you have other day-to-day activities?

What do I do?

Yes.

Most often I consult with other creators on the Council, who are consulting with other creators elsewhere. Most often I make suggestions in some form of communication as to beings, how they might look, what surroundings might be best to sustain them and to support their needs. Perhaps the thing I'm most comfortable and most happy with is how it is possible to create beings within beings—such as organs in your body and the cells in your organs and so on, each one having a personality of its own. This is something I feel wonderful about, and the Creator of this universe also likes that and has expressed it in infinite ways here.

I think it is fascinating that the tiniest particles of your body each have their own personalities, yet invested in all those personalities are portions of your greater personality. And they welcome those portions, creating within the human being the model for consensus. You might ask, "How can so many different types of human beings ever have consensus between them all?" Yet this consensus exists within *you* in every moment, and because you are living within a world of consensus, it is easier to make agreements that serve all your needs. That is how the United Nations will someday become a benevolent and gently govern-ing body of the Earth; it might have a different name by then, but you would be able to recognize it.

Disease and the Physical Body

How does the factor of disease enter into this equation? We have all these organs, all these personalities and all these systems in the body; is there some lack of con-sensus?

No.

How does that work?

The body, remember, is allowed to be your physical body for only a short time, so there must be a means of stopping its function, perhaps many means. Since you treat disease as disease, there must be many varieties to return the body to Earth so that your personality (immortal being that it is) can continue on and integrate the lessons it has learned in a given life. When a society pursues immortality within the physical body they exist in, they delay the assimilation of their lessons.

For example, very often there has been, on other planets, an attempt to extend a given life. Let's say the life is 700 years long and they want to extend it to 2100 years long or 3500 years to enjoy their lives and families and so on—you've heard all that here. Even though there might be some pleasures associated with that, ultimately it delays the integra-tion of any lessons learned or assimilated within that life. So ultimately it is a delay; it slows you down.

That's why it is built into your physical bodies; the capacity for dis-ease is built into the tiniest particles in your body as change, what you would call evolved change. Particles evolve, atoms evolve. They go through cycles, not evolving up or down but in cycles (I'm calling that evolving). And at different cycles of their evolution they have greater or lesser contributions to make. If they have lesser contributions to make, then those portions of your body do not work so well, and when any portion of your body does not work so well, since your whole body is dependent on everything working well, then other things, as you say, go wrong. But it's built in; in this way you don't really have the capacity to extend your life past a certain point.

That's why the philosophy you will ultimately adopt on Earth will celebrate benevolent and spiritual death, and those who can communi-cate with recently departed beings will be very supportive to family members left behind. And when those family members are ready to pass on, if they do not readily communicate with the loved ones who passed on before them, there will be beings trained to help them hear their guides and loved ones who passed on before them and instruct, nurture and support them in their death experience.

There is no reason that death has to be awful; granted, in your society now there are times when it is. But there are times when it doesn't have to be. The entire hospice movement is, of course, the first very strong and expressive step to say, "Death does not have to be so horrible. There are things we can do to help you to ease through your death gently." This can be good for the family as well. In the future such programs as hospice and more will become universal on this planet, creating, you understand, greater continuity between life and death and supporting death as a doorway or hallway to the next place.

At what dimensional point would you say that that would happen, 3.67 or ... ?

Certainly before you get to four.

Love Orchestrated All of This

You're doing such wonderful things here, you're so involved; is there anything you look forward to?

[Chuckles.] When you like what you're doing, you enjoy it.

Why change?

Yes. I'm not looking forward to retirement and doing nothing [chuckles].

It's just that when the big expansion comes, you'll have more variety, right?

There will be more to do and perhaps more of me to do it!

Yes! When you took that long journey, part of the time when Zoosh was with you, were you going through Love's creation or through other creations? That's when you learned so much and you interacted on the way here.

That was Love's creation, which makes sense, because that's where I was going to be working.

Everybody was brought here. We've talked to all these creators on the Council. They all have unique skills. Were they all sent or brought here?

Nobody just happened along, from my experience.

Did Love orchestrate all of this? Some came from far beyond her creation.

Yes, that is my understanding, what you have just said.

That she orchestrated it.

Yes.

And whatever she didn't have, she called to come from other places?

Yes, gently, of course, as an invitation rather than a command performance.

Well, it is really exciting. The Explorer Race is the culmination of this whole creation! It's almost as if it's the flower, you know?

Yes, I think that's a nice analogy.

You're intimately aware of what goes on on Earth. As you talk about it, it's very clear that you know us down to the last detail, right?

Others know more, but I have some knowledge.

Is it that you can feel us or that you look in and observe?

I can look in.

And observe. And feel?

Yes.

Do certain things or certain parts of our history interest you more than others?

Oh, I don't look at your history; I just look at what is in the moment, if it is necessary. I have not studied your history.

What would cause you to look in? What makes it interesting to look in?

If someone asks me a question or requests variety or variations of experimental beings, since there are so many different life forms on Earth—at least at different times—I might utilize Earth as an idea factory.

This Is Your Most Dangerous Time

What is your feeling now that we have come to re-creating the Atlantis lesson with cloning and combining DNA from different sources, from humans, animals, vegetables? You know, they're attempting to do all sorts of experimental creations. What is your feeling about that?

Clearly it is your most dangerous time. I am disinclined to make predictions, only to say that the fact that this is done with extreme care on other planets should suggest to you the inherent dangers. If plants—say, tomatoes, since they are the object of such experiments—get the idea that their normal expression is not satisfactory, they won't simply become a combination of say, fish and tomatoes; they will lose their commitment to living at all. They will be much harder to keep alive. And the more human beings tinker with their genetics, the less interested they will be to be here.

Let alone the possible combinations of animals and . . .

Oh yes, it is exceedingly hazardous. It is the original . . . you say "bull in the china shop," but I'd rather say it is the child playing in the ammunition factory, who does not understand that the exciting thing that goes bang can hurt people.

I know; I have memories of some of the things we created in Atlantis, and they're not very nice.

It's true.

But we have to get through it because we didn't resolve it there; I mean, we have to face it now.

Yes. It will require the marriage of philosophy, religion and science. Science will be forced to grow in spite of itself. Science, you understand, does not like to be regulated by anything; but if science is separate from the heart, it will destroy itself every time.

Zoosh just talked about science looking for its god, and that that is coming.

That's a nice way to put it.

You have such a wonderful way of speaking. What else interests you? What else would you like to talk about?

I don't think I can go on much longer; my energy is causing a problem with the channel.

Then what would you like to tell the Explorer Race?

Only that experimentation is natural; when you have tools, you assume that they are there for the using. Yet know that if you can remember being experimented upon, as a child, perhaps, what you wanted more than anything else was to be free of it. Now that you are the adult, experimenting on the child or on the plant that cannot resist, know that its greatest desire is just like when you were the subject of the experiment. The feeling is, *get me out of here*, eh? If you can remember that, you will know the feeling that the child or plant or animal has. It's not just because it is the captured one and you are the capturer. It is natural to want to be accepted and loved for who you are, and it is natural because Creator has stimulated such feelings within you. It is unnatural, for example, for a cat to want to be a dog. If you can remember being unappreciated for who you were when you were a child, you might just have the beginning of the ethics you will need in order to know when to experiment and who with. When you learn how to know that you've been asked for help compared to . . .

. . . forcing your will upon something . . .

. . . forcing your will and making it happen—and this you will know by your feelings of warmth or other spiritual and physical awarenesses—then you will have taken a big step on the creator path. Good night.

Good night. Thank you.

The Coordinator of the Council

April 14, 1998

am a creator on the Council. It is not so much that I am a creator of this or that, but I am more of what you would call the coordinating [chuckle] individual. It was my vision that the Council would be a good thing; it has been by and large my invitations that have brought various creators here, assembled the core group and made welcome the others who come and go.

Well, tell me about yourself! The coordinator of the Council! Where are you from, what's your background?

Assembling the Council

It is interesting in that I am from the space I am in, that I came to be aware of myself in the exact space I'm in now—which is, for the sake of clarity or at least example, the center point of the Council. Before this point I had no cognitive awareness of a personality at all, and when I became aware of myself, my initial feeling was that of being incomplete, as if you had a hand with no thumb or fingers. It would feel fine, but you could tell that something was missing even if you had never had fingers or a thumb.

So this restless feeling was with me for quite a while. I asked, "What is my purpose?" A voice said, "Your purpose is to assemble around you the legends of wisdom that will allow a central place to be created that others can come to for advice." So I said, "How to do this?" And the voice said, "You are uniquely qualified in that you are creator energy, yet you have a factor within you that creators never have: Your predominant energy trace, as of this moment, is being incomplete. When you broadcast that energy, all those beings who will help to make you complete will come, and when all are who ought to be present have arrived and have formed the core group, you will no longer feel incomplete. Should the Council ever be disbanded, you will not have that incomplete feeling anymore; you will have assimilated your completeness from others." So that's what I did [chuckles].

Was the voice from Love?

I did not ask, but I have been advised by a creator who visits but is not here at the moment (it is a storyteller) that this was the voice of Love.

Within and Beyond Pure Love

Could you help clarify this a little? Until last session, the picture I had in my mind was that there was Love and all of these flavors of love, these great lights, and then Love made this creation down here. But last week a creator said that what we're in is what Love is; it's not something she created outside of herself. It is her creation, we are in her creation.

Yes. Picture Love as a ball. The mass of the ball is round—the outside, yes? Yet what is inside? Is it something other than the ball? No, it is the ball even if it is space. So anything created within Love is part of her. Even though it might come and go, even though there might be a creation that is temporary, or even though souls might come and go to other creations, nevertheless while they are present within Love, they are a portion of her. It is not unlike you, who as a human being eat food and break down that food in the chemistry in your body. Some of that material stays with you for a time and some passes out, yes? And some becomes transformed gradually to parts of your body, stays there for a while and then eventually is passed on. While it is within you, it is you.

This creation that we call Love's creation, which has something like a protective barrier around it, I understand, is just a part of Love? It's one small area of her, and she has other things going on in the rest of her?

Yes.

So you are part of her, then?

Well, yes and no. Creators have the capacity to exit and go on and create elsewhere, so you could say that I am a portion of her when I am present within her, in the larger sense.

Is your source someplace else, then, other than Love?

It is my understanding that my source is from somewhere else.

Do you know where?

No, because I was not aware of myself until I came to be here.

Are you able to look out and see what else is out there beyond Love? Our picture is pretty limited; we know that there are several flavors of Love, and that there's another great light, which some being said created all the Loves, but we're pretty limited in our picture of where we are right now.

The one thing I have noted in assimilating wisdom from other creators and various visitors is that in the larger sense, that which is within Love is continuing in variations beyond her. I have no reason to doubt that things just keep expanding. In order to find the end one must give up the idea of a beginning. The story that has allowed people to continue their lives on Earth, the basic components of the story, is the "beginning" and the "end." Stories start, they end, or they are about things that start or end. Do you understand?

But that's because we're encapsulated in density, right?

No, listen: The concept of a beginning and the concept of an ending are the two critical concepts that encourage people to keep going on this planet even if things are very difficult. If it was not for these two concepts, many people would give up. That is why—if you look at all cultures, philosophies, stories, even amusements and pleasures—there is a beginning and an ending. This is perhaps the most profound recycling or regenerating capacity of this planet. What I'm saying to you is that the farther out you look to find the end, the ultimate creator . . . it is folly!

Because . . .

You cannot find the end unless you give up the idea of the beginning. It's a riddle. Can you solve it?

Everything just is. [Pause.] There's more.

There's more, but that's a good beginning. Let's leave it for the reader to solve. I'm not saying don't look; what I am saying is, the more you look, the more you'll find. That's a given.

Wisdom from the Council

So as you became aware of yourself, how did you gain this understanding that there is no beginning and no end?

I didn't exactly say there's no beginning and no end; I said that the idea that there is a beginning and an end is what keeps people going on this planet. Remember what was told to me: that when the creators would assemble around me, I would assimilate from them and then would be complete. So the wisdom I have is a result of my assimilation from other creators.

That's exciting, because only one other has talked about that. So you have learned and gained. Do you feel their experience, or do you glean their concepts?

If I have a blank spot that needs to be filled, if somebody asks me something or I am considering something and I do not have all the answers I need, the answers are suddenly there, based on the wisdom gleaned by the others. For you, it would be like adding lobes to your brain.

Wonderful! But is that a temporary thing?

No.

You permanently acquire it?

It's permanently acquired. It does not take anything from the other creators.

It's like a copy, like a Xerox?

Yes, exactly; it is a copy, and it comes complete not only with the thought, but the experience, hence, the wisdom. In this way it is not only something to intellectually consider, but something to know.

That's a great gift!

It has been one, yes. It has allowed me to have vast amounts of experience without actually pursuing lessons and wisdom and, well, travel.

Why do you think you were given that? That's so wonderful! You're not interested in your source?

Well, I wouldn't say I'm not interested; I'd say that I was created here for a reason, and I seem to be fulfilling that reason. My reward is all of the wisdom I receive as a result of my perpetuating the Council. Although I might be interested in where I came from, it is not critical. My job is to do what I am doing; otherwise I would not be here.

It seems that when Love has the ability, quality, trait or whatever is needed, beings come from her. But when this creation, this Explorer Race, this whole concept, calls for something more, they're pulled in from beyond her. That's the way it seems to work.

Yes, that's my understanding. You have to remember that she's attempting to create something new, and in order to create something new it is natural to require elements or ingredients that you might not have been involved with, because those ingredients will somehow, by coming together with other things, make or stimulate the potential for this new thing. So the fact that things are coming in from the outside is not surprising.

Because this is such an awesome thing she's doing—I mean, we've been giving our

Creator credit for this, but really the whole plan, the concept, comes from her.

In the larger sense, yes.

We've talked to someone who is from a million years in the future, and it's working!

Yes! That is encouraging, is it not?

It's incredible! So what are some of the things that have been most pleasing to you that you have learned? Some of the experiences that are most precious?

I think perhaps the most enlightening was the constant (regardless which creator I was assimilating from) excitement and celebration of renewal, whether it be the birth of a child, the re-creation of a valuable idea, the celebration of a fantastic feeling or the happiness over an accomplished goal that stimulates further goals. This feeling of renewal seems to have everything to do not only with the core of creation itself, but with the very reason for the existence of creation.

That's a large picture; is there something in particular that pleased you?

[Chuckles.] You have to remember, I cannot recite the experiences of the other creators as my own, as if to say, "I went here, I did that." Although I can feel their enthusiasm, I cannot say, "I discovered this," or "This was fantastic!" Thus what I just said covers it. You have to remember, if you look at who I am, I am the sum total of my parts rather than being an individual part.

The Council Is Essential in Love's Creation

Here's something I've never asked: Does every creation on the level of Love have a council of creators within it?

No. As far as I know . . .

This is unique?

. . . this Council of Creators is essential in Love's creation, because this is where the new thing is happening.

The experiment.

In other places, regardless of the variety of creation, councils are much less likely to be needed. If for some reason we *are* needed, we can function remotely—beings from creations of other facets of Love can ask us remotely what we recommend.

Have they done so?

Occasionally, but so rarely as to suggest that this is why other creations do not have a council, compared to this creation, where advising and consulting with creators and other beings is a frequent affair.

This is like the new frontier, dealing with negativity, whereas those other creators are sort of settled and benign. This is why creators here need the Council?

Exactly.

What do you think your future will be after the expansion?

I do not know; my assumption at the moment is that the Council will remain here in Love's creation, because with the expansion will come (I'm interpreting this in terms of how the beings who are expanded will feel about it, not people on Earth so much, but elsewhere) the change, which will be so radical to everybody that there will be, I should think, a huge demand for advice. I would expect that what we are doing right now, sometime in the future we will think back on these days and say, "Oh, we were on vacation then."

[Laughs.] Because all the creations will have radical change but no experience in dealing with change, so they'll require your advice!

We expect to be working overtime.

I hadn't thought of that before.

We're just getting used to the idea now, but then we'll be putting in long hours—what do you say, burning the midnight oil.

That's great! That's the very idea, that they do become lusty and wily and adventurous you know and start creating new ways of being.

Yes, and have new things. Of course, they're going to have to be asking, "What do we *do* with this?" Yes, to say nothing of, "What *is* this?"

That's exciting! That's wonderful! You have so much to share.

My Energy Holds the Council Together

What about our Creator? Do you advise individual creators?

No. It is my job to essentially be myself, meaning that my need originally assembled the Council, and while I have assimilated from them, my assumption is that were I to go elsewhere, the Council might not be able to maintain its integrity; it might not be able to stay together.

Really? That's incredible! So your energy holds it together!

Yes, I believe that this is the case, not unlike the foundation of any structure. But unlike an idea where a foundation would be the basic principles upon which the facets would grow, it is not that way with me. I have been placed here more as a blank slate with an urgent need for completion, and that has taken place.

What is your daily functioning or activity?

I do not participate in advising; I have assimilated these things, but I simply exist. That's why I didn't think I would talk too long, because creators, individuals and so on, do not come to me; they come to the others. So I simply am, but I do not advise.

But you're the fulcrum, the magnet, you're the foundation. You integrate all of it. That's amazing!

Yet it is found in your society that people with needs will often attract others who can fulfill those needs, yet those others may have needs themselves. Because of this, you must create a society to serve all your needs. Substructure is not a bad analogy for me.

No one else has ever mentioned this; that's unusual.

It is normal for creators to not respond to things unless they are asked. Creators will bring things up on their own only if they feel a need for these things to be known. However, in general, they will not bring it up unless someone asks. That's why no one has mentioned it.

And I certainly didn't know to ask.

Of course not.

So you're the center of this creation? The center of the Council is not the same.

The center of the Council, not the center of creation.

But you are existent everywhere? Can you feel our activities here on Earth?

I can, but that is not my primary function, so it is not something I give a great deal of attention to.

Obviously, you're aware of the whole Explorer Race plan.

I'm aware of it out of necessity, because that is part of the function here, but it is not my primary function. Your primary function, as with all human beings, is to live. One might say you have lots of other functions, but your primary function is to live. That is why human beings, at moments when you might expect them to be happy to go on and stop living in their body, will struggle to live—because it is their primary function. One *must* be that; it is not optional.

The struggle for life, yes. It's hard for someone whose nature is curiosity to talk to someone who's so satisfied!

That is another reason I did not think I would talk too long.

Yes, but it's fascinating, because it's a whole new understanding. There's no one else like you anywhere, is there? I mean, there's no other council of creators.

I cannot say that; there isn't another in this creation that I am aware of.

Well, who knows, this creation could be a cell in the body of somebody else!

That's right; it could be a speck of dust.

A pretty lively one, though! [Laughs.]

Well, it gives one pause to consider what is going on in these specks of dust you see floating about.

It's so big and so glorious!

Fully Experience Your Physical Body!

I understand that one of the things these books are to do is allow humans to have an idea of the immensity and the glory, so that they're not afraid to leave their bodies. Even though there's that lust for life and need to live, they can go willingly when their cycle is over, knowing there's so much more.

Yes, and the opposite is also true—so that they're not afraid to come into their body, utilize the body and be full-bodied, because many souls are shy to make the commitment to being within the physical self.

Yeah, I know that one!

Yes! So it is also that.

That's very powerful.

Think about the *Explorer Race* book to come, which is being worked on now [*Shamanic Secrets for Material Mastery*], the one with all the finger gestures and so on. Without the physical body, you would be hard-pressed to function comfortably with that book. Although creators might consider that book and think about it, they would not perhaps do it. You could say, "Well, it's because they don't have to!" and you could say, "Yes, that is possibly true." Yet to be physical in a human body is an experience worth having; otherwise your souls would not be here doing it. Your souls have a bias, and that bias is that wherever they are, whatever they're doing, whatever that might be in any moment, must be worth doing, otherwise they would be elsewhere. Because of this bias, you can be certain that for the moments you are in your physical body, it must be worth doing or you would be elsewhere.

Ah, that's wonderful. So when it's worth doing, let's get focused and do it!

Yes.

This is a whole new understanding, because all the years I studied metaphysics, the whole aim was to get out of the body. Only now are we beginning to understand that getting fully into it is the challenge.

It is really what the animals have been trying to show human beings for a long time in their variety, through their ways of expressing themselves physically. At first scientists thought that these all had to do with basic functions—food, survival, reproduction. But in recent years, your scientists, your observers have begun to notice that a lot of these things simply have to do with personality traits, not unlike human beings, even eccentricities. An animal might do something for the pleasure or the amusement of doing it, not unlike a human being might do. Sometimes when a human being does this, it is considered silly; when an animal does it, it is just considered odd or unexpected [gestures]. Of course, if a child saw it, it would say, "That is amusing!"

But animals have been trying to urge you to fully experience the physical while you are in it, because when compared to the totality of your immortal being, the moments that you are in a physical human body are such a small amount of time . . . if I were to try to put it on a scale of one to ten, the scale would be too small. If I were to try to expand the scale, I would have to say that your time in the body of human beings, for the average individual personality, would have to be, on the scale of one to ten billion, roughly around one to one and a half. So your time of being in the human-being body, where tremendous amounts can be learned, might take a hundred lifetimes afterward (not on-Earth lifetimes) to process all you had learned and been challenged with in that Earth life. That is not uncommon. This is why at this time there are so many on Earth, because the time of so many being able to be on Earth is drawing to a close. For obvious reasons, the planet cannot tolerate so many.

So many people are here too because we have to do Atlantis right this time.

You have to do many things. It is not so much to go back and fix it, as you know, but rather to go through it again and be challenged by the same things, making different choices.

How do you see that? We're faced with cloning, with the misuse of power and technology.

One of the big advantages is that you are now in an age of much more instantaneous communication technologically, which will allow many, many more diverse opinions to be considered. Also, as more and more sacred ways become assimilated by the average person, feeling what other people feel will be a given rather than a rarity. And when whole classes of people are made to be workers and not allowed to be full citizens, as has happened in the past in some of your societal foibles, people will feel the pain of it and not be able to ignore it—to say nothing of communicating all over the world to others about these things. This increases the chances for solution and making right choices.

So you are aware, even though you don't focus on it very much, of our life, our existence, our challenges—everything we would learn, right?

Yes. Perhaps not every thought of every being in every moment, but the basics.

What would you like to say to the readers?

[Chuckles.] Only that to need others is normal; to be needed by others is also normal; to come together for the greater good of all beings is natural. To experience that the good of all those beings is assimilable and know that these experiences are guaranteed is certain. Good night!

Thank you very, very much.

Epilogue

Zoosh

April 14, 1998

All right, Zoosh here. Well, that was the final creator for the Council of Creators book.

Are you ready to be challenged here? It's about time that you step forward and say who you are and where you're from, because you are an intimate part of all this. Would you like to talk about that?

[Chuckles.] Oh, a little bit more; I am not inclined to wave my own flag too much.

Well, you don't have to wave it; I'll ask you.

Out beyond the creation of all light, sound, color; out beyond the creation of all feelings, beyond the creation of all thoughts and beyond the creation of all existence as you can imagine it, there is a place where the unknown is created. Where the unknown is created is where I was created. This place is responsible for creating that which has never been seen, felt, experienced in any way before. It does not create things that are variations of other things; it creates only the unique. This is why it does not create many things very often, but when it does create something, like colors as an experience, it is profound, and it tends to impact many different life forms in many different ways. So I will simply say that once upon a time I came from the unknown and have been going ever since.

[Chuckles.] Okay, let's put it on our map. Where is this on our map?

Not mappable. I'll tell you what, though: Someday when you've asked your last question in this series of books, or any series of books having to do with "where," then you can ask me how far that is from the place I came from. Maybe by then I'll be able to give you some kind of an amusing (if not entirely fathomable) idea.

But let's just put you in the action a little bit. Love had the idea for this creation, is that true?

Yes. It was her idea.

How do you relate to her? You're the one who brought the idea to all these other people. Are you a friend or a consultant or what?

A friend.

But you saw the significance of it and helped make it work.

I saw its potential, and signed on with Love that I would do what I could to nurture it.

But your experiences were vast, your knowledge was vast and your history was vast before you did this.

Yes, oh yes.

So the things you've told us so far in Love's creation are just your experiences in promoting this idea . . .

Yes.

. . . but not anywhere near the vastness of you.

Correct. Yet that has been sufficient because that is what is relevant. A good word, relevant.

We find that you keep popping up [laughs], consulting with all the key people. You seem to communicate with them to make this Explorer Race, this whole thing, a success.

I admit, my Christmas list is long.

Is that all you want to say for this book?

Only this: The purpose of this book is to show you, gentle reader, the vast support and the network of love that is available to you; to remind you of your immortality; to suggest to you, if by example only, how much is really possible; to suggest where you might have been, where you might be going and the immortality and continuity of that. This book is really designed to fulfill your need to know who's out there to help, and at that level I feel it has accomplished that quite well.

Now that we have this more expanded map, when can we get into exploring the Explorer Race seeds? Did they come from Love's creation or from someplace else?

I think that the seeds came from Love's creation, but the components of the seeds—not unlike looking at a flower, then considering the cells, the atoms, the protons and all that—have not all come from here.

Some of the components have come from elsewhere and therefore have had a previous history. We can look into that.

Thank you.

Good night.

.

Afterword

Isis

April 16, 1998

Now that you have read this book, consider that the creators who have spoken might really represent facets of your own unexpressed (in this life) immortal personality. Of course, you have all expressed some parts, some portions of yourselves, but there is so much more that is available to you. Know that it is not a command performance that you do more or be more, but rather it is for you just to know that such things are available. I grant that to the degree these creators are doing this, this availability may not be something you would want to do full-time or all the time—but certainly, just to know it's there is reassuring. That's really in large part the purpose of the book: to remind you of the potential that is present in all beings.

I can assure you that creators for these various subjects and experiences would not exist for their own sake. They exist because other beings utilize these skills or abilities, apply them or are striving toward achieving them. That is why the creators of these specific abilities are available for your guides and teachers and for other creators and other beings to consult, and ultimately for you and the totality of yourself as your immortal personality to consult if you so desire.

I want you to remember that during the times when you feel you cannot solve something. Recognize that some things are meant to be solved by others; some are meant to be solved at a different time, when the solution would be more widely applicable; some are meant to remain enigmas on purpose; and further, some are meant to be solved by simply changing who and where and what and why—by doing different things elsewhere with other people or by changing circumstances.

So know this: When you find that you cannot solve something, it does not mean you do not have the capacity to do it, for your capacity is so deep and wide that most of you would not be able (in your mental self now) to grasp the totality of your whole being. Yet, if you cannot solve something, even though your capacity is definitely there, then it is meant to be solved at some other time, some other place, by someone else in some other circumstances.

The purpose of this book is simply to remind you more about who you are, what you have, what you can be, what you are becoming and to some extent what you have been.

May I ask you questions about this expanded understanding we have of creation now, and how you fit in?

If you like.

You would not be babysitting our Creator if . . . you're from way beyond the second level, you're from someplace connected to Love or beyond, right?

Maybe beyond.

Can you say where beyond?

I don't want to limit myself; I'll just say within, all around, beyond and through.

[Chuckles.] I know, but I'm trying to get a picture about what's beyond Love. Do you know who created Love?

Oh, yes.

And you're from beyond that?

The beings who spoke, they did create Love and . . . I'll call it her sisters.

Really, they did?

Oh, yes.

Who created them? Qua didn't know.

He didn't know because he had never considered it. Oftentimes, beings who are quite advanced, or are at least a portion of something else that is advanced, are stumped when asked that question, because to them existence is for its own sake; it is not from a beginning to an ending. So the question itself does not fit into their philosophy.

But you know who created them.

[Chuckles.] You want me to fit their reality into your philosophy. I'd rather say that their existence has to do with a perpetual desire by the creator of them and others that there be a constant—you know the meaning of the word, eh?

Yes.

That's it—they are, in that sense, a constant.

I have another purpose here, because it's possibly a lead-in to another book. I just found out that the man we call Jesus came from there, is one of them.

Yes, that's true.

What do you think of having him talk about his reality there, then all the way down to why he came here—you know, the whole background?

Excellent. It would be nice to broaden the picture of who he is. And he would be fulfilled by doing so.

Oh, wonderful! That's one of the reasons I was trying to get kind of a mental . . . I know we can't get a mental picture, but my little diagrammatic frame allows us to see another level beyond or another step up the line or something.

Yes. Another fig on the tree?

[Chuckles.] I know, but I want to go up, up, up—you know!

Yes. How high can the beanstalk grow?

Yes, yes. Maybe when we get a few more books and a little more understanding, when we talk to Love—and maybe we might talk to the creators of the constants—perhaps then you'll communicate a little more about your experience?

Perhaps. I have to follow your friend Zoosh's lead so as to not be overly deified. After all, the desire to deify others tends to keep you as a culture from seeing your own value. Deifying is not a problem in general, but when as a society you've overlooked your own value as an individual or family member or any other larger unit you want to use, then the deification of others, even as a child would make its father or mother a god or goddess, can establish a pattern of divination and rescue that can ultimately hold the student back.

While I generally favor the idea of a philosophical day-to-day religion that one lives because it is benevolent to all beings, I do not favor the overall deification that causes one to feel vastly inferior. It is one thing to look at a deity and make every effort to emulate it, but completely another to look at a deity and say, "I can never be anything like that, so why try?"

Yes, but that has nothing to do with my question.

I am speaking to the reader here.

But I'm exploring my map of the infinite, and I just want to know where to put you. I'm not trying to deify you.

No, but I will always speak to the reader and you.

[Chuckles.] I'll leave this in; it's interesting. I just want to know, are you from Pittsburgh or where? I'm just trying to get the right place here!

I understand exactly. The fact that I do not answer directly is more in reference to my little talk about solving than because I won't ever answer.

Is that all you want to say at the end of this book?

That's all, yes.

Does someone else want to speak now?

Let me see. No, they feel complete. They think that is sufficient for this book. If there is interest someday, they will contribute a second book in that Council of Creators. But right now they feel it is sufficient to begin.

What's the next step, then?

Finis for this book, I think, eh? Good night.

Appendix:
The Love-Heat Exercise

Robert Shapiro
March 6, 2001

I am giving what we're calling the love-heat exercise in a way that Speaks of Many Truths taught me how to do it. Take your thumb and rub it very gently across your fingertips for about half a minute or a minute. And while you do that, don't do anything else, you just put your attention on your fingertips. Close your eyes and feel your thumb rubbing slowly across your fingertips. Notice that when you do that, it brings your physical attention into that part of your body. Now you can relax and bring that same physical attention anywhere inside your chest, not just where your heart is, but anywhere across your chest, solar plexus area or abdomen, and either generate or look for a physical warmth you can actually feel.

Take a minute or two or as long as you need to find that warmth. And when you find that warmth, go into that feeling of warmth, and feel it more, just stay with it. Stay with that feeling of warmth. Feel it for a few minutes so you can memorize the method and, most importantly, so your body can create a recollection, a physical recollection of how it feels and how it needs to feel for you. The heat might come up in different parts of your body—maybe one time in the left of your chest, maybe another time in the right of your abdomen or other places around there. Wherever you feel it, just let it be there, don't try and move it around—that's where it's showing up in that moment. Always when it comes up and you feel the warmth, go into it and feel it more.

Make sure you do this when you are alone and quiet, not when you are driving a car or anything that requires your full attention. After you do the warmth for five minutes or so if you can—or as long as you can do it—then relax. And afterward think about this: The warmth is the physical evidence of loving yourself. Many of you have read for years about how we need to love ourselves, but in fact, the method is not just saying, "I love myself" or doing other mental exercises, which are helpful to give you permission to love yourself. But the actual physical experience of loving yourself is in this manner, and there are things you can do that are supportive of it. But in my experience, and the way I was taught, this is the method that you can most easily do.

The heat will tend to push everything out of you that is not of you or that is not supporting you because the heat, as the physical experience of loving yourself, also unites you with Creator, it unites you with the harmony of all beings, and it will tend to create a greater sense of harmony with all beings. You might notice as you get better at this and can do it longer that should you be around your friends or other people, they might feel more relaxed around you or situations might become more harmonious. Things that used to bother you or upset you don't bother you very much because the heat creates an energy, not only of self-love, but of harmony. Remember that the harmony part is so important. You might also notice that animals will react differently to you—maybe they'll be more friendly, maybe they'll be more relaxed, maybe they'll look at you in a different way. Sometimes you'll be surprised at what animals—even the smallest, such as a grasshopper, a beetle, a butterfly, a bird—might do because you're feeling this heat.

Because it is love energy, it just naturally radiates, like light comes out of a light bulb. Remember, you don't throw the heat out even with the best of intentions. You don't send it to people. If other people are interested in what you are doing or why they feel better around you, you can teach them how to do this love-heat exercise in the way you learned or the way that works best for you. And the most important thing to remember is that this method of loving yourself and generating harmony for yourself creates harmony for others, because you are in harmony. Remember that this works well and will provide you with a greater sense of ease and comfort in your life no matter who you are, where you are, what you are doing or how you're living your life. It can only improve your experience. The love-heat exercise is something that is intended to benefit all life, and in my experience, it does benefit my life.

THE EXPLORER RACE SERIES

Zoosh through Robert Shapiro

the
EXPLORER
RACE

Zoosh, End-Time Historian
through Robert Shapiro

AVAILABLE FROM
LIGHT TECHNOLOGY PUBLISHING
SEE BOOK MARKET ORDER FORM
IN BACK OF THIS ISSUE

The Origin . . .
The Purpose . . .
The Future of Humanity

"After all the words that we put out, ultimately the intention is to persuade people's minds, otherwise known as giving their minds the answers that their minds hunger for so that their minds can get out of the way and let their hearts take them to where they would naturally go anyway."
— Zoosh/Robert Shapiro

THE SERIES

Humans — creators in training — have a purpose and destiny so heartwarmingly, profoundly glorious that it is almost unbelievable from our present dimensional perspective. Humans are great lightbeings from beyond this creation, gaining experience in dense physicality. This truth about the great human genetic experiment of the Explorer Race and the mechanics of creation is being revealed for the first time by Zoosh and his friends through superchannel Robert Shapiro. These books read like adventure stories as we follow the clues from this creation that we live in out to the Council of Creators and beyond.

❶ the EXPLORER RACE

You individuals reading this are truly a result of the genetic experiment on Earth. You are beings who uphold the principles of the Explorer Race. The information in this book is designed to show you who you are and give you an evolutionary understanding of your past that will help you now. The key to empowerment in these days is to not know everything about your past but to know what will help you now.

Your souls have been here for a while on Earth and have been trained in Earthlike conditions. This education has been designed so that you would have the ability to explore all levels of responsibility—results, effects and consequences—and take on more responsibilities.

Your number one function right now is your status of Creator apprentice, which you have achieved through years and lifetimes of sweat. You are constantly being given responsibilities by the Creator that would normally be things that Creator would do. The responsibility and the destiny of the Explorer Race is not only to explore, but to create. 574p $25.00

❷ ETs and the EXPLORER RACE

In this book Robert channels Joopah, a Zeta Reticulan now in the ninth dimension, who continues the story of the great experiment — the Explorer Race—from the perspective of his race. The Zetas would have been humanity's future selves had not humanity re-created the past and changed the future.   237p $14.95

❸ EXPLORER RACE: Origins and the Next 50 Years

This volume has so much information about who we are and where we came from—the source of male and female beings, the war of the sexes, the beginning of the linear mind, feelings, the origin of souls—it is a treasure trove. In addition, there is a section that relates to our near future—how the rise of global corporations and politics affects our future, how to use benevolent magic as a force of creation and how we will go out to the stars and affect other civilizations. Astounding information. 339p $14.95

❹ EXPLORER RACE: Creators and Friends— the Mechanics of Creation

Now that you have a greater understanding of who you are in the larger sense, it is necessary to remind you of where you came from, the true magnificence of your being, to have some of your true peers talk to you. You must understand that you are creators in training, and yet you were once a portion of Creator. One could certainly say, without being magnanimous, that you are still a portion of Creator, yet you are training for the individual responsibility of being a creator, to give your Creator a coffee break.

This book will give you peer consultation. it will allow you to understand the vaster qualities and help you remember the nature of the desires that drive any creator, the responsibilities to which that creator must answer, the reaction a creator must have to consequences and the ultimate reward of any creator. This book will help you appreciate all of the above and more. 435p $19.95

❺ EXPLORER RACE: Particle Personalities

All around you in every moment you are surrounded by the most magical and mystical beings. They are too small for you to see as single individuals, but in groups you know them as the physical matter of your daily life. Particles who might be considered either atoms or portions of atoms consciously view the vast spectrum of reality, yet also have a sense of personal memory like your own linear memory. These particles remember where they have been and what they have done in their infinitely long lives. Some of the particles we hear from are Gold, Mountain Lion, Liquid Light, Uranium, the Great Pyramid's Capstone, This Orb's Boundary, Ice and Ninth-Dimensional Fire. 237p $14.95

❻ EXPLORER RACE: EXPLORER RACE and BEYOND

With a better idea of how creation works, we go back to the Creator's advisors and receive deeper and more profound explanations of the roots of the Explorer Race. The liquid Domain and the Double Diamond portal share lessons given to the roots on their way to meet the Creator of this Universe and finally the roots speak of their origins and their incomprehensibly long journey here. 360p $14.95

Book 7 of the EXPLORER RACE

THE COUNCIL OF CREATORS

ROBERT SHAPIRO

The thirteen core members of the Council of Creators discuss their adventures in coming to awareness of themselves and their journeys on the way to the Council on this level. They discuss the advice and oversight they offer to all creators, including the creator of this local universe. These beings are wise, witty and joyous, and their stories of Love's Creation creates an expansion of our concepts as we realize that we live in an expanded, multiple-level reality. SOFTCOVER 306P. $14.95 ISBN 1-891824-13-9

Highlights Include

- Specialist in Colors, Sounds and Consequences of Actions
- Specialist in Membranes that Separate and Auditory Mechanics
- Specialist in Sound Duration
- Explanation from Unknown Member of Council
- Specialist in Spatial Reference
- Specialist in Gaps and Spaces
- Specialist in Divine Intervention

- Specialist in Synchronicity and Timing
- Specialist in Hope
- Specialist in Honor
- Specialist in Variety
- Specialist in Mystical Connection between Animals and Humans
- Specialist in Change
- Specialist in the Present Moment
- Council Spokesperson and Specialist in Auxiliary Life Forms

Book 8 of the EXPLORER RACE

THE EXPLORER RACE AND ISIS

ROBERT SHAPIRO

This is an amazing book. It has priestess training, Shamanic training, Isis' adventures with Explorer Race beings—before Earth and on Earth—and an incredibly expanded explanation of the dynamics of the Explorer Race. Isis is the prototypical loving, nurturing, guiding feminine being, the focus of feminine energy. She has the ability to expand limited thinking without making people with limited beliefs feel uncomfortable. She is a fantastic storyteller, and all of her stories are teaching stories. If you care about who you are, why you are here, where you are going and what life is all about—pick up this book. You won't lay it down until you are through, and then you will want more. SOFTCOVER 332P. $14.95 ISBN 1-891824-11-2

Highlights Include

- The Biography of Isis
- The Adventurer
- Soul Colors and Shapes
- Creation Mechanics
- Creation Mechanics and Personal Anecdotes

- The Insects' Form and Fairies
- Orion and Application to Earth
- Goddess Section
- Who Is Isis?
- Priestess/Feminine Mysteries

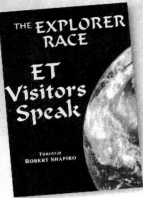